UNRAVELING THE GARMENT INDUSTRY

Social Movements, Protest, and Contention

Series Editor: Bert Klandermans, Free University, Amsterdam

Associate Editors: Ron R. Aminzade, University of Minnesota
David S. Meyer, University of California, Irvine
Verta A. Taylor, University of California, Santa Barbara

For more books in the series, see page 246.

UNRAVELING THE GARMENT INDUSTRY

Transnational Organizing and Women's Work

Ethel C. Brooks

Social Movements, Protest, and Contention
Volume 27

 University of Minnesota Press
Minneapolis • London

For Farhan and Charu

In memory of my parents

All photographs in the book were taken by Ethel C. Brooks.

Published by the University of Minnesota Press
111 Third Avenue South, Suite 290
Minneapolis, MN 55401-2520
http://www.upress.umn.edu

Library of Congress Cataloging-in-Publication Data

Brooks, Ethel Carolyn.
Unraveling the garment industry : transnational organizing and women's work / Ethel C.
Brooks.
     p.   cm. — (Social movements, protest, and contention series ; v. 27)
   Includes bibliographical references and index.
   ISBN-13: 978-0-8166-4485-8 (hc : alk. paper)
   ISBN-13: 978-0-8166-4486-5 (pb : alk. paper)
   1. Antisweatshop movement. 2. Protest movements—International
cooperation. 3. Women—Developing countries—Social conditions.
4. Women—Developing countries—Economic conditions. 5. Working
class women. 6. Social conflict. I. Title.
   HD2337.B76 2007
   331.4'25--dc22

                                                            2006030911

Printed in the United States of America on acid-free paper

The University of Minnesota is an equal-opportunity educator and employer.

12 11 10 09 08 07   10 9 8 7 6 5 4 3 2 1

Myth does not deny things, on the contrary, its function is to talk about them; simply, it purifies them, it makes them innocent, it gives them a natural and eternal justification, it gives them a clarity which is not that of explanation but that of a statement of fact.

—Roland Barthes

They are selling the poverty of the country. The factory owners do it, as do the unionists, NGO people, and academics, too.

—Former Salvadoran garment worker

Contents

Acronyms

AAFLI	Asian-American Free Labor Institute
AALC	African-American Labor Center
ACTWU	Amalgamated Clothing and Textile Workers Union
AFL–CIO	American Federation of Labor–Congress of Industrial Organizations
AIFLD	American Institute of Free Labor Development
AIP	Apparel Industry Partnership
ASIC	Asociación Salvadoreña de la Industria de la Confección (Salvadoran Garment Industry Association)
ASTTEL	Salvadoran Association of Telecommunications Workers
ATEMISA	Association of Mandarin International Workers, the company union at Mandarin International
BGMEA	Bangladesh Garment Manufacturers and Exporters Association
BIGU(F)	Bangladesh Independent Garment Union (Federation)
BRAC	Bangladesh Rural Action Committee
CAFTA	Central American Free Trade Agreement
CBI	Caribbean Basin Initiative
CENTRA	Centro de Estudios del Trabajo (Center for Labor Studies in San Salvador)
CEP	Council for Economic Priorities
CISPES	Committee in Solidarity with the People of El Salvador
CLR	Campaign for Labor Rights

CNTS	Centro Nacional de Trabajadores Salvadoreños (National Center of Salvadoran Workers)
CODEH	Committee for the Defense of Human Rights in Honduras
COSDEMA	Coordinating Group for Dignified Employment in the Maquila
CSWA	Chinese Staff and Workers Association
CTD	Central de Trabajadores Democráticos (Democratic Workers' Central)
CTS	Central de Trabajadores Salvadoreños (Salvadoran Workers' Central)
EPZ	export processing zone, sometimes called free trade zone (FTZ), or *zona franca* in Spanish
FEASIES	Federación de Asociaciones y Sindicatos Independientes de El Salvador (Federation of Independent Associations and Unions of El Salvador)
FENASTRAS	Federación Nacional Sindical de Trabajadores Salvadoreños (National Union Federation of Salvadoran Workers)
FLA	Fair Labor Agreement
FMLN	Frente Farabundo Martí de Liberación Nacional (Farabundo Martí National Liberation Front)
FTUI	Free Trade Union Institute
FTZ	free trade zone, also known as export processing zone (EPZ), or *zona franca* in Spanish
FUSADES	Fundación Salvadoreño de Desarrollo Económico y Social (Salvadoran Foundation of Economic and Social Development)
GMIES	Grupo de Monitoreo Independiente de El Salvador (Independent Monitoring Group of El Salvador)
GSS	Gonoshahajjo Sangstha, Bangladeshi children's advocacy organization
ICA	Inter-Church Action for Development, Relief, and Justice
ILGWU	International Ladies' Garment Workers Union
ILO	International Labor Organization
IMF	International Monetary Fund

INS	U.S. Immigration and Naturalization Service, now the U.S. Department of Homeland Security
ISSS	Instituto Salvadoreño de Seguridad Social (Salvadoran Social Security Institute)
JIT	just-in-time production system of flexible subcontracting
MAM	Movimiento de Mujeres Mélida Anaya Montes (Mélida Anaya Montes Women's Organization in El Salvador)
MOU	memorandum of understanding to phase out child labor from the Bangladeshi export-oriented garment industry
NACLA	North American Congress on Latin America
NGWF	National Garment Workers Federation of Bangladesh
NIDL	new international division of labor
NLC	National Labor Committee
NMASS	National Mobilization against Sweatshops
SETMI	Sindicato de Empresa de Trabajadores de Mandarin International (International Factory Union of Workers of Mandarin International)
SITEMSAL	Sindicato de Empresa Maquila de El Salvador
Tk	taka (Bangladeshi currency)
UBINIG	Bengali acronym for Research on Alternatives to Development
UNITE	Union of Needletrades, Industrial, and Textile Employees
UNITE HERE	Product of the merger between UNITE and the Hotel Employees and Restaurant Employees International Union (HERE)
UNOC	Unión Nacional Obrero Campesino (National Worker–Peasant Movement)
UNTS	Unión Nacional de Trabajadores Salvadoreños (National Union of Salvadoran Workers)
UPD	Unidad Popular y Democrático (Popular and Democratic Unity)
USAID	U.S. Association for International Development
USAS	United Students against Sweatshops
USDOL	U.S. Department of Labor
VIM	vertically integrated manufacturing

Introduction

Since the middle of the 1990s, the globalization of manufacturing has given rise to the globalization of industrial protest. Movements to improve working conditions have organized cross-border campaigns, bringing together labor activists and consumers in the United States and Europe with labor organizers, workers, and activists in manufacturing sites to protest labor violations in factories that subcontract production for large, multinational retailers. Like the corporations they oppose, the tactics of transnational campaigns increasingly work to affect a product's image and the way it is marketed and consumed; furthermore, antisweatshop campaigns themselves employ third world women garment workers—their bodies, labor, representations, and testimonies—in the production of transnational protest.

This book focuses on three protest campaigns against abusive labor practices in international garment manufacturing, an industry that exemplifies the most advanced forms of globalization, vertically integrated manufacturing and subcontracting, labor intensity, and corporate image making. By concentrating on working conditions on shop floors, in garment production regimes, and in transnational activist coalitions, my research examines the logic, origins, objectives, and consequences of transnational campaigns for workers' rights. I am among the first to investigate transnational industrial protest through a multisite study.

I take the discursive and material formations of globalization and transnationality in order to put forth a critique of new imperial formations and to explore the gendered, sexual, raced, and classed subjectivities that are both remainders and reconfigurations of earlier colonial formations.

Methodologically, this work is centered on multisited ethnography and combines it with analyses of political economy as consumption and production, transnational activism, gendered agency, and the possibilities of new forms of labor organizing. I explore hegemonic representations and mythologies of globalization and the place of the local, the problematics of political economy and method, and the formation of modernity as technology, as constitutive outside, and as contradiction. I address broader issues such as the particular historical contexts and localities of garment production and protest and the notion of rights within movements that attempt to bridge divides between the first world and the third world within a context of transnational activism. Throughout, I maintain an analysis of women's bodies as central to production, consumption, and protest; I question the ways in which gendered, raced bodies of third world women are portrayed as victims or models and what the relation of such representations is to criteria of consumption and production.

I chose to focus on transnational protest in the garment industry for a number of reasons. First, for the past two decades, the garment industry has been at the center of scholarship around the new international division of labor and the feminization of the shop floor.[1] Second, transnational labor protest, with few exceptions, has targeted garment retailers, citing their piece-rate payment system, exceptional mobility, and the complex levels of subcontracting through which production goals are met. For both activists and scholars, garment production has been emblematic of globalization, both in its exceptionally mobile production practices and in its dual identity as a producer of clothing, or goods, and fashion, or images. Third, both sides of the dual identity of garment production—fashion and clothing— have relied on women as producers, consumers, retailers, and models. The garment industry and the fashion industry have depended on, reproduced, and shifted gender stereotypes and gender relations in all aspects of everyday life. My aim is to connect these aspects of women's work—production, globalization, transnational politics, gender identities, and the relations between consumption and image making—to relations of gender, class, race, nation, and sexuality in three transnational protest campaigns in the garment industry.

I explore transnational, consumer-oriented protest campaigns against labor violations of mostly women workers at an export processing zone (EPZ) in El Salvador, against the use of child labor in Bangladesh, and against immigrant sweatshops in New York City. In these campaigns, I focus on the relationship between garment workers, transnational protest campaigns, and the coalitions of consumers and activists sponsoring the campaigns. The purpose of transnational protest is to connect corporate image with labor practices in order to improve the latter. Therefore, a study of how garment workers are represented in the protests and of the material effects of cross-border organizing campaigns on shop floors is central to an assessment of their effectiveness. My study of transnational campaigns for labor rights, and the coalitions that they engender, sheds light on questions of "global," and even cross-border, civil society. In fact, it calls into question the possibilities of creating long-lasting transnational social movements or efforts to widen citizenship on a transnational scale.

Since cross-border protest highlights the relationship of production sites to retail outlets and corporate headquarters, companies find it more difficult to leave areas where labor abuses have been documented. However, I shall argue that a protest model that depends on criteria of consumption and public relations campaigns does not necessarily make garment manufacturers more publicly accountable or improve working conditions. Although these tactics of protest seem to fit the new configurations of production, how are workers' concerns addressed in these tactics? If what we are witnessing is a new, global politics arising in response to new business tactics, whose concerns are being represented and which issues are being left out of the protests?

The three campaigns in this study brought together consumers and activists from the North with women workers from the South, and, through media-savvy use of workers' testimonies, targeted corporations that subcontract in the third world in order to improve labor practices on shop floors. Recently, corporations have become quite susceptible to attacks on their images, their brands, and their corporate reputations. In the past, companies like Sears Roebuck and United Steel were not subject to the same kind of vulnerability to their images and brand names. As more and more areas of life become commodified—with stores like Niketown, which in themselves are leisure destinations, and Disney Worlds circling the globe from Florida to Paris, from California to Japan—branding and advertising are an ever larger part of companies' expenses, profit margins, and expansion.[2] This study opens up questions around the commodification of images and the new ways in which women's bodies are commodified in garment production, advertising, and protest.

Part of the expansion of advertising paradigms is that the image itself has become commodified: the image of the brand and retail outlet sells products, and it is that image that corporations try to protect, develop, and foster. We see this in the example of Wal-Mart, with its "Made in the USA" advertising campaign alongside its exploitative subcontracting practices, its refusal to pay minimum wage to disabled workers in its stores, and its legal and public relations–focused attempts to avoid brand damage after the discovery of undocumented workers being locked into Wal-Mart retail outlets after hours to clean the store. It is this production of corporate image that activists now target, rather than production relations on the shop floor. However, the very focus on image has its limits in terms of what changes can be made and who can participate in change. How do relations of gender, race, sexuality, nation, and class operate in these corporate-focused, consumer-oriented campaigns?

When I began my research, I was inspired by the possibilities presented by coalitions that would cross the boundaries of nation, gender, race, and class. My aim was both political and scholarly and informed by my position as a white, leftist feminist academic from a working-class background. I proposed to analyze and evaluate the ways that everyday production relations, through transnational consumer-targeted activism, were being incorporated into the spaces of retail outlets and boardrooms, bringing the spaces of EPZs and sweatshops into contention with Madison Avenue and Wall Street. While I began with a specific political concern about the labor rights of manufacturing workers under globalization, my research has shown that the position of women workers in both production and protest is complex, shifting, and very much dependent on new relations of empire, location, and hegemonic contingency.

This cross-border form of protest has come into being through the formation of what Margaret Keck and Kathryn Sikkink call "transnational advocacy networks." In the case of global antisweatshop activism, the linkage of production through layers of global subcontracting, what Gary Gereffi and Miguel Korzeniewicz call "commodity chains," has been incorporated into the repertoires of contention employed by social movement activists. In the formulation of Keck and Sikkink, various networks that have pushed for the enforcement of international labor codes and improved working conditions in garment factories throughout the world have emerged within a particular context, in circumstances where the "channels between domestic groups and their governments are blocked or hampered or where such channels are ineffectual for resolving a conflict." This work explores the relation of such transnational advocacy to ongoing forms of local advocacy and organizing among garment workers and activists in the global North and the South: Who participates in transnational advocacy networks? What opportunities are created through transnational advocacy? What possibilities are foreclosed? What is the role of class in Keck and Sikkink's formulation of the transnational?[3]

In globalized garment production, countries or areas looking to promote corporate investment and create employment for their people will turn a blind eye to and often actively promote labor violations, as I document in later chapters. The most common violations include withholding pay, union busting, mass firings and lockouts, and even limiting bathroom trips and forcing the pregnancy testing of workers. Most garment workers are too afraid of losing their jobs to complain, unionize, or protest violations. When garment workers do protest, they are fired, lose wages, and in some cases the police or paramilitary troops have been called out to violently protect the private property of the factory owners and export processing zones.[4] Transnational networks have brought worldwide attention to some instances of labor violations and worker abuse through NGO contacts, mailing lists, meetings and conferences, the Internet and e-mail, and protest actions.

When garment workers who are at the center of the transnational protest campaigns have been blocked from resolving their grievances, advocacy groups have stepped in and used their privileged networks, citizenship status, and access to language to carry out campaigns in support of labor rights. The work of the transnational networks supporting garment workers' rights is an example of what Keck and Sikkink call a "boomerang pattern" of political activity. This boomerang pattern is used when traditional channels for political action are blocked and domestic NGOs "bypass their state and directly search out international allies to try to bring pressure on their states from outside."[5] How does such a boomerang pattern work in labor organizing?

Keck and Sikkink focus their study on human rights campaigns, and a similar pattern has emerged among many transnational labor activists. In some of the campaigns in this study, however, it was Northern activists, rather than Southern NGOs, who initiated networks for political action in support of garment workers, unions, and NGOs in the South. When protest originates among Northern NGOs, focusing on problems in the South, older imperial and colonial relations are drawn on, reproduced, and often reinforced even though the explicit goal of the organizers is stated to be otherwise. Because of such relations, the origin of the protest often has had a considerable effect on reactions to and the effectiveness of transnational campaigns in the target areas.

The initiation of protest by consumers, rather than by garment workers, raises a central question about a labor protest model that does not necessarily involve shop-floor organizing and protest by those in whose name contention is carried out. What is the effect of consumer-oriented protest on production practices? Under what conditions do consumer-oriented transnational networks step in, especially in the garment industry, where the local groups consist mostly of poor, working women? I have looked at the ways that local relations of gender, sexuality, and class get taken up in the campaigns.

In garment factories throughout the world, women make up the majority of the workforce. The feminized shop floor is both a new phenomenon and, especially in the garment industry, the way things have always worked. Early in the twentieth century, ready-to-wear garment and shoe production was carried out by mostly immigrant women in U.S. cities like New York, Lowell, and Philadelphia.[6] The globalization of production has led to a "new international division of labor" (NIDL) that has been taken up in the current period by producers and protesters, both of whom rely on third world women's bodies for their maintenance, reproduction, and survival.

In the twenty-first century, garment factories are still sites of feminine labor, and garment production continues to be seen as women's work. The garment industry continues to employ immigrant women in large numbers, causing some nonimmigrant groups of workers and union members in the United States to target immigrant and offshore workers for taking U.S. jobs. Just as retailers have employed "Made in the USA" as a defense against the taint of the sweatshop, unions and workers in the United States have at times used nativism and racism in attempts to protect their own jobs.

Garment factories in the United States have used disciplinary mechanisms of immigration status, racism, sexuality, and gender hierarchies, such as holding employees' immigration papers and employing people without papers, in order to keep them working at piece rate, without overtime, and often in illegal factory sites with locked doors.[7] Through such mechanisms of control, local relations of race, gender, sexuality, citizenship status, and nation are put to use in the name of production imperatives. Their work on the shop floor, because it is in addition to maintaining their homes and raising their families in full-time, non-wage labor, means that women garment workers have to negotiate various sets of overlapping, conflicting demands on their time and energy on a daily basis.

Women on the various shop floors are relegated to the lowest-paid jobs,[8] jobs that are considered to be naturally women's work. The garment jobs that are given to women in EPZs, in factories, and as homework are seen by managers and the women themselves as being similar to housework—sewing, cleaning, and other jobs that require nimble fingers, docility, and care and attention to detail. Thus, patriarchal gender roles and representations are depended on to maintain high-intensity, hyperexploitative production relations inside the factories that produce clothing for the retail market.

These everyday, gendered realities, both at the level of the local garment factory and on a global scale, have proved to be serious barriers to women's organizing on shop floors and in communities. Two new aspects of garment industry protest campaigns have arisen in response to local organizing difficulties. Globalized garment protest is not necessarily shop-floor-based in that it involves transnational organizing and coordination; at the same time, it is very much focused on women's bodies and production practices. However, consumer activism and attacks on corporate reputation have become central to transnational campaigns, making the shop floor secondary to protest tactics. What dilemmas are posed to scholars and activists when principal protest tactics include the threat of consumer boycott, protests outside company headquarters in the United States, picketing and leafleting of retail outlets in the United States and Europe, and the promotion of media coverage on television, radio, and in newspapers? What are the effects of regimes of vertically integrated manufacturing, just-in-time production practices, and subcontracting in the garment industry on the push for living wages, fair trade, and human rights?

Productive and Symbolic Politics

Scholars have identified the current period of flexible, JIT production systems and the new international division of labor as being marked by an increased globalization of production and finance.[9] The literature of globalization has also focused on space as socially and historically produced, whose organization may shift over time.[10] Such categorizations are useful in understanding the period of transnational finance and manufacturing as something new. However, a theoretical focus on symbolic exchanges and signs leads us to view globalization as something that takes place outside of everyday relations and production regimes.[11] By exploring the relationship between transnational organizing and shop floors, I investigate the quotidian manifestations of what are seen as symbolic exchanges on the one hand, and their differentiation from relations of production on the other. In this way, I interrogate the notion of a global-local split, which, along with the material conditions of subcontracting processes, has made it easier for companies to pack up production and move elsewhere in the face of labor unrest or attempted unionization. This mobility of corporations, in turn, has become an even larger barrier to political organizing and contestation by women who work in export-oriented garment factories.[12]

To combat the difficulties in pinning down global chains of production and subcontracting in order to enforce labor rights, activists have targeted the sweatshop as a site of both material and symbolic production. This focus has helped to reinforce the sweatshop as the ultimate other of more benign, more virtual forms of capital accumulation, reproduction, and circulation, such as those of technology, media and cultural production, the welfare state, and, quintessentially, Fordist production practices. This singling out of the sweatshop—with its young, third world women employees—creates a site of exception to the day-to-day normal functions of business, a site of abject materiality that can be located—and bounded—outside the consumption centers of the United States.

The tactics of singling out the sweatshop have, furthermore, appropriated signs that depend on the languages and practices of consumption with a double-sided granting of agency, creating the sweatshop as something to be consumed by both activists and consumers. Because the tactics are directed at consumers of ready-made garments in the United States, privileged agency is given to consumers of signs and commodities; the very appropriation of the sweatshop as part of the system of signs that circulate in advertising and public relations puts forth the notion that it is only through the consumption of the sweatshop that activism can be carried out. The protests, as they have been conducted with regard to garment workers' rights, have employed sweated labor and consciousness-raising over strikes or other tactics of shop-floor-level organizing.

In other words, there is an assumption that those who consume have the right to act as political agents through the fact of their purchasing power. This double granting of agency has material repercussions in everyday events and relationships among consumers and activists, garment workers and activists, and consumers and garment workers.[13] As such, the tactics reproduce the very class, race, and, in the case of New York–based garment factories, immigration status distinctions against which they were mobilizing.

The Nation-State and Globalization

Not only have the tactics of transnational organizing reinforced a split between the material and the symbolic and between production and consumption practices, but they have also maintained an analytical split between the nation-state and the economy and between technological innovation and production practices. While social science literature on globalization has moved away from an exclusive focus on financial flows and technological innovation to examine the nation-state and its position within global capital formations and metanational governance regimes, much of this research has worked within the paradigm of national versus regional or global autonomy.[14] Saskia Sassen argues:

> Economic globalization has mostly been represented in terms of the duality national-global, where the global gains power and advantages at the

expense of the national. And it has largely been conceptualized in terms of the internationalization of capital and then only in the upper circuits of capital, notably finance.[15]

Dani Rodrik's conception of safety nets is one example of this duality; he advocates a certain level of state intervention in order to solve the problems associated with allowing capital too much sway.[16] The duality of the nation-state versus flows of capital helps to reinforce hierarchical notions of capital as something above or outside the nation-state that can be reined in by bringing corporations back home, to a certain degree, to the realm of the national. The literature pointing most emphatically to the current period of decline of the nation-state and the renewed sovereignty of capital exemplifies this top-down perspective.[17] The relationship between the national and the global is not easily defined. Rather than seeing the global and the national as separate spheres that either compete or complement each other, it is important to explore the ways in which one constitutes the other and how the split between the global and the local is continually being delineated and reconstituted politically.

With regard to the concept of the state and its relationship to society, Timothy Mitchell argues, "we need to examine the detailed political processes through which the uncertain yet powerful distinction . . . is produced." Similarly, the global-local distinction leaves unexamined the ways in which national trade laws can be used to facilitate movements of corporations among places and across nation-state boundaries, or how the United States, for example, is able to maintain sovereignty in the face of labor market pressures regarding its immigration law. Mitchell writes:

> The distinction must not be taken as a boundary between two entities, but as a line drawn internally within the network of institutional mechanisms through which a social and political order is maintained. The ability to have an internal distinction appear as though it were the external boundary between two separate objects is the distinctive technique of the modern political order.[18]

Because of this distinction, politics of transnational protest in the garment industry—when transnational retailers are called on to act as corporate good citizens—is often unable to address questions of governance or accountability. When appeals are made directly to corporations, in the arena of the retail outlet and the stock exchange, they help legitimize finance capital as something both outside and above the workings of the nation-state. Corporations, in this model, become the final authority and are accorded the ultimate power to grant concessions in their labor practices.[19] In some cases, when appeals, supported by the threat of U.S. or international law, are made to corporations, they bring the state back in as an arbitrator. While acknowledging activists' claims against corporate domination, this maintains an apparent division between the global, seen as the corporate; the national, or the laws of the nation-state; and international regimes.

Commodity Chains and Labor Flows

Gereffi and Korzeniewicz examine commodity chains under global capitalism, historically and in the contemporary period, and look at the ways that retailers and buying considerations shape production networks globally. They are able to demonstrate the various stages that production networks go through in order to produce a commodity that is then marketed by one company. Gereffi's description of the workings of commodity chains is composed of material, spatial, and political components:

> Global commodity chains have three main dimensions: (1) an input-output structure (i.e., a set of products and services linked together in a sequence of value-adding economic activities); (2) a territoriality (i.e., spatial dispersion or concentration of production and distribution networks, composed of enterprises of different sizes and types; and (3) a governance structure (i.e., authority and power relationships that determine how financial, material, and human resources are allocated and flow within a chain).[20]

Sassen looks at international labor flows, maintaining that U.S. investment and immigration policy attract migrants and that they help to explain the creation of and changes in world labor markets.[21] The consumer campaigns put such labor market questions at the center of politics and put commodity chains firmly on the policy table. By highlighting workers' concerns, the campaigns attempt to call attention to the labor flows and working conditions, discussed by Sassen, in order to influence the governance structure of commodity chains. The problem with consumer-oriented campaigns is that, after documenting labor violations carefully and calling for workers' rights, the campaigns place authority back into the laps of transnational corporations by appealing to them for clemency and labor patronage. In so doing, the protests normalize the concept that corporations—and not governments or unions—make all of the decisions about workers' rights and that the only route to change is to appeal to corporate beneficence and self-interest. For example, high-profile protest depends on corporate vulnerability to shifts in retail position and public image. Such vulnerability shows that Gereffi and Korzeniewicz's commodity chains can potentially work both ways: conditions or grievances inside the production network can affect the policies of retailers and corporate buying decisions. As Miriam J. Wells argues, "economic configurations—too often portrayed as the inevitable and value-neutral outcomes of changing global economic structure—may instead be primarily the result of local sociopolitical conflicts."[22]

Cross-border organizing in the garment industry arises out of the specific combination of transnational production and capital flows in a world of nation-states.[23] While the nation-state and the international system determine labor and trade law, they also provide an iron cage of law that allows corporations transnational mobility and the freedom to act *as if* they are not subject to the boundaries of the nation-state. This combination allows corporations and capital the freedom to act globally, while individual citizens are subject to immigration barriers on the one hand and an increasingly ineffectual labor law on the other. These factors, along with the small amount of capital needed for garment production and the relatively quick time needed to complete orders, allow businesses to shift manufacturing sites to other countries in the event of widespread local protest, the enforcement of national labor laws, or rising wages.[24]

An increasingly common goal of garment industry protest has been to push companies to adopt codes of conduct for labor rights and to establish a system of independent, third-party monitoring of working conditions by local NGOs and human rights and religious groups.[25] Ideally, cross-border protest that attempts to focus on production sites and retail outlets as well as corporate headquarters would make it rather pointless for companies to leave areas where labor abuses have been documented.

The three case studies I present exemplify the organizational methods of this transnational movement. Each case demonstrates new tactics of protest in the garment industry and in industries with similarly transnational production practices as employed by a number of coalitions that focus on labor rights. The El Salvador campaign was carried out by a combination of U.S.-based solidarity organizations and religious groups along with human rights organizations in El Salvador. The Bangladesh agreement was the result of a coalition between U.S.-funded Bangladeshi labor unions, the U.S. Embassy, UN-based organizations, and local garment manufacturers. The New York City case brought together U.S.-based nongovernmental organizations and labor unions. All three protests depended on consumer boycotts aimed at corporations with lax labor standards and relied on third-party monitoring to enforce labor regulations, but in each coalition, workers were represented in different ways.

Members of the U.S. Congress and the U.S.-based Child Labor Coalition began the Bangladesh campaign in 1992 in order to end the use of children's labor in garment factories producing for U.S. manufacturers such as Wal-Mart and JCPenney. The organizers of the campaign were pushing the U.S. Congress to threaten economic sanctions if Bangladesh failed to enforce anti-child-labor laws in its garment industry. Pressure on the U.S. Congress was combined with a media campaign in the United States to encourage a consumer boycott of clothes produced by children in foreign countries. After the threat of sanctions and the consumer boycott, the Bangladesh Garment Manufacturers and Exporters Association (BGMEA) fired ten thousand child workers in the space of two weeks, thereby invoking censure, protest, and open letters in the press from children's rights organizations and labor activists throughout the country. In light of a threatened expulsion of its ambassador from Bangladesh, U.S. Embassy officials met with officials from the government of Bangladesh, UNICEF, and the ILO (International Labor Organization) to present a compromise to the BGMEA. Over the course of a year, the compromise was rejected, renegotiated, and finally accepted on July 4, 1995. Negotiations ended in a memorandum of understanding (MOU) that created schools and stipends for the garment workers who had been fired, along with phasing out child labor from the garment export industry and a system of monitoring by the signatories to ensure compliance.

The El Salvador campaign was carried out by the National Labor Committee (NLC) and other U.S.-based NGOs and U.S. and Salvadoran labor and religious organizations against the mass firing of unionized workers and the violation of labor codes at the Mandarin International factory in El Salvador's San Marcos free trade zone. Mandarin subcontracts production for the U.S. manufacturer Gap Inc., which owns the retail outlets Gap, Old Navy, and Banana Republic. The El Salvador protest and its resolution involved a unified push by labor unions, U.S. and Salvadoran religious and human rights organizations, and solidarity networks to improve working conditions at Mandarin. The tactics in this case included consumer boycotts of Gap clothing, protests at retail outlets, and a tour of the United States and Europe by Salvadoran garment workers to educate consumers about working conditions. This campaign succeeded, by 1996, in setting up a "Code of Conduct for Labor Rights" for all manufacturers of clothing for Gap Inc. and in forming an independent monitoring group at the Mandarin factory to enforce labor law and support the right to worker organization in the factory. The consequences for labor organizing, however, were troubling. The Sindicato de Empresa de Trabajadores de Mandarin International

(SETMI), the garment workers' union, was left out of the negotiation process, and by the end of the 1990s its membership had dwindled. A company union, Association of Mandarin International Workers (ATEMISA), which was created during the corporate campaign, in the meantime has seen its membership grow into the hundreds.

The New York case is part of the "Stop Sweatshops" campaign. The campaign brought UNITE (Union of Needletrades, Industrial, and Textile Employees), the U.S. garment workers' union, together with immigrants' rights groups to protest the abuse of immigrant workers and the sweatshop conditions under which clothes are produced for retailers like Wal-Mart. Celebrity labels such as the Kathie Lee Gifford clothing line have been targeted in media campaigns carried out by UNITE and the NLC. The factories have also increasingly been targets of U.S. Department of Labor raids on illegal sweatshops throughout New York City. Results of these campaigns have included advertisements and lobbying by Gifford and Governor George Pataki of New York that focus on the elimination of sweatshop production of garments. Gifford was shown publicly handing out wads of money to garment workers from factories in New York making her clothing line. Since the Kathie Lee line also produced clothing in Honduras under similar conditions, for the first time labor violations in New York City were linked in the media to those offshore in the manufacture of garments sold by the world's largest retailer.

NIDL in Production and Protest

The new international division of labor that marks global production practices often is reproduced in the politics of protest. U.S.- and European-based activists define the tactics of transnational protest that, in turn, are focused on corporations with retail outlets and headquarters in the North. Furthermore, the target audiences of the campaigns are the U.S. and European consumers who buy the clothing made in garment factories throughout the world. The women who produce clothing also provide the raw material of their testimony, which is then incorporated into particular repertoires of contention chosen to appeal to consumers and to affect corporate image.

Keck and Sikkink, borrowing from Alison Brysk, have developed a typology of tactics that transnational networks employ in "their efforts at persuasion, socialization, and pressure" that consists of

> (1) *information politics* [that] . . . quickly and credibly generate politically usable information and move to where it has the most impact; (2) *symbolic politics* [that] . . . call upon symbols, actions, or stories that make

sense of a situation for an audience that is frequently far away; (3) *leverage politics* [that] . . . call upon powerful actors to affect a situation where weaker members of a network are unlikely to have influence; and (4) *accountability politics* [that] . . . hold powerful actors to their previously stated policies or principles.[26]

While these politics of information, symbol, leverage, and accountability are tactically powerful, they account for the actions of people in only one site of the transnational social movement. Those in other sites do the work of making the clothing that consumers wear, as well as that of shop-floor organizing. They provide the impetus, information, and testimonies for U.S.-based activists who then carry out the politics within the boundaries of the United States. This complicates the notion of class for Keck and Sikkink and in the tactics and politics of garment industry protest.

Women in garment factories around the world, whether or not they have been involved in organizing protest on the shop floors, are the ones who "quickly and credibly generate" the information that is then used by the Northern activists to target Northern corporations. Although the information generated is intended to be used to improve working conditions in the factories that are the focus of protest, its generation by one group and narrativization by another tends to privilege the agency of the activists who are in control of the information's use and dissemination. Many of the women and men who work in the factories that are at the center of transnational protest and of much scholarly work on globalization have carried out extensive community and shop-floor-organizing projects in their own localities. Their agency, however, is often defined by and circulated through transnational protest and academic publications, such as this one. This lays bare some of the problematics of activist and scholarly transnationality, since opportunities for participating in spaces that are marked as transnational are already determined by one's access to U.S. media outlets, retail spaces, language formations, and dollars that can be used for consumer subjectivity.

While transnational campaigns have had a number of positive effects, within individual factories and for the industry as a whole, it is important to examine them as productions. This study, while keeping in mind the benefits gained through transnational labor activism, will analyze the production practices and labor relations that make up the campaigns in order to expose the problematics of global production and protest as parallel and mutually dependent formations. Within the globalized politics that results from consumer-focused, transnational labor organizing, the agency that comes from acts of witnessing and testimony and from shop-floor and feminist organizing is reshaped to fit the demands of image making and knowledge production. As I will demonstrate, the politics of information privileged in tactics emphasizing brand name and corporate reputation creates inequalities within each particular movement, even one whose goal is to break down inequalities on shop floors and in retail spaces and neighborhoods throughout the world.

Achievements and Symbolic Politics

The anti-child-labor campaign succeeded in providing schooling for children under the age of fourteen who had been working in the garment industry in Bangladesh.[27] The MOU that resulted from the Bangladesh campaign required that export-oriented garment factories be inspected regularly for child workers, and most factories have been found to comply. Since the 1995 signing of the MOU, ILO, UNICEF, the government of Bangladesh, and the BGMEA have worked together to further the access to schooling for garment workers through the Earn and Learn program. In June 2000, all parties signed a second memorandum of understanding that would continue and expand the provisions of the 1995 MOU and maintain the factory inspection and schooling program. The Bangladesh program was replicated among soccer ball producers in Pakistan, with mixed results.

The achievements of the NLC-Gap campaign included the institution of an independent monitoring group at the Mandarin factory, which provided a model for NGO and human rights–centered monitoring in factories throughout the worldwide garment industry. At the end of the campaign, Mandarin rehired 35 of the 350 fired union members and provided greater bathroom and drinking water access at the factory while ending conditions like forced birth control. The campaign also had an effect on production practices and working conditions in the greater garment industry. As a result of the Mandarin publicity, Gap Inc. promised to examine the working conditions in factories of its other subcontractors on a regular basis. My research shows that the 1995 Gap campaign, the 1996 Kathie Lee campaign, and the 1995 signing of the MOU on child labor in Bangladesh were part of a larger series of antisweatshop protests that called attention to worldwide labor violations. As we recognize these achievements, it is important to explore other consequences of the campaigns, their effects on the shop floors and neighborhoods of garment workers and on global production practices, and the possibilities for agency in each site—shop floors, neighborhoods, and unions, as well as retail outlets, stock markets, NGOs, and development agencies in both the third and first worlds.

The "symbolic politics" employed by transnational activists also has had perverse consequences, since the symbols, actions, and stories that are called on have particular histories of race, gender, class, and nation that often go unrecognized in their appropriation. In the case of the transnational labor campaigns, the target audience is made up of consumers who, while being conscientious, rely on the logic and signs of advertising regimes on the one hand and on colonial legacies of race, gender, and sexuality on the other. Transnational activists' strategies of focusing on advertising, corporate reputation, and consumption raise two serious concerns. First, the very language of consumption and consumer agency takes buying as its main practice, and its actors are those with the money to shop. Since people who make the clothing at the center of transnational labor activism do not have access to the disposable income—or, often, the retail outlets—necessary for consumer action, they are left out of the symbolic and material political activism that is at the heart of consumer-directed protest campaigns. At the same time, advertising regimes rely on exclusions and performances of identity that are bounded by particular nation-spaces through the circulation of national currency, and, in the United States, they depend exclusively on gender, race, and class discourses that idealize particular notions of womanhood. This dependence circumscribes the potential for agency that lies outside of the ideal and outside of a nation-space bounded by dollars. If political action takes the form of a boycott or embargo of products of a particular brand or country, the action itself depends on people with access to money and sites from which to buy the boycotted or embargoed product.

Within the idealized notion of consumption relations, shopping often becomes central to desire and longing for the familiar while at the same time bounding difference in ways that are easily consumed. Agency that takes place outside this consumption paradigm—in productive work, shop-floor organizing, or "fair trade" initiatives—is framed in ways that make it politically appealing in the North, often mirroring both advertising images and colonialist tropes. This transnational frame, in turn, determines the forms that production and consumption take, both symbolically and materially, within the discourse of the global. These frames of globalization and transnationality, which at the same time focus on the retail, also determine which actors and which forms of agency are privileged and which are naturalized or ignored.

Even as I take on the discursive production of globalization and transnationality centered on consumption, I do not assume that the category of consumers is a monolithic one or that it is homogeneous in terms of race, class, sexuality, gender, or geographical location. Rather, I look at the ways in which consumption practices, with all of the contradictory, overlapping, and messy relations and meanings they entail, inform the transnational politics of labor in the garment industry. How does the discourse of labor rights combine with that of conscientious consumption to bring forth this new, transnational politics?

In the case of Bangladesh, the everyday struggles of the child workers themselves—and their positions as actors and agents in their homes and on the shop floors—are downplayed in order to highlight their victimhood in the face of transnational capital and abusive local factory owners. In the same way, organizing among women and the multiple responsibilities and challenges that women garment workers negotiate at all times are de-emphasized in favor of highlighting their identities as workers in the new sweatshop.

The campaigns' emphasis on the victimhood of women and children who work in the garment industry raises questions about agency among garment workers and campaign organizers. Much of the force of the trans-national labor organizing comes from the testimonies and witnessing of women garment workers from the factories that are at the center of the campaigns. The act of witnessing is a courageous one and an essential part of the political activism of women and of garment workers in the trans-national arena. Because the interpretation of testimonies and the activ-ism on the world's shop floors and in various localities are then performed under the auspices of (Northern) public relations imperatives, the courage and complexity of those testimonies are often sacrificed in exchange for sound-bite appeal.

I look at testimony as both living proof and production, keeping in mind the legacies and politics of witnessing within various forms of activism—from shop floors, communities, and activist organizing, to re-tail sites, media outlets, and corporate imperatives. Within the discourse of the transnational, where are Northern consumers and activists placed, how are garment workers and their activism shown? Often, the consumers and activists are presented within the frame of protest as acting in solidarity with—rather than determining—protest on the shop floor, and garment workers are portrayed as unmediated agents doing direct battle with trans-national corporations. Within the official narratives of transnational orga-nizing, there is no portrayal of the history—of consumption, production, and activism, and differences of class, gender, race, nationality, colonialism, and privilege—that has mediated representations of garment workers and their agency.

Similarly, the politics of leverage and accountability discussed by Keck and Sikkink depends on appealing to and calling on powerful actors—in the case of transnational labor protest, corporate heads and celebrity spokespeople—to implement and advocate the demands of the transnational campaigns. Not only does the reliance on powerful actors grant those with power a privileged political position precisely because of their own compromise with and maintenance of capital relations, it also depends explicitly on the patronage and sense of noblesse oblige of retailers and stockholders to concede to consumer demands. In other words, consumer-based protest depends on corporations seeing the effects on their bottom line and voluntarily becoming good global citizens. The sustained agency of women in local communities, as garment workers, consumers, participants, and activists, is often sacrificed, and in some cases curtailed, in favor of corporate-directed "global" politics.

Finally, transnational labor protest has relied on consumer activism working within a political economy of signs and symbols where value is reproduced and added through the promulgation of brand names and trademarks. The very attacks on corporate image may serve, in the end, to reproduce the primacy of brand name through regimes of conscientious consumption. By naturalizing the "new" political economy, with its globalized circuits of capital and corporate reputation, we grant credence to the assumption that we are all equally victims of the totality of capital—moneyed consumers, exploited workers, and well-intentioned corporate heads. This denies the continued hierarchy of nation-states and the fact that, even in the discourse of the transnational and the global, there still remain concentrations of power that draw from notions of modernity and difference on the one hand and the privileges of capital on the other. The everyday struggles and negotiations of transnational capital and the meaning of those struggles are often downplayed in favor of a political focus on the metaphenomenon of globalization. Is it, in fact, inevitable that market forms of justice prevail over other alternatives in the form of the globalized political participation of conscientious consumption?[28]

This particular form of globalized political participation has come about with the reinvention of the sweatshop as what Mitchell calls the "constitutive outside" of capitalist modernity. His discussion of "the displacements opened up by the different space of the non-West and the ways in which this space is made to appear different" is helpful here. The sweatshop performs a double role, being both central to capitalist production relations in certain manufacturing sectors and incompatible with the progressive rationalization of production and the humane treatment of workers. Mitchell argues with reference to modernity: "Elements that appear incompatible with what is modern, Western, or capitalist are systematically subordinated and marginalized, placed in a position outside of the unfolding of history. Yet in the very processes of their subordination and exclusion, it can be shown, such elements infiltrate and compromise that history."[29]

The different space of the sweatshop within the history of a progressive, rationalized capitalism is performed both in corporations' own narratives of their production practices and in the conceptualization of the global sweatshop held by U.S.-based consumers, scholars, and activists. In this different space, workers themselves are viewed as outside progressive capitalist narratives, and their agency as producers is thus circumscribed. Because of this conceptualization of the sweatshop, it is only through practices of consumption, in sites that are within the realm of the modern, or postmodern, that agency can be recognized as such.

This project focuses on six major questions and implications of transnational protest in the garment industry. In chapter 1, "Children, Schools, and Labored Questions," I look at specific issues of agency and citizenship within the context of the U.S.-sponsored campaign against the use of child labor in Bangladesh's export-oriented garment industry. The campaign, which brought together U.S. politicians, the U.S. State Department, and UN organizations, pushed to end the employment of children under the age of fourteen in Bangladesh's export-oriented garment industry. It was resolved in 1995 with the signing of the MOU that phased out child labor by placing underage garment workers, with the support of a monthly stipend, into nonformal schools set up by local NGOs and regularly inspected by signatories of the MOU. The proposed consumer boycott, the U.S. congressional legislation, and the MOU had unforeseen effects in Bangladesh. I explore the anti-child-labor campaign and its consequences through an analysis of the symbolic politics of child labor and the notions of agency that informed the campaign and its resolution. To determine who participated and how in the anti-child-labor campaign involves examining various assumptions about the position of children, women, garment workers, and citizens in Bangladesh, the United States, and other sites of export-oriented industrialization throughout the world.

Chapter 2, "Organizing in Times of (Post)War," addresses the possibilities of transnational labor organizing and the legacies of the 1980s civil war in El Salvador. Through an analysis of the 1995 Gap campaign carried out by the New York–based National Labor Committee, I explore the position of the shop floor within the parameters of globalized production and protest. My research in this chapter includes interviews, factory visits, and participant observation to look at the on-the-ground consequences of coalition politics that organized around issues of workers' rights at the Mandarin International garment factory in El Salvador. I argue that the shop floor is incorporated into the campaign as part of a conceptual and material split between the local and the global, which has implications for both the sites and methods of transnational organizing and depends on the denial of multiple histories of organizing, militarism, and counterinsurgency and gendered agency.

Chapter 3, "The Ideal of Transnational Organizing," takes up the question of symbolic politics by looking at the ways that gender, race, class, and celebrity came together in a widely publicized antisweatshop campaign in New York City. I analyze the 1996 NLC-UNITE protest campaign against the labor practices of Wal-Mart subcontractors producing the Kathie Lee line of clothing in Honduras and New York City. A century ago, questions of child labor, sweatshops, and working conditions featured prominently in consumer-based, government-directed campaigns and in shop-floor organizing initiatives in the garment and textile industries. The current antisweatshop movement differs from its predecessors both in its global focus and in its increasing focus on brand names and advertising image. I explore the ways in which Kathie Lee Gifford and her line of clothing were used to increase profits and then to protest working conditions in the garment industry.

In chapter 4, "Disciplining Bodies," I explore questions of labor regulation and discipline on the factory floor and in protest campaigns. I focus on sweatshop conditions in different sites of garment production and the ways in which they are addressed politically. Specifically, I look at the manifestations of Fordist regulation in El Salvador's Lenor factory, the deployment of immigration status in garment factories in New York City's Chinatown, and the lockout of more than five thousand workers from the Youngone factory, a Bangladeshi EPZ. These methods of discipline and regulation employ both typically Fordist methods and methods that have been categorized as post-Fordist. This chapter demonstrates that consumer campaigns are not necessarily a new solution to the old problem of sweatshops; in fact, methods of labor discipline are often redeployed and reinforced within the very actions taken to contest them.

Chapter 5, "Women First?" looks at the gender makeup of the industry and the problematic of the new international division of labor within transnational labor campaigns. I investigate gender relations on the factory floors and among participants in the protest campaigns. In this chapter, I return to Mandarin and compare it to a campaign that was organized around an incident in which hundreds of women at the DINDEX factory in El Salvador collapsed in the space of a few hours. Both of these cases from El Salvador resemble the ongoing efforts to organize women being carried out in Bangladesh by the activist research group UBINIG (a Bengali acronym for Research on Alternatives to Development). While all three organizing efforts have been successful in a number of ways, I argue that local relations and histories matter as much as, if not more than, the organization of labor campaigns at the transnational level.

In chapter 6, "Living Proof," I explore the uses, meanings, provisions, and circulation of living proof by garment workers that is manifested in testimony and witnessing, in their gendered and raced bodies, in their production relations and their possibilities for consumption, and in their discussions of their hopes, pain, and agency within both transnational protest and production. I also address my position as a North American researcher and call into question my own complicity in circulating testimony and living proof by putting forth a critique in the name of radical practice while building my career on theorizing garment workers' subaltern subject positions.[30]

Finally, in the epilogue, I discuss the circulation of images, commodities, and gender in the production, marketing, and protest of the garment industry. I further explore the three central themes of this study: how the global-local split present in the discourse of globalization is reproduced in transnational labor protest; the use of symbolic politics in the campaigns and on the shop floor, as well as at the centrality of relations of gender, race, class, and nation to global garment production and protest; and a reaffirmation of the need to focus on the many-layered negotiations and contestations of politics in all localities, and the equally important need to place women at the center of protest over the new global sweatshop. Activists and scholars alike have to investigate ways to shift transnational organizing paradigms away from globalized discursive formations that retain power in metropolitan centers and deny the privileges of the nation-state and to redistribute resources, access, representations, and labor practices in more inclusive, encompassing ways. We have to work against and within the contingencies of hegemony. One step toward that goal would be to recognize that women garment workers, on whom the entire network of economic, political, and social relations is based, are subjects of transnational protest and producers of the global even as they are taken up in the service of Other agendas, imperial and otherwise.

1

Children, Schools, and Labored Questions

The labor of women and children is at the center of production within and protest against the new sweatshop. As both producers and consumers— and, since the late 1970s, as activists—women and children throughout the world have been increasingly crucial participants in the political economy of globalization. The urban spaces in which they work, furthermore, can be seen as a challenge to dominant paradigms of the global city. Cities like Dhaka (Bangladesh), San Salvador, Brooklyn, and Queens produce and reproduce the discursive and material formations of globalization just as centrally as do Tokyo, London, and New York.[1] Because of the effect of the global-local split, globalized production and protest have tended to appeal to and naturalize power as created, maintained, and wielded at the uppermost strata of society. The very centrality of third world migrant women and children to globalization discourse rests on the notion that they are coming into the global political economy from the outside. That children especially are conceived as innocent, pre-rational, and pre-economic, and therefore as extreme victims of global political-economic flows, makes space for activism and protest by children and about children.[2]

Why has there been such a strong focus on child labor as particularly emblematic of the new sweatshop? Activists and policy makers have pushed for the elimination of child labor in the export-oriented garment industry precisely because of its appeal as an issue that can be supported by a large and diverse number of people throughout the world.[3] By looking at the manifestations of U.S. anti-child-labor activism in Bangladesh, however, the very neatness of child labor as a political issue is called into question. As

I will demonstrate in this chapter, the focus on child labor to the exclusion of other violations leaves out a number of factors, including the myriad consequences of action in one part of the world on relations in another. Within the discourse of child labor, no space is allowed for dynamics that are both internal to Bangladesh and that are part of the relationship of Bangladeshis to capital, transnational processes, and empire. One result of the U.S.- and European-based child-labor activism and threatened boycott is that class, gender, and age relations on the shop floor and in communities disappear in favor of straightforward protest against the use of child labor. The campaign, therefore, led to unforeseen class alignments within Bangladesh and a large-scale protest against U.S. protectionism, along with longer-term resentments of U.S. imperialism in Bangladesh.

The anti-child-labor campaign began in 1992 with a united effort by consumer groups, U.S. politicians, the U.S. State Department, and UN organizations. Their goal was to end the employment of children under fourteen years of age in Bangladeshi garment factories producing for U.S. manufacturers such as Wal-Mart and JCPenney. Their tactics included a call for U.S. and European consumer boycotts of clothing and other goods produced by child laborers in exporting countries and the threat of an embargo of Bangladesh by the U.S. government that would encourage the enforcement of anti-child-labor laws. U.S. legislators and activists also pushed for the promise of alternative schooling programs for children working in Bangladesh's garment industry, to be funded by U.S. labor unions, UNICEF, and the ILO. On July 4, 1995, an MOU was signed to phase out child labor from the Bangladeshi export-oriented garment industry. As a result of the agreement, former underage garment workers were placed in nonformal schools and a group of monitors from the ILO, the BGMEA, and the government of Bangladesh were employed to enforce it.

In fieldwork carried out in Dhaka during 1996 and 1998, I interviewed garment workers, visited their homes, and spent time at factory sites, union centers, NGOs, and government and international organization offices. Through the interviews, participant observation, and analysis of industry trends and data, I explored the implications and consequences of the MOU for the people who work in Bangladesh's export-oriented garment industry. I examined the child-labor campaign's relationship to Dhaka's garment industry and to the people who participate in it.

I focused on the everyday manifestations of the anti-child-labor campaign in order to grasp what Foucault called the "capillary form of existence" of the MOU and the "synaptic regime of power, a regime of its exercise *within* the social body, rather than *from above* it."[4] My analysis of the shop floors, streets, and garment workers' schools in Dhaka questions the prevalent assumption of globalization as a metamovement, something that occurs outside of everyday relations and is more related to itself than to anything occurring in specific locales among groups of people. This notion of globalization as something both omnipotent and omniscient leads scholars to view it as the inevitable "end of history"[5] and an often unintentional assumption that people are the unwilling recipients of action from above, with no recourse other than acceptance of the terms of the global economy. This effaces the multiple forms of agency practiced by women, children, and men garment workers in Bangladesh, El Salvador, New York City, and other sites, as well as the agency practiced by factory owners and managers, union organizers, consumers, and the first world organizers of transnational activism.

The children in Bangladesh's garment industry are neither passive victims of capital nor active agents of protest. In the case of the anti-child-labor activism, the proponents of the consumer boycott and the MOU offered them as models to be applied to other countries and other industries; at the same time, others have criticized the Bangladeshi experience as a protectionist ploy on the part of U.S. unions and business interests. I will problematize both positions in order to look more closely at how the campaign has been constructed and narrated through the relationships between U.S. and European activists, international organizations, Bangladeshi garment workers, and business representatives. As such, I push to reframe our thinking around agency, activism, and hierarchy within the discourse of transnationality.

Through my exploration of the protests against child labor and the signing of the MOU, I question the naturalization of the industry as a whole. Part of this naturalization includes viewing Bangladesh and South Asia as the particular site of the problem, creating the necessity for U.S. and European consumers and government officials to act in the name of garment workers in Bangladesh in order to normalize these particularly aberrant shop floors.

At the same time, I do not intend to downplay the achievements of the NGOs and international agencies involved in the creation, signing, and implementation of the MOU or the resulting changes in working conditions between 1996 and 1998. I wholeheartedly support legislation banning the use of child labor in production and its enforcement—whether export-oriented or not. However, I maintain that looking at the campaign to eradicate child labor in Bangladesh's garment industry—in Dhaka's neighborhoods, schools, and garment factories—will help us understand the everyday effects of policies that seem by nature to be transnational.

By focusing on the manifestations of protest and capital in these everyday spaces of conflict, we can begin to get a picture of the complexities involved in what seem to have been straightforward questions of solving problems or fighting for social justice.

Discourses of Globalization and Transnationality

Sweatshops, export processing zones, and garment workers have been frequent subjects of scholarship and activism since the 1980s. Increased flexibility in sourcing and production, along with the compression of temporal and spatial relations to the point of near-instantaneity, have been described as new, post-Fordist methods of capital accumulation.[6] In keeping with these new methods, the garment industry has taken advantage of its low start-up costs and capital investment ability to produce in sites scattered throughout the world and to move wherever labor is cheapest and labor organizing least likely.[7] A central aspect of the post-Fordist model has been the development of the new international division of labor, where, as Mies argues, "Developing countries increasingly become areas of production of consumer goods for rich countries, whereas rich countries increasingly become areas of consumption only. . . . [C]orporations must mobilize consumers in the rich countries to buy all the items produced in Third World countries. In both strategies the mobilization of women plays an essential role."[8]

Within the context of the NIDL, one recurring puzzle has been addressed by scholars and activists: how to fight for, and guarantee, workers' rights in particular sites when factory and company owners can simply move to other areas where labor guarantees do not exist.[9] An increasingly widespread answer to the problem of the combination of transnational production and capital flows in a world of nation-states has been to organize transnational campaigns based on consumer boycotts that support the rights of the people producing garments for the "world" (U.S. and European) economy.[10] In both production and consumption patterns and in the protest campaigns, the central position of women and children as consumers, producers, and activists has raised questions about citizenship and participation in the global political economy.[11] Do notions of citizenship become divided along the lines of race, gender, social class, nation, and age in much the same way as those of the new international division of labor?

Such a questioning is especially important in light of Nancy Fraser and Linda Gordon's critique of T. H. Marshall's 1949 essay "Citizenship and Social Class." With specific reference to the history of Great Britain, Marshall defines three stages of citizenship: civil citizenship, corresponding roughly to the eighteenth century; political citizenship, arising over the course of the nineteenth century; and social citizenship, developed in the twentieth century in the guise of the Keynesian welfare state. Fraser and Gordon argue: "When questions of gender and race are put at the centre of the inquiry, key elements of Marshall's analysis become problematic. His periodization of the three stages of citizenship, for example, fits the experience of white working men only. . . . His conceptual distinctions . . . presuppose, rather than problematize, gender and racial hierarchy."[12] If scholars and activists could bring questions of transnationality and citizenship into debates over labor rights, we could begin to do the work of making hierarchies of gender, race, class, and nation central to debates over agency.

For example, in Bangladesh, as elsewhere, the majority of workers in export-oriented industries are women.[13] There is a complex, multifaceted debate about the role of the garment industry among scholars who work in the fields of Bangladeshi, gender, and labor development. Several studies have been written about whether the garment industry is good for the women who work in it and whether it allows them access to the same citizenship practices traditionally enjoyed by men. Some scholars have argued that the garment industry's influence in Bangladesh has been a liberating one, bringing women into the public sphere. Although these scholars have reservations, they laud the fact that it has drawn women out of their homes and into factories, provided independence and a means of support, and offered them the option of not contracting an arranged marriage or of not accepting undesirable offers of marriage.[14] Other Bangladeshi feminist scholars have tried to temper the notion of empowerment through wage labor by pointing out the drawbacks associated with factory work, the nonliberating aspects of wage labor, and the complicated relationships that are involved on the factory floor and in homes for the women who work.[15]

U.S.-based debates over citizenship would be enriched by such discussions of the public/private split and the role of the social in garment workers' lives, even though such discussions are not necessarily couched in the language of citizenship or liberal rights from whence they are drawn. The language of empowerment, often employed in mainstream developmental discourses that center on the agency of women outside of the United States and Europe, could be productively placed in conversation with that of development in order to decenter the position of U.S. and European liberalism, discourses of the rational individual, and human rights through a focus on the everyday struggles of Bangladeshi women working in the garment industry. European and U.S. consumers and activists who participated in the boycott of Bangladeshi garments and pushed for the abolition of child labor have limited the potential of such an engagement by staking their protests on a single issue: the ages of the people working in the garment factories.[16]

The Origins of the Campaign in the United States

The trajectory of the campaign against child labor in Bangladesh begins in the United States within the context of a North American union movement on the defensive in light of 1980s Reaganomics and its continuation under the neoliberalism of George Bush and Bill Clinton into the 1990s.[17] Not only was union membership in severe decline, but the early 1990s marked the culmination of corporate downsizing in the United States and the export of U.S.-based manufacturing jobs to offshore production sites that would guarantee cheap labor and a nonunionized work force. According to Richard Barnet and John Cavanagh, "By 1991 more than half of all U.S. exports and imports were transfers of components and services within the same global corporation, most of them flying the American flag." They go on to cite the following figures: "In 1950 about a third of all American jobs were in manufacturing; by the mid-1980s factory employment accounted for only 20 percent of the work force, and by the early 1990s only 16 percent."[18] Often, rather than blame neoliberal policies and a corporate-focused nation-state, conventional wisdom blamed offshore workers for taking jobs from U.S. workers.

The early antisweatshop movement played on such fears while at the same time trying to focus more blame on rapacious corporations whose race to the bottom hurt all workers. In this period of U.S.-based manufacturing decline and severe drops in union membership, the AFL-CIO and U.S. politicians began to focus on the use of child labor in foreign manufacturing industries. The Bangladesh campaign became the first that brought together U.S.-based unions and politicians to address the effects of globalization on working conditions in the United States and abroad. The campaign was launched by introducing Senator Tom Harkin's 1992 bill that proposed "to prohibit the importation of goods produced abroad with child labor."[19] In so doing, the proposed Child Labor Deterrence Act of 1992 combined an invocation of the 1959 UN Declaration of the Rights of the Child[20] with an assertion that "adult workers in the United States and other developed countries should not have their jobs imperiled by imports produced by child labor in developing countries."[21] The proposed 1992 act was subsequently tabled. It was followed, however, by a 1993 call by the AFL-CIO international division, the Asian-American Free Labor Institute (AAFLI), and a group of forty U.S. NGOs, all under the umbrella of the Child Labor Coalition, for U.S. consumers to boycott clothing produced in Bangladesh.[22]

U.S. politicians, NGOs, and labor unions organized the Child Labor

Deterrence Act[23] and the call for boycott based on research being carried out by AAFLI on the number of factories employing children in Bangladesh, which was later published in its 1994 *A Report on Child Labor in Bangladesh*.[24] Politically, it is important to note that the campaign took place in the context of other efforts by both liberals and conservatives in the United States, backed by unions and labor NGOs, to promote trade protectionism as a solution to downsizing, massive layoffs, and diminishing union membership in manufacturing sectors.[25] For example, the National Labor Committee produced *Paying to Lose Our Jobs* in September 1992, which looks at how U.S. taxpayers' money subsidized U.S. Association for International Development (USAID) programs to create export processing zones in the third world, which gave tax incentives to corporations producing offshore for the U.S. market.[26]

The proliferation of reports on child labor laid bare the contradictions between the position of the U.S. nation-state as labor champion and promoter of trade liberalization. Of course, the focus on child labor helped to obfuscate these neoliberal problematics. We can see evidence of this in mid-1994, with the July publication by the U.S. Department of Labor of *By the Sweat and Toil of Children*, vol. 1, *The Use of Child Labor in Manufactured and Mined Imports*.[27] The evidence presented in the chapter on Bangladesh is based heavily on the AAFLI report, making an even stronger case for connecting the use of child labor abroad with the loss of jobs at home. In September 1994, a hearing on child labor was held for the U.S. Senate Subcommittee on Labor.[28] *By the Sweat and Toil of Children* used evidence from the AAFLI report, which was then backed up by the congressional hearings, which included key testimony on Bangladesh from Nazma Akther, a garment worker and labor organizer from Dhaka. Akther went on to become an organizer and leader of the Bangladesh Independent Garment Union (BIGU). With support—financial, logistical, and organizational—from AAFLI, BIGU was founded in 1994 because, its founders argued, "Many [garment] workers were dissatisfied with the existing unions which claimed to represent the interests of garment workers. These unions were either extensions of political parties, ineffective or corrupt and more often than not, a combination of all three."[29] Thus, by the end of 1994, the case for boycotting Bangladeshi exports to the United States was strongly built up with the support of government, NGO, and union groups in both the United States and Bangladesh.

The Use of Child Labor in Bangladesh

Images of children working in factories in Dhaka and Chittagong first appeared on U.S. television and in newspapers in 1993, with accusations that Wal-Mart used children in its Bangladeshi subcontracting plants. The most famous coverage was a *Dateline NBC* piece featuring a Wal-Mart production site in Bangladesh. The *Dateline* story showed a factory in Dhaka employing children to work in its Wal-Mart production line, operating machines and trimming garments. In the *Dateline* piece, a Wal-Mart representative responded to allegations of the factory's employing child labor by saying that because Bangladeshis were so malnourished, full-grown adults appeared to be children and, in fact, all of the workforce had reached adulthood despite appearances to the contrary.[30]

Wal-Mart's response to the *Dateline* footage is a mirror image of the coverage itself and of the positing of Bangladesh's "problem" as one of child labor. In both conceptions—the first, of children toiling in the factories of multinational capital, forced there by the callousness of the society in which they live, rather than by the drive to push wages down as far as possible by large retailers and buyers in the United States and Hong Kong; or the second, of midget-sized adults without the nourishment to develop into normal size, working at jobs for which they are forever grateful—is the implicit notion of Bangladesh as a site of eternal failure and of Bangladeshis as forever victims, children, or (gendered) others. Development, it would seem, just has not worked for Bangladesh—leaving space for Wal-Mart, *Dateline,* and U.S. and European conscientious consumers to have a try at Bangladesh's salvation. As we can see from this example, the debates over child labor were more about Foucauldian biopolitics than about protecting workers in either space.

After the *Dateline* piece, Bangladesh became a signifier for child labor; in the United States, especially, some segments of the population began to associate Bangladeshi-made garments with exploited children. Levi Strauss & Co., which had implemented a corporate code of conduct for labor conditions in 1992 after being accused of using bonded labor in Saipan, began requiring ID cards with dates of birth for all employees in Bangladesh in order to avoid the "taint" of child exploitation associated with Bangladeshi production sites.[31] Wal-Mart's response was its "Buy American" campaign, which combined the politics of ethics with those of consumption, featuring large signs throughout the stores with arrows pointing to racks of clothing and other merchandise that carried tags proclaiming themselves "Made in the U.S.A."[32] Nativism and the shopping were thus reconciled with social conscience. *Dateline* producers, with U.S. activist and corporate supporters, posited oppressing children in the name of exports as a Bangladeshi problem, one that could be easily solved by avoiding clothing produced outside the United States.

A common factor in both companies' responses—not to mention the subsequent consumer boycott, threat of legislation, and television coverage—is the value of a brand name. Levi Strauss tried to protect its corporate reputation and curtail protest by instituting a code of conduct in 1992. The company publicly carried out inspections of its Bangladeshi factories, checking for age and placing underage garment workers into schooling programs. On its Web site, Levi Strauss published an anecdotal story about its attempts to rid its factories of child labor and its "innovative solution" to the discovery, by the company's internal auditors, of the presence of children under fourteen years of age working at two of its Bangladeshi factories: "Rather than dismiss the girls, which would have put them at risk of exploitation and economic hardship, Levi Strauss & Co. teamed up with the contractors. . . . The contractors agreed to stop employing underage workers, and to continue to pay a salary for the girls, provided that they attended school." Levi Strauss agreed to pay for the girls' "tuition, books, and school uniforms. The contractors, in turn, pledged jobs for the girls after completion of their schooling."[33] Production imperatives were not disrupted, since the girls would eventually return to the factories, and Levi Strauss was able to portray itself as a global corporate good citizen by providing schooling for its underage employees. From the beginning, consumer advocate groups and policy analysts lauded Levi Strauss for setting an example of fair production practices; no thought was given to the interests of the girls who would eventually return to the factories after their few years of schooling.[34]

Instead of placing child workers in schooling programs, Wal-Mart adopted a strategy that would dissociate its brand name completely from Bangladesh, child labor, and the taint of foreignness. Although Wal-Mart continued to carry a number of products made in Bangladesh and other areas of the world, it launched its "Made in the U.S.A." ad campaign in newspapers and throughout its stores on labels, ad copy, and even bumper stickers for sale that celebrated "Buying American." Though the tactics were different, both companies were asserting the purity of their brands and their trademark as compared to the unclean or impure Bangladeshi products.[35] This moral purity through the corporate provision of (nonformal) education to third world children allowed for a focus on the "child behind the label"; Levi Strauss and Wal-Mart in this way were able to use child labor for both production and advertising purposes.

Nationalist Responses in Bangladesh to the Anti-Child-Labor Campaigns

The consumer outcry and corporate response over offshore production practices had come shortly after Senator Tom Harkin and Representative George Brown introduced the Child Labor Deterrence Act of 1992 in

Congress. Although the now-famous (at least in Bangladesh) Harkin Bill was tabled year after year, more consumers in the United States and Europe were boycotting Bangladeshi-made garments in support of children's rights. In Bangladesh, however, NGOs such as UBINIG criticized the boycotts. Shirin Akhter and Farida Akhter, founders of UBINIG, argued that the boycotts were organized by "the U.S. trade protectionist lobby, acting to protect U.S. business interest groups." UBINIG took the position that "Bangladesh should not rely on the North for influencing social issues; rather, they should be addressed by ourselves so that we can focus on the issues that are important in the context of our own socio-economic circumstances."[36] UBINIG was attempting to reconfigure the hierarchies of transnational cooperation through its insistence on Bangladeshis setting their own socioeconomic agendas without influence from the global North.

UBINIG, along with other NGO and activist groups in Bangladesh, charged authors of the Harkin Bill and the consumers who would boycott Bangladesh-made goods with protectionism and imperialism. The reasons given for these charges were several: First, activists argued, such campaigns implied that Bangladeshis are the problem, since they were either stupid innocents unable to defend themselves from corporate greed or fiends who would sell their own children to labor in the factories subcontracted by multinational corporations. Second, since child labor is not the only socioeconomic problem in Bangladesh—and children in the garment industry are only 10,000 of a population of 120 million—a focus on that issue while ignoring others becomes a waste of both resources and energy. Third, because workers' families, the entire cities of Dhaka and Chittagong, and the country as a whole depend on garments for needed income, a boycott would create a loss much larger than its proponents had calculated. Finally, the question of outside interference was central: many argued that these initiatives were depriving the people most affected of the chance to come up with solutions applicable to their own situation. UBINIG and others argued that the ramifications of North-South actions should be taken into serious consideration, and that those people affected by activism should have a say in when and how action should be taken.

The language of U.S. consumer and government imperialism brought together unlikely groups, from leftist feminist groups such as UBINIG to garment factory owners, child labor activists in Bangladesh, and Bangladeshi government officials. The garment factory owners and managers, and their allies in the government, wanted to avoid compliance with labor laws and ILO conventions against the use of child labor so that they could pay lower wages. Therefore, factory owners and government officials were more than willing to act on the protests initiated by NGO, women's, and activist groups. They wanted to keep employing child workers to keep labor costs down for everyone in the industry and to maintain factory discipline through competition between child and adult workers for wages and jobs.

Child workers and their families, along with Bangladeshi children's rights NGOs, protested the U.S. boycotts of Bangladeshi export clothing by writing an open letter to the national Bangla and English language newspapers protesting the dismissals.[37] Although they were exploited in export-oriented factories, children working in garment factories were afraid of losing much-needed income for their families unless they accepted alternative employment as domestic workers, brick makers, or sex workers. Other garment workers and the country's major unions, faced with losing jobs and members in the face of an industry-wide boycott, also protested what they perceived as U.S. consumer protectionism.

The national political parties were threatening *hartals,* or general strikes, in light of the U.S. consumer boycott because all sectors of society—from rickshaw drivers to shopkeepers to the national electric company—would be affected by cuts in clothing orders. Garment factories buy electricity from the electric company, some workers ride rickshaws to and from work, and food stalls sell food to garment workers entering and leaving the factories. By getting an idea of the importance of garments to various parts of society, one can better understand some of the problems involved with the threat of boycott.

In this way, the rhetoric of child labor was employed—materially and symbolically—among various classes not only in the United States but in Bangladesh as well. In Bangladesh the Harkin Bill was shown to be part and parcel of U.S. protectionism and imperialism by labor, feminist, and child welfare organizations, as well as by garment factory owners, government ministers, and bankers throughout Bangladesh. The language of imperialism was especially powerful in Bangladesh, given its history as part of the British Empire until 1947 and then its subordinate role as East Pakistan to West Pakistan until its war of independence, which ended with the founding of the People's Republic of Bangladesh in 1971. Garment production has served as a development model in independent Bangladesh, and women's work has been seen as central to that model. This is especially visible in the geography of Dhaka, even to a first-time visitor.

Garments in Dhaka: A Map of the City

Dhaka is a garment town; its geography can be laid out in garments—or at least that is how I perceived it on my arrival in June 1996. Early in the morning, between 6:00 and 8:00, the streets are filled with women going to their jobs in garment factories. At noontime, garment workers are again out in the areas around the factories—in Mirpur, Mohammadpur, Malibagh, and Kalabagan—shopping or doing errands during their hour-long break. Thousands of young women, mostly under twenty-five years of age, walk around or board buses, in groups, in neatly pressed clothing, with oiled hair and makeup. The men who work in the garment factories are less recognizable as a distinct group, since men have always been part of the city landscape. The advent of garment production brought large numbers of women into the urban workforce for the first time in Bangladesh and the streets of Dhaka.

An estimated one million people are employed in the export-oriented garment industry in Bangladesh, 80 percent of whom are women.[38] Garment production is centered in Dhaka and Chittagong, the largest port city, with the majority of the factories located in city centers (although in the past few years, with increasing unionization attempts among workers, garment production has been moving out of the city and into export processing zones).[39] Garment factories in Dhaka are clustered in neighborhoods with relatively easy access to rail lines and highways; its Sarvar export processing zone is on the west side of the city, with easy access to both the rail lines and the highway to Chittagong (Map 1).

Other signs of the garment industry can be seen on billboards and street signs throughout Dhaka, which display advertisements for bobbins, zippers, thread, sewing machines, and textiles—not to mention garment manufacturers and buying companies. These billboards, and the garment factories themselves, provide a backdrop for rickshaw stands, open-air markets, and everyday life in the city (Figure 1). The garment industry also marks the city with its transport vehicles, and the countryside in turn is marked by the superhighway that links Dhaka's factories to the Chittagong port.

The garment industry has been the biggest source of foreign exchange for Bangladesh, after remittances: in 1995, of the $3.2 billion total export earnings of Bangladesh, garments brought in over $2 billion.[40] A 1994 USAID report on Bangladeshi development prospects concentrates on the growth of EPZs and garment production as the key to financial success. Garment production has served, in the last decade, as a principal development model for Bangladesh; exports have been a central mode of national income generation, with garment exports at the forefront. Finally, garment workers—girls, boys, women, and men—provide much-needed income for themselves and for their families. According to a survey by Hameeda Hossain, Roushan Jahan, and Salma Sobhan, 63 percent of women and girl garment workers spend between 501 and 3,000 taka per month on family

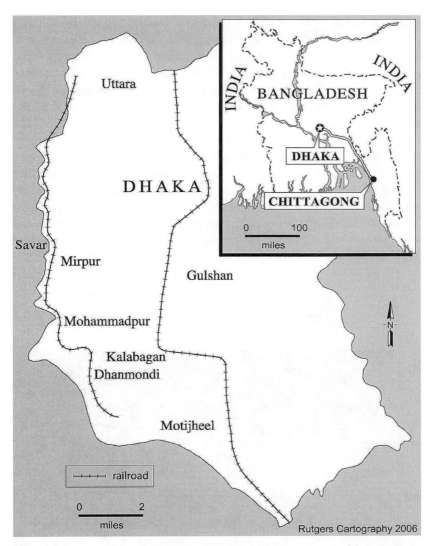

Map 1. Map of Dhaka, Bangladesh, featuring the most significant garment producing neighborhoods. The inset map of Bangladesh highlights the Dhaka-Chittagong highway and the country's major rivers. The nearby railroads, highways, rivers, and port of Chittagong are significant modes of transport for Bangladeshi garment exports. Courtesy of Rutgers Cartography.

expenses, and most women and girl garment workers spend less than 400 taka a month on personal expenditures and savings and the rest on family support.[41] One twelve-year-old girl I interviewed in 1996 told me that she had to support her mother and her brother with her factory job. She said that the family still would not have enough to eat unless she could find money to buy a chicken, whose eggs could be both eaten and sold by the family.[42]

Within the context of the country, its two major cities, and the families of a million people relying on garments for a large percentage of income, the child labor boycott is called into question. The larger familial, local, and national contexts show that the boycott is not a simple question of right versus wrong; an exploration of the boycott within various contexts can help to interrogate relations of power in various ways. One way we can examine the dynamics of the campaigns, and the phenomenon of transnational organizing in general, is to keep in mind Gayatri Chakravorty Spivak's caution:

> Belief in the plausibility of global alliance politics is prevalent among women of dominant social groups interested in "international feminism" in the comprador countries. . . . On the other side of the international

Figure 1. Billboard for zipper manufacturer near a rickshaw stand, Dhaka. Billboards advertising all aspects of garment production, along with those calling attention to the work of various NGOs and development organizations, are the backdrop of much of Dhaka's cityscape.

division of labor, the subject of exploitation cannot know and speak the text of female [or child] exploitation even if the absurdity of the nonrepresenting intellectual [or politician or activist] is achieved.[43]

The implausibility and absurdity analyzed by Spivak can be seen in the union meetings I attended in Dhaka in 1996 and 1998 in which organizers would ask garment workers about their complaints of factory life. When women workers would begin to talk about, for example, their need to buy groceries for their families, the organizers would guide their complaints into ones that were more easily translated into the language of exploitation and workers' rights. How, then, can we translate a young girl's need for a chicken and its eggs into the language of transnational labor activism? Into the campaign against child labor? Into the discourse of exploitation? Into the pages of this text?

Part of the absurdity rests in the ways in which the experiences of workers—and the subjectivity of intellectuals—is rendered transparent in the recounting of labor abuses. In the campaigns and legislation, there was a move to contain factory spaces as neutral, ones that should be free of innocent Bangladeshi women and children workers. In this way, Bangladeshi women and children were defined as "outside" what Mitchell, in *Colonising Egypt,* calls the process of "enframing" the Bangladeshi factories of transnational capital. While Mitchell argues that enframing is central to the disciplinary methods of producing a colony, it is also central to producing globalization. I would point to its power in producing "normal" global factory spaces, without child labor, that are outside the particular Bangladeshi context and legal jurisdiction. Mitchell argues:

> Enframing is a method of dividing up and containing, as in the construction of barracks or the rebuilding of villages, which operates by conjuring up a neutral surface or volume called "space." . . . (It is no accident that the beginnings of this method in rural Egypt coincide with origins of private landownership, in which space becomes a commodity.) . . . The plans and dimensions introduce space as something apparently abstract and neutral, a series of inert frames or containers. . . . Within these containers, items can then be isolated, enumerated, and kept.[44]

In efficient Fordist production practices, workers and factory space are accounted in the name of efficiency and coordination. This differentiates, materially and symbolically, factory space from what are posited as cultural practices of child labor. Western consumers, U.S. policy makers, and Bangladeshi factory owners can thus come together to reinscribe this enframing, placing Bangladeshi garment workers at the center of anti-sweatshop discourse as aberrant bearers of culture rather than as agents with whom one has to work. The relationship of garment production and protest, in this context, becomes a direct one between U.S. and European consumers and the transnational corporations that sell clothes, while the subjects/objects of this seemingly direct relation are women and children who work in Bangladeshi factories. At the same time, the complexities of compradors-as-subcontractors, the complicity of the U.S. and Bangladeshi governments on both sides of the discourse, and the work done by garment workers in the factories and the campaigns are elided in imperatives of protest and production.

The relationship, thus defined, reflects the advertisements placed in trade journals by the Bangladesh Export Processing Zones Authority and the Bangladesh Board of Investment. The advertisements invite potential investors and foreign companies to "Discover Bangladesh and let your business boom!" and to invest in the EPZs of Bangladesh "for optimum profit." By investing "directly" in Bangladesh, one can take advantage of the "most inexpensive but productive labour force," examples of which are shown in the photos of young women bent over sewing machines in factories producing for export. Finally, investors are encouraged to "Buy a garment from Bangladesh, help a poor woman to work and save her children."[45]

The Crisis

After the original tabling of the Harkin Bill in the U.S. Congress, the campaign to stop child labor became more sporadic and did not pick up again until late in 1994; it was reinvigorated by the beginning of other anti-sweatshop activism that I discuss later in this book. Since nearly 50 percent of all Bangladesh-made garments are destined for the United States,[46] the BGMEA became intransigent in the light of the threatened boycott. In 1993, in response to the Child Labor Coalition–AAFLI boycott threat, the BGMEA announced that, in the two thousand factories under its jurisdiction, it would fire without compensation all of the child workers under fourteen years of age beginning October 31, 1994. By May 1995, the majority of the child workers in garment factories were laid off permanently from their jobs, and local NGOs and unions were protesting the mass firings.[47]

Negotiations between the BGMEA, the government of Bangladesh, and the U.S. Embassy continued, but when thousands of dismissed children appeared on the streets of Dhaka, Bangladeshi NGOs, unions, and activist groups began protesting U.S. involvement and imperialism. This cry was also quickly taken up by the BGMEA. At this point, the ILO and

UNICEF entered into the negotiations—with considerable backing from U.S. ambassador to Bangladesh David Merrill, who feared being thrown out of the country by its government because of the resulting diplomatic incident.[48] Under the guidance of the Bangladeshi children's advocacy organization Gonoshahajjo Sangstha (GSS) and other children's NGOs, the fired child workers wrote "open letters to the U.S. Embassy, the Government of Bangladesh, and Senator Harkin that were published in leading English and Bangla dailies asking for support for their families, and for their jobs back, if necessary."[49]

The Signing and Implementation of the MOU

In these instances of protests by garment workers, child-labor activists, and feminist groups, we can see that the agency of garment workers is quickly effaced in the signing of the "Memorandum of Understanding on the Use of Child Labor in the Export-Oriented Garment Industry in Bangladesh" (MOU). The MOU called for a survey of the two thousand garment factories in Dhaka and Chittagong to determine the number of children employed there, their ages, and schooling and income needs. A school system for dismissed workers was to be set up on the model of nonformal schools in Bangladesh's rural areas and would be supported financially by the signatories of the MOU. The children attending the garment worker schools would be eligible until they reached the age of fourteen and would be provided with a monthly stipend of 300 taka, or about half of their current monthly salaries. Money for the schools and for the stipends would come from the ILO, UNICEF, the BGMEA, and the U.S. Embassy. The verification for compliance of the provisions of the MOU would come from inspection teams made up of members of the ILO, BGMEA, and Bangladesh's Ministry of Labor. Each team would inspect the schools and factories in light of the MOU's provisions. In addition, local NGOs, the Bangladesh Rural Action Committee (BRAC, the world's largest NGO), and the GSS would run the garment worker schools according to their community schooling models.

The garment worker schools begun as part of the MOU, along with the schools set up and run by garment worker unions such as BIGU, offer a curriculum of written and spoken Bangla instruction, mathematics, and some English, along with singing, poetry recital, and dance. Many of the songs and rhymes recited by the students were written by the teachers and the children themselves. The poems and songs address subjects such as the children's unwillingness and outright refusal to return to the factory and the happiness they have found in school. They talk of their hopes for the future and their eagerness for further education. The children—95 percent girls, from what I saw in the schools I visited, which matched the numbers people provided in interviews—also sang, danced, and recited poetry about Bangladesh's war of liberation *(mukhti gan)* and read and sang poetry by Rabindranath Tagore *(Rabindra sangeet)* and other national poets. The children in the schools range in age from toddlers to teenagers, and all are extremely motivated and quick to learn (Figures 2 and 3). Since the schools are usually located not far from children's homes, they walk in groups back and forth between home and school.

Because the implementation of the agreement was slow in happening, by 1996 only 250 of the proposed 500 schools had been set up. In 1997 all of the schools were finally up and running, and approximately 9,600 children were participating.[50] However, when the children reach the fourteen-year-old working age, they become ineligible for participation in the school program. The U.S. Embassy and UNICEF proposed a Learn to Earn plan in 1997, whereby children over fourteen could continue school for part of the day, without a stipend, while the rest of the day could be spent working in factories through an arrangement with the BGMEA. The purpose of the schools—and their long-term effects—is left out. These schools are not part

Figure 2. Former child garment workers, now enrolled in the BIGU garment workers' school in Dhaka, perform skits at the school's end-of-the-year pageant. They are accompanied by their teachers and a researcher-organizer; in the background is a painted mural featuring the Bangladeshi flag and Dhaka's language martyrs' memorial, a symbol of Bangladeshi independence.

Figure 3. Audience of former child garment workers and their teachers at the end-of-the-year pageant, BIGU garment workers' school, Dhaka.

of the graded mainstream school system, which means that the students cannot continue on to higher levels of education. In the schools, the children learn reading, writing, and mathematics, equipping them to be better, more efficient garment workers.

Results?

Taken out of the context of Bangladesh, without considering what happens to the students after they turn fourteen, the garment worker schools are an admirable accomplishment. Certainly, educated garment workers are better able to have access to and read labor law for themselves and perhaps are even more likely to join unions.[51] By 1998, according to ILO figures, fewer than 10 percent of factories in Dhaka and Chittagong employed workers under the age of fourteen. But what about working conditions?

Inspections for child labor in Bangladeshi factories and to monitor the school programs were carried out daily with a team of five ILO-trained inspectors, although they only had the authority to look for children. If fire hazards, union busting, worker abuse, or the withholding of wages is discovered during any of the visits, there is no space on the inspection sheet for reporting it, and there is no way to rectify the abuses or change the conditions. However, according to ILO, BGMEA, and government of Bangladesh factory inspectors,[52] general conditions such as fire hazards and access to potable drinking water have improved over the last year or so.

Even now, hundreds of Bangladeshi workers continue to die annually from factory fires. Workers, unions, and NGO members with whom I spoke said that withholding of wages, lack of health insurance, and the threat of dismissal for joining a union remain widespread practices.[53] In some factories, there has recently been a greater compliance with labor laws because of the requirements of transnational garment retailers. In order to protect the reputation of their names and the integrity of the brands, many retailers are requiring more stringent enforcement of labor laws and improved factory conditions before signing contracts with factories.[54] This is an echo of Marx's critique of industrial capitalists. Marx points out that the beginnings of modern industrial capitalism can be found in "Colonial system, public debts, heavy taxes, protection, commercial wars . . . the necessity of child-stealing and child-slavery for the transformation of manufacturing production into factory production and the establishment of the true relation between capital and labour-power." According to Marx, while the origins of the "industrial capitalist" can be found in colonialism and child labor, among other things, the very sources of this genesis are concealed from view because of institutions such as national debt and international credit. Marx argues: "With the national debt arose an international credit system, which often conceals one of the sources of primitive accumulation in this or that people. . . . A great deal of capital, which appears to-day in the United States without any certificate of birth, was yesterday, in England, the capitalised blood of children."[55]

Bangladesh after the MOU

Since the MOU was first signed in 1995, Bangladesh has been portrayed as successfully eradicating child labor in official statements by UNICEF, the ILO, the government of Bangladesh, and the U.S. State Department; the absence of child labor has also been used by the BGMEA to advertise Bangladesh as an attractive site for garment production. Senator Harkin himself went to Bangladesh in January 1998 and, in a widely covered televised press conference, pronounced himself impressed with the implementation of the MOU. U.S. consumer groups, such as the Child Labor Coalition, have congratulated Bangladesh—and themselves—for being the first to come up with a viable solution to eradicating child labor. The Bangladesh "brand" has been saved by the signing and implementation of the memorandum of understanding—and is now free for the shopping and investing of everyone.

With the success of the campaign and the MOU, Bangladesh has become a paradigm for success in labor rights for the ILO, the U.S. and Bangladeshi governments, and retailers who subcontract clothing manufactured in Bangladeshi factories. The child labor model that has come out of the MOU negotiations was applied to soccer ball production in Pakistan, and ILO officials were debating whether it could be applied in other countries and industries where child labor is still employed.[56] The garment industry of Bangladesh is now seen as a model, in contrast with its former image as the locus of oppressive, exploitative working conditions and use of children to work long hours for little pay.[57] Whereas before we knew about Bangladesh's beaten workers, women and children, with marks of labor on their bodies and the factory floor in their souls, now we know about its potential as a growth model for the rest of the world.

Success Stories

According to Neil Kearney, the general secretary of the International Textile, Garment, and Leather Workers Federation, in 2003 Bangladesh was still primarily dependent on the garment industry. In his discussion of the end of garment quotas in 2005, Kearney pointed out: "Garments account for 75% of all exports. The industry employs 1.5 million workers and provides 70% of all formal sector employment for women. Bangladesh is totally dependent on its export trade with the European Union and the US which take 95% of all [its] textile and clothing exports."[58] Nearly a decade after the signing of the MOU, garments are still the biggest source of employment for women workers and a significant source of the nation's gross domestic product. It would appear that the signing of the MOU saved both Bangladeshi workers and the Bangladeshi garment development model.

The success story, however, is not as seamless as it appears. According to Kearney, the situation in Bangladesh's garment industry for the workforce, made up of mostly young women, is dismal: "Most work 7 days a week often 12 to 14 hours per day. Existing labour legislation is largely ignored. Health and safety is of little consideration. Hundreds of workers were burnt to death in factory fires in recent years."[59] In fact, one month after the original signing of the MOU to eradicate child labor in garment production, a switchboard fire in the Lusaka garment factory on August 6, 1995, in Dhaka killed nine people. All of those killed were between the ages of twelve and sixteen years. Although the fire only lasted a few moments, those nine died and more than fifty people were injured while attempting to escape.[60] In August 1996, I visited a factory that was producing sweaters in a burned-out shell of a building that had been destroyed by fire two weeks earlier. Because the factory owners did not want to miss production deadlines, they continued production by using two floors of the building that had blown-out windows and a destroyed interior.

Just as child labor is not the only problem with Bangladesh's garment industry, children working in the export-oriented garment industry were never the only child workers in Bangladesh. According to ILO figures, 96 percent of working children in Bangladesh are in the informal sector and 4 percent in the formal sector—fewer than ten thousand work in garments. However, with the signing of the MOU, the ten thousand former garment workers were allocated a budget in the millions of dollars, while the ILO allocated a total of only $600,000 to all the other working children programs in Bangladesh.[61] At the time that the MOU was signed, Fakrul Islam calculated that 75 percent of Bangladeshi children below twelve years of age were malnourished and that 85 percent of the population of Bangladesh and 60 percent of that of Dhaka lived below the poverty line. Islam went on to cite Abu Taher, saying that in 1991, in Dhaka alone, more than 400,000 children worked in the formal sectors. This figure did not include child workers in the nonformal sectors, in rural areas, or in other cities, like Chittagong.[62]

These figures, along with the fact that most families need the incomes of their children to survive, were not included in the debates over child workers in the garment industry. If wages were raised to a livable level, many children would not have to work in the factories. Also, of jobs available in Dhaka, those in garment factories often have better pay and better working conditions than alternative jobs, such as those in domestic work or brick making.

Were Bangladeshi child garment workers victims of exploitation or models of antisweatshop organizing? They were both and neither. The only actors that participated in the Bangladesh child labor solution—and present in the negotiations—were consumers from the United States and Europe, factory owners from Bangladesh and the BGMEA, and representatives from international organizations. The children who took to the streets, the GSS who had advocated on behalf of the child workers, UBINIG, BIGU—all were left out of the agreement. Although the signing of the MOU, the campaigns, and their results are laudable, it remains difficult to see which problems were solved by its implementation other than those of guilty consumer consciences, the maintenance of brand purity, and the pressures of protectionism on the part of U.S. labor unions. The politics of capitalist production and subcontracting in the garment industry returned to business as usual, with the ten thousand former child workers as the exception to the rule.

During Senator Tom Harkin's 1997 visit to Bangladesh, he was quick to congratulate the BGMEA on its efforts on behalf of the workers and former child workers. The BGMEA attempted to cash in on the praise and to take on the role of champion of working rights in order to raise its quotas for the export of garments to the United States.[63] The women and children who worked in the factories and the people who are the subjects/objects of protest were still shown as silent, despite the fact that they continued to work long hours and that they had been out on the streets and in union offices organizing workers and protesting the original firing of the 9,600 children from the factories. Scholars and activists have to read these apparent silences, interrogate the building of the campaigns, and question the violence and erasing of difference that they entail and their ultimate failures in creating the very categories they seek to establish.

Why has there been such a strong focus on the problem of child labor as emblematic of the new sweatshop? Why does this violation become the only issue around which consumer protest in the United States is organized? Of all the countries where the use of child labor is prevalent, why did Bangladesh—and in particular the Bangladeshi garment industry—draw so much attention?

Certainly, the use of children—to produce garments or for any sort of wage labor—is both morally wrong and financially unnecessary, despite factory owners' claims to the contrary. Another answer could be that the campaigns are a replication of developmentalist discourse that portrays Bangladesh as a "basket case" and children as uniquely innocent.[64] In the case of the everyday workings of the garment industry, children—and women—need to be shown as innocent, young, and possessing nimble fingers, in contrast to the rationally calculating individuals who are adult (male) garment workers, factory managers, corporate heads, and ministers or secretaries of labor. In the case of child garment workers, we—consumers, development experts, labor organizers—would protect them from the evils of exploitation until they reach the age of "consent" to sell the products of their labor. This age of consent ranges from fourteen to eighteen years old, depending on national labor law and ratification of ILO conventions.[65] This is precisely the "benevolent imperialism" pointed to by Spivak.[66]

The appeal to an ethics—against child labor and exploitation, for example—apparently outside of capital becomes problematic in an interrogation of the discourses of globalization and transnationality. By viewing (third world women and) children as outside power, we reframe the debate as one among white adults about brown children in the developing world. Although activists should by no means ignore the very real problems faced by families that make them send their kids off to work, the debate among

U.S. and European activists and consumers as it is currently framed precludes discussion of the challenges faced by entire communities and the communities' own responses to challenges.

The problem of labor abuse in garment production is never just about the single, young brown women and children working in garment factories, despite the emphasis on these individuals. This focus precludes discussion of other jobs taken up by children—jobs that are outside the export sector and therefore outside the reach of reforming consumers in the United States and Europe. Finally, the concentration on child labor in current debates over sweatshops elides discussions of age, gender, racial, and sexual relations on the shop floor, in the union hall, in the NGO office, and among the organizers of these transnational campaigns.

Because of these elisions, the effects of the Harkin Bill and the signing of the MOU in Bangladesh and the United States are mixed. In the period since the introduction of the Harkin Bill, the language of protest against the use of child labor has slipped from that of saving U.S. jobs and unionist protectionism to solidarity with workers throughout the world. The particular juxtaposition of "imperiling the jobs of adult workers in the United States" against protecting the universal "rights of the child" is telling—and has made the Harkin Bill a synonym for U.S. protectionism throughout Bangladesh's garment-producing cities of Dhaka and Chittagong.

The children working in the factories are in a seemingly unmediated relationship to activists, to consumers, and even to corporate heads. They have no families, no friends, no union organizers or neighbors; they have no acquaintance outside the country or even the neighborhood in which they work. Class becomes monolithic, unproblematic, and unquestionable; race disappears in the redeployment of imperialist relations; and people are reduced to subjects ignorant of the outside world, of their position in the world or in their communities and families, and of rights—and thus they are objects for salvation. This process of salvation in solidarity's name is, then, a reenactment of earlier (colonial) salvations—of an entire history of "taking up the white man's burden." Is child labor the only issue on which labor protest can be successfully organized? If that becomes the case, then the possibilities of transnational agency by gendered, raced third world subjects become impossibilities, and we are left with globalization and the triumph of the market(place); the only possibility is then to fight against the worst abuses in the name of innocents.[67]

By focusing on the issue of child labor, other questions of working conditions were left out of the equation, though with the implicit notion that the industry in Bangladesh is "bad."[68] By contrasting "good" working conditions with "bad" ones, U.S. and European activists and consumers have contributed to the vilification of Bangladesh as a space of aberration and backwardness in the normalcy of progress—of capital, of the West, of modernity. In this way, singling out Bangladesh (and now, Pakistan and India) as the bastion of child labor serves as a distant echo of the 1971 U.S. State Department description of Bangladesh as the world's quintessential basket case. Bangladesh itself becomes an unruly—ungovernable—child to be disciplined, and in the process of the implementation of the MOU, it returns to garment production and to the docile, disciplined, and productive site expected by imperialist players in the Bangladeshi solution.

2

Organizing in Times of (Post)War

If globalization has become the trope of the post–cold war period, the new sweatshop has symbolized its worst abuses. From the perspective of the shop floors of garment factories throughout the world, the politics of globalization works to frame interrogations of current productive and labor-market practices. Here I will examine the phenomenon of cross-border, consumer-oriented protest campaigns that push for labor rights on behalf of women workers in garment factories in El Salvador and the United States.

This chapter's title both questions the notion of "post" in the Salvadoran context and references a 1980s song from Nicaragua by Luis Enrique Mejía Godoy, "Amando en Tiempo de Guerra" (Loving in time of war).[1] In El Salvador, 1993 officially marked the end of the fourteen-year-long civil war. Wartime development policies and postwar reconstruction alike depended on the construction and proliferation of export processing zones, free trade zones, and bonded areas.

What is the relationship of globalization and neoliberalism to war? During the postwar period, what have been the challenges for union organizing and the promotion of labor rights in El Salvador? What are the legacies of war for labor activism? What is the postwar role of the El Salvador solidarity movement in the United States? What are the problematics of cross-border organizing between the United States and El Salvador in light of the history of official U.S. support for the Salvadoran military and the large-scale solidarity movement of many popular groups in the United States with the people of El Salvador? Finally, what form can social change take when it is carried out within the parameters of globalized production and protest?

In order to address some of these questions, I will look at the anti-sweatshop movement in the United States and its cross-border organizing work with El Salvador in the middle of the 1990s. The latter half of the 1990s was marked by the rising importance of protests against sweatshop abuses. Antisweatshop protest has often been combined with various calls to dismantle the top-down relations that have marked corporate restructuring, the breakdown of welfare states and corporatist pacts, and the increasingly rapid, worldwide movements of finance and productive capital. Consumer campaigns against sweatshops have called attention to abuses by transnational capital through a coalition politics of consumers in richer metropolitan areas with workers (mostly women) in the world's garment sweatshops.

I collected my data from interviews, factory visits, and participant observation in NGO and union offices and focused on the on-the-ground consequences of transnational coalition politics organized around issues of workers' rights in a global industry. I argue that the forms of repertoires of contention, specifically their contextualization as *transnational,* delineate which issues may be addressed in the name of labor rights and depend on deployments and meanings of power through the discourses and materialities of globalization, transnationality, and legacies of U.S. unionism, the nation-state, and the solidarity movement in El Salvador.[2]

In particular, I investigate the New York City–based NLC campaign against Gap Inc. carried out in 1995 and 1996 to protest sweatshop conditions at the Mandarin International garment factory. The NLC campaign drew on tactics and networks from the 1980s solidarity movement to address labor abuse, union busting, and child labor at Mandarin International, a garment factory located in an export processing zone on the outskirts of San Salvador.

The National Labor Committee's 1995 campaign against Gap Inc. drew from earlier research it had carried out in Central American export processing zones at the beginning of the 1990s. Mandarin International was a garment factory in San Salvador's San Marcos export processing zone that produced clothing for Gap Inc. and for companies such as JCPenney and Eddie Bauer. Nearly three-quarters of Mandarin International employees, mostly women between the ages of fifteen and thirty-five, joined together to form a union (SETMI) on the factory site in 1994. The union was registered with the Salvadoran Ministry of Labor in early 1995. The company refused to recognize the union, in direct contradiction to the provisions of El Salvador's national labor code, and began firing employees who were members. The Ministry of Labor did not enforce labor law in the face of worker appeals; rather, the Mandarin International workers were categorized under El Salvador's Law of Free Trade Zones, which was written to supersede national labor and trade laws in the specified free trade zones/EPZs and bonded areas—individual factories that are bonded to conform to the rules of free trade zones.

Once the firings began, and it was clear that the union would not be officially recognized by the factory or the government, SETMI, along with local human rights groups, contacted the NLC to inform them of the firings. During the first six months of 1995, the NLC organized a transnational campaign protesting labor violations at export-oriented factories—*maquiladoras*—in Honduras and El Salvador.[3] The campaign was directed at U.S.- and European-based activists and consumers, bringing Mandarin International, its workers, and El Salvador directly into U.S. retail outlets, corporate headquarters, and neighborhood spaces long dominated by consumption practices, advertising, and profit making.

In the official narratives of participants in the campaign and its resolution, and in the narrative of the larger antisweatshop movement, the NLC-Gap campaign has been used as the principal model for transnational labor protest as well as the solution to the problem of the sweatshop.[4] Rather than judge the NLC-Gap campaign in terms of its success or failure in any absolute sense, I examine its concrete achievements in the everyday lives of Mandarin International workers and in the larger political context of El Salvador.[5] My analysis differs from official narratives of the campaign and its resolution in that it keeps a focus on the local contexts of the campaign—the Mandarin International shop floor, Salvadoran political economy in the wake of civil war, and activist and solidarity politics in the United States. In this way, I posit a critique of dominant notions of globalization that take it as an abstract entity resting on and above everyday, messy relations and practices within specific localities.

Within the larger context of transnational protest, there are three possible aims of transnational labor protest tactics. First, they could seek to improve the working conditions in the particular sites targeted. Second, they could seek to improve working conditions in other sites, industries, or sectors in a number of countries, including those in the United States and Europe. Third, they could seek to educate consumers in the United States about sweatshop conditions in the global garment industry.[6] The NLC-Gap campaign of 1995 and the organizing model coming out of it certainly have raised U.S.-based consumer awareness of working conditions worldwide and the labor violations that go into making brand-name clothing. The effects of the NLC-Gap campaign of 1995 in the United States were widespread, informing activists and consumers alike about the commodity chains of transnational garment production and the labor abuse built into the current system. What about its effects in El Salvador and in the worldwide garment industry as a whole?

Evidence from interviews I carried out in El Salvador, Bangladesh, and New York between 1996 and 1998 shows that consumer campaigns for labor rights have been incorporated into an ongoing process of factory-level discipline. For example, retailers regularly adopt codes of conduct for sourcing and subcontracting that are available on most of their corporate Web sites. Nike's code of conduct, for example, says that its business "was founded on a handshake" and that it commits itself to working with subcontractors who share its commitment to "best practices," including "Management practices that respect the rights of all employees, including the right to free association and collective bargaining."[7]

The particular set of repertoires of contention[8] around struggles for labor rights in the garment industry that have been built up in the course of transnational organizing have defined and delineated the issues to be addressed and the violations to be ameliorated. Sweatshops can be excoriated; the regular workings of capital, however, are not open to question. The accepted repertoires of contention for transnational labor organizing include a focus on the use of child labor, bathroom access, and low hourly wages; they often call for the incorporation of a corporate code of conduct and independent monitoring of labor conditions within subcontracting factories; they use worker tours from sites around the third world and videotaped testimonies, often by young, brown women workers, framed with commentary by white U.S.- and European-based activists. These repertoires have also predicated the organizations, companies, or individuals on which claims may be made, such as Wal-Mart, Disney, and Gap Inc., and the people and groups that have the authority to carry out protest actions in the name of garment workers, such as NLC representatives themselves and their networks in the third world and the AFL-CIO and its international allies.

The National Labor Committee

In order to understand the U.S. context and the development of tactics and repertoires of contention in the NLC-Gap campaign, it is important to understand the origins of the National Labor Committee in the Reagan era of proxy war and people-to-people solidarity that marked U.S. relations with Central America in the 1990s. The NLC was first founded in 1980 in New York City as the National Labor Committee in Support of Democracy and Human Rights in El Salvador by David Dyson, a staff member of the

Amalgamated Clothing and Textile Workers Union (ACTWU), along with other union activists. At the time of its founding, the group focused on protesting U.S. intervention in the civil war in El Salvador. Despite its critical stance, the NLC had been founded as part of the larger umbrella of the U.S. union movement under the leadership of the AFL-CIO. By the 1990s, the NLC had become an organization independent from the AFL-CIO. As a central part of their protest of U.S. policy toward Central America, the NLC criticized the AFL-CIO's role in U.S. foreign policy, its cold war support of U.S. interventionism in El Salvador, and its central role in the international anticommunist unionism that supported counterinsurgency throughout Central America.

The NLC gained the support of many within the U.S. union movement who opposed U.S. military intervention, whether in Vietnam or Central America. The NLC became a nexus of protest against the AFL-CIO's cold war policies, through which it grew into a national entity that included in its membership presidents of twenty-three U.S. unions. With funding coming from U.S. unions and contacts in the Salvadoran labor movement through its ties to the North American Congress on Latin America (NACLA), the NLC began fact-finding trips to El Salvador in the 1980s to investigate the deaths, disappearances, and human rights violations of union leaders by the Salvadoran government and paramilitary death squads. Based on this information, the NLC issued press releases, wrote reports, and took out newspaper advertisements denouncing human rights abuses and the anti-union repression policies of the Salvadoran military regime.[9]

After the signing of the 1992 peace agreements that ended the civil war in El Salvador, the NLC maintained its ties with Salvadoran labor groups, human rights organizations, religious organizations, and other nongovernmental organizations. At the same time, the NLC began to shift its focus toward "the economic issues that [have shaped] conditions for democracy and social justice in the hemisphere, particularly trade policy, job exports, and international labor standards."[10] The NLC's activist tactics continued to send fact-finding missions—throughout Central America and the Caribbean and eventually into Asia—and to produce press releases, reports, and paid newspaper ads. In addition, the NLC began to make videos of its fact-finding missions and to hold televised press conferences about labor and trade policy in the region. As a result, NLC campaigns were often featured on television news shows like *Hard Copy* and *60 Minutes*.

In the early 1990s, after the Central American peace agreements, the end of the cold war, and changes in the U.S. foreign policy agenda, the concerns of both the NLC and the AFL-CIO shifted, bringing them more in line with one another. The NLC's focus on the relation between offshore garment production and job loss from corporate downsizing in the United States firmly connected issues of dwindling union membership at home with the policies of USAID in Central America. The NLC was able to appeal to activists and consumers alike through its critique of USAID's funding strategies for the promotion of neoliberalism in the name of free trade and wartime pacification. The NLC backed up its critiques by providing data on garment industry shifts, labor conditions, and production information. Its members would circulate copies of ads placed in trade magazines like *Bobbin* that promoted offshore subcontracting for U.S. retailers. These ads highlighted the low wages, tax benefits, and docility of the labor force in countries throughout the Caribbean and Central America.

The first report to be published by the newly independent National Labor Committee, *Paying to Lose Our Jobs,* appeared in 1992; its followup, *Free Trade's Hidden Secrets,* came out the following year. Even though the NLC was nominally independent from the AFL-CIO, it continued to work closely with the U.S. union movement, as shown in these reports that supported the protectionism that marked early 1990s U.S. unionism. The reports provided documentation of the role that USAID played in setting up export processing zones in Central America and the Caribbean—in effect, using U.S. tax dollars to subsidize companies' moving offshore in search of a nonunion workforce, low wages, and low or no taxation. *Paying to Lose Our Jobs* documented plant closings in the United States and the funding by USAID that facilitated U.S. businesses moving their production to offshore production sites. The reports that were featured on *60 Minutes* became effective tools for pushing the reform of USAID. They led to the eventual passage of an amendment to the 1993 Foreign Appropriations Bill "conditioning all U.S. foreign aid on respect for internationally recognized worker rights."[11]

The NLC-Gap Campaign

The NLC-Gap campaign in El Salvador served to call attention to poor working conditions and grievances inside the production network. Within the master frame of the campaign, however, the organizing efforts of the women who worked inside the Mandarin International factory were underplayed in favor of highlighting their victimization in the face of corporate greed. The history of relations inside Mandarin International that led up to the long unionization drive was, for the most part, left out of the language and images of the transnational protest campaign. Nor did the resolution acknowledge that most people who had worked at Mandarin International were left out of the entire negotiation process.

Because of the effect of the global-local split, the NLC campaign emphasized its own lack of resources and its subordinate position—at the global scale—relative to a corporation like Gap Inc. As a result, in subsequent campaigns, the NLC was labeled "the mouse that roared" in the press. At the same time, the U.S. activists did not appear to understand their own high level of political and social influence in the various localities in which they worked. Because of geopolitical and socioeconomic hierarchies among nation-states, regionally and internationally, actions by groups without much power inside the United States can have large-scale repercussions in third world countries like El Salvador. This is especially the case given the wartime history of U.S.–El Salvador relations. In other words, the NLC took action as a small, local activist group, while its effects in El Salvador often had a number of unintended, undetected consequences.

Forms of Protest

The tactics employed in the NLC-Gap campaign come out of particular local, national, and international histories of protest and contention. In her chapter in *Transnational Social Movements,* Jackie Smith (1997) presents a table of possible tactics of "Transnational Social Movement Organizations," organized according to target of activity.[12] The tactics employed in the NLC-Gap–Mandarin International campaign fall under all three of Smith's categories (individuals, national governments, and intergovernmental organizations) but primarily targeted audiences in the United States and Canada, especially consumers of Gap Inc.'s clothing. Tactics included protests at retail outlets and at Gap Inc.'s corporate headquarters in San Francisco, accompanied by calls for consumer boycotts of Gap Inc. and letter writing by consumers and activists to Gap Inc., the Salvadoran Ministry of Labor, and the management of Mandarin International. A main goal of the campaign's tactics was to educate U.S. and European consumers and others through what Keck and Sikkink call "information politics." These attempts to educate key audiences were, as Keck and Sikkink point out, "what human rights activists . . . call the human rights methodology: 'promoting change by reporting the facts.'"[13]

The politics of information employed by the NLC, and by the antisweatshop movement as a whole, is the product of particular histories of repertoires of contention that use testimonials of individuals combined with news articles and other forms of documentary to tell the "truth" about a situation. As Keck and Sikkink point out, this tactic was employed to great effect in the antislavery movement and "foreshadowed many of the modern publications of transnational networks, both in its scrupulous attention to reporting facts and its use of dramatic personal testimony to give those facts human meaning and motivate action."[14] More recently, the tactics of witnessing were employed by the Central American solidarity movement in what Christian Smith calls a "symbolic battle to construct and define reality." The battle became one of the relative "potency of contending 'packagings' or 'framings' of Central American reality."[15]

In the antisweatshop movement, this battle over the potency of framing reality has become one between antisweatshop activists and clothing retailers in an attempt to shape the imagination and conscience of the U.S.-based consuming public. The packaging of truth as a tactic of protest, while useful as an educational project, has led, in the case of garment workers, to a scripting of reality and a recycling of images that potentially deny agency to the very people with whom it is standing in solidarity. At Mandarin International, garment workers had organized a union, registered it with the Ministry of Labor, and even taken over the free trade zone at San Marcos by force, but none of this history shows up in the U.S. version of the story; Salvadoran garment workers in the United States are seen as victims of U.S. retailers and U.S.-based capital. The complexities and ambiguities in transnational gender, class, race, and social relations and the strong histories of activists have no room in the official story of cross-border labor coalitions.

Christian Smith analyzes the struggle to control the interpretive packagings—what social movement theorists would call the frames of contention—of Central America by the 1980s solidarity movement and the Reagan administration. A focus on these interpretive struggles helps to shed light on the particular cross-border tactics being used in the battle over Gap Inc.'s labor practices that constitute its subcontracted production at Mandarin International in El Salvador. First, many of the antisweatshop activists working on the NLC-Gap-Mandarin campaign had participated in the solidarity movement during the 1980s period of civil war in Central America. Second, and more important, the tactics of witnessing were borrowed, often directly, from the 1980s solidarity campaigns by the antisweatshop movement. As Christian Smith points out:

> Any analysis of the battle to use the mass media to define the Central American "reality" for the American public and Congress must recognize that the mass media itself is not an open, impartial, and transparent vehicle of communication. Instead, mass media institutions are characterized by definite interests, biases, norms, and practices that significantly condition what and how material gets published and broadcasted to mass audiences.[16]

The current effect of global-local separation is an essential part of that conditioning, so that problems in current structures of consumption, production, and communication are seen simply as blips within the seamless flow of globalization, as particular localities that can be fixed without interfering with the process of globalization itself.[17]

Part of the effect of the split between the global and the local is its definition of an inside and an outside: for globalized protest (and globalized production), the inside is made up of Sassen's "global cities," the retail and media outlets, and the centers of commerce that they contain. Just as the public relations machine of the U.S. government under Reagan was large and well funded, the public relations and advertising budget of Gap Inc. and other retailers is enormous; it is this side of production that is performed within the global. The outside of the global in this formulation includes garment factories—in El Salvador, Honduras, Bangladesh, or in Brooklyn, the U.S. prison system, or parts of Los Angeles—sites of what Lash and Urry call "post-Fordist ghettoes."[18]

Because, according to Lash and Urry, such spaces are framed as "ungovernable," they are seen as too messy to be contained within the frame of the global and are thus relegated to local sites of aberrance. We can see this in the coverage of labor abuses in garment factories throughout the world: abuses that are systemic, such as the illegality of union organizing within the bylaws of export processing zones, along with those that are locally produced, such as forced birth control, are alike viewed as local problems that can be rectified while maintaining the efficient running of the commodity chain as a whole. Once these problems are fixed, consumers and corporations alike can go back to the business of retail without many qualms.

The discourse of aberrance and ungovernability cannot account for various types of contextualized agency and activism within these post-Fordist ghettoes; rather, the language of the local has been deployed as that which is victim to the global, in a parallel to discourses about the victimization of garment workers. Contextualized agency ranges from the spirit possession of women workers in Malaysian EPZs documented by Ong in *Spirits of Resistance and Capitalist Discipline* to the community soup kitchens and other self-help organizations organized by women workers in urban communities throughout the world.[19] This framing of the local as outside, or as the Other, of the global cannot capture the overdetermination of agency in particular moments and places or within particular relationships, communities, or socioeconomic relations.[20] The protest tactics in the NLC-Gap campaign focus on the site of globalization—media outlets, shopping malls, and the stock market, and specifically in the United States among Americans with disposable incomes. These global sites are reproduced as universal rather than particular, thus potentially limiting which aberrations are to be seen and which problems can be addressed.

Gap Inc., Mandarin International, and El Salvador: The Official Story

Information politics, a reliance on the tactics of the 1980s Central American solidarity movement, and the maintenance of a global-local split played a key part in the NLC's repertoires of contention, both around Gap Inc.'s labor practices at Mandarin International and in its other attempts to cast the spotlight on labor violations in garment factories throughout Central America and the Caribbean. Such information politics included the making of a 1994 documentary video about the garment industry in Honduras, *Zoned for Slavery,* and a subsequent tour of the United States by former Honduran garment worker Lesly Rodríguez, who testified at a Senate hearing on "Child Labor and the New Global Marketplace."[21]

In the wake of attempted unionization and the formation of SETMI at Mandarin International, 350 suspected union members were fired and barred from entering the factory or San Marcos. The lockout and firings at Mandarin International in 1995 pushed the NLC to build on its tactics of information politics by issuing regular reports to its network of activists and the press about the situation at Mandarin International. It also sponsored a tour of the United States by two young women garment workers from factories in El Salvador and Honduras.

Where does the focus on globalization by the NLC leave the 350 Mandarin International workers who were fired in 1995? What follows is my reconstruction of what happened between January 1995 and June 1998. I pieced this particular narrative together from interviews I carried out in San Salvador with members of SETMI and Grupo de Monitoreo Independiente de El Salvador (GMIES), managers of Mandarin International, Salvadoran unionists, and NGO participants and through the NLC's press releases and news articles covering the Mandarin International situation for audiences in the United States.

The corporate-targeted, consumer-activist campaign that was carried out by the NLC in 1995 against Gap Inc. centered on working conditions at Mandarin International. The campaign was initiated after more than 350 workers were fired for forming a union at the factory in January 1995.[22] The factory first opened in 1992 in the Zona Franca San Marcos, on the outskirts of San Salvador. SETMI was formally recognized by the Salvadoran Ministry of Labor in 1995. In the three intervening years, workers at Mandarin International formally lodged several complaints and filed suits regarding violations within the factory. Workers had claimed, among other things, of being forced to work overtime without pay, of not being allowed to go to the bathroom when needed, and of not having access to drinking water on the factory site. Reports of verbal and physical abuse of workers at Mandarin International were also common.

There had been a couple of earlier attempts to unionize the factory before the registry of SETMI with the Ministry of Labor. Each time a union had been started, Mandarin International's management offered money to the union leadership or the federation in exchange for the names of people who had joined. One member of SETMI recalled: "The first two times workers tried to organize Mandarin International, the labor federation they had joined with, FENASTRAS, sold the names of the union members to the owners and everyone was fired."[23] Those who had joined the union in each case were not only fired, they were blacklisted and unable to find work in the garment industry.[24] The potential of transnational activism is clear when we understand the industry-wide challenges for women whose employment options are already so limited. However, this very crucial need for transnational solidarity is foreclosed with the elision of the everyday agency of women in their contribution to both garment production and protest.

The NLC-Gap campaign in the United States began in mid-1995 with a letter to Gap Inc. signed by Salvadoran NGOs, unions, individuals, and religious groups. After eight months of firings and harassment of union members, after hundreds had lost their jobs for joining SETMI, labor activists in El Salvador faxed news articles about the firings to the National Labor Committee in New York.[25] According to a member of SETMI's directorate who had been fired in 1995:

> We couldn't move, couldn't organize. People had already tried organizing a union two times before, because of the hitting, shouting, and mistreatment by management. I didn't know what a union was, but soon realized that it was a good thing. In 1995, we joined up with the CTD [Central de Trabajadores Democráticos], began organizing in hiding, until we got the paper from the Ministry of Labor. The directorate was formed, and the Ministry informed the Mandarin International management that SETMI had been organized at the factory.[26]

The Mandarin International management refused to recognize SETMI, even after it had registered with the Ministry of Labor, and tried its usual tactics to break the union. One SETMI leader recalled: "The manager called us in one by one and offered us money to end our organizing, saying that other leaders had left in exchange for payment. I refused and said to the manager, 'How cheaply they sold themselves.'"[27] SETMI leadership was then barred from entering either the factory or the San Marcos EPZ after the union refused to back down from its request to be recognized. In February 1995, when the guards of the EPZ enforced a lockout of the Mandarin International workers and refused to allow SETMI leaders inside the zone to talk with management, workers in other factories in the EPZ demanded that the Mandarin International workers be allowed to enter the factory. The head of security at Mandarin International hit one SETMI member and made her nose bleed; other security guards began to beat union members, and a widespread fight ensued within the San Marcos EPZ.[28]

The factory started firing suspected union members. A SETMI member described it to me: "They started firing people in groups of six or ten, saying that they were losing work and needed to let people go." Before, she recalls, "we needed a ticket to go to the bathroom, and when they would refuse to give pregnant women permission all of us would defend her, [but] now we were powerless against the firings. That has got to stop, we said."[29] Between February and May 18, 1995, the estimate of those fired totaled 150. By June 28, the total was an estimated 200, and by July 21, 1995, a total of 350 workers had been fired for union organizing at Mandarin International.[30]

The remaining nine hundred Mandarin International workers were locked out of the factory and the zone by management, and five thousand workers from other factories in San Marcos went on strike to support the Mandarin International workers.[31] SETMI and its supporters took up positions outside the EPZ gates, eventually pushing through and occupying Mandarin International and blocking access to the San Marcos EPZ.[32] The director general of Mandarin International, Pedro Mancía, recalled that during those days in February, San Marcos was "practically closed down by the conflictive actions of the union." Mancía went on to describe his version of the events: "For thirty-six hours, the workers held the management hostage and took over the factory. They planned to move from Mandarin International and form unions in Jatex, Amitex, S y C Apparel, Lindotex, GABO, Hangchan, Maquisaltex [garment factories operating in various EPZs in El Salvador]."[33] During the course of our discussion, Pedro Mancía showed me photos of the women workers from Mandarin carrying two-by-four sticks of wood with nails sticking out as they patrolled the EPZ during the takeover. Mancía showed the photos to me as evidence of what he called the "stubbornness and brutality" of the SETMI workers, but refused to let me copy them or even hold the photos in my hand. For me, the photos were evidence of the courage and agency of the SETMI workers, compared to the three levels of armed guards and body searches that marked the everyday security of the EPZ.

For three days, SETMI and its supporters occupied Mandarin International and closed down the San Marcos *zona franca*. A member of SETMI's directorate pointed out: "When we took over the factory, in February 1995, they had armed guards and we had scissors. They beat us, but in the end we had to make them come to an agreement and sign, so that if they fired someone, all bets were off. After the agreement [in February], there was no more physical abuse, but they still didn't respect us—especially the women.[34] Not only did the women at Mandarin International have to fight the management of the factory, the EPZ, and transnational political economic formations for their right to work without being abused, they had to fight to organize a union at their work site. The SETMI members were fighting for recognition as women and breadwinners, as many were single mothers supporting entire extended families. The production practices of the garment industry, along with traditional labor organizing models, tend to focus on people's identities as workers to the exclusion of all else. The photos shown to me by Pedro Mancía, the stories told by SETMI workers, and the evidence of their everyday struggles to care for their families, make garments, and organize a union in the face of violence, however, cannot be contained in the monolithic category of worker.

In July 1995, the NLC sponsored a tour of the United States and Canada by Judith Viera, a former Mandarin International worker, along with Claudia Molina, a worker from the Orion plant in Honduras. From July through September 1995, Viera and Molina traveled around the United States along with Charles Kernaghan and Barbara Briggs of the NLC, talking about their experiences as garment workers and union members in Central American maquiladoras. Viera and Molina were presented to the U.S. audience as both typical workers and exploited teenage girls. Both women had talked about their unpaid overtime, limited bathroom breaks, and the verbal and physical attacks from supervisors at their respective factories. Bob Herbert's op-ed pieces in the *New York Times* provided comprehensive coverage of the tour, followed by his own trip to El Salvador to interview garment workers and factory owners in order to put added pressure on Gap Inc. to resolve the situation at Mandarin International. Herbert asks in one editorial: "Claudia Molina and Judith Viera have been brought to the United States by the National Labor Committee to tell their story. How long can we, like the big apparel companies, refuse to hear them?"[35]

Through press releases and news coverage, the garment worker tour, and mailings to its activist network, the NLC called U.S. consumer attention to the situation at Mandarin International and helped organize protests outside Gap Inc.'s headquarters in San Francisco and at retail outlets all over the United States. In the meantime, according to one SETMI member, the factory managers "had made up a list of the workers—those of us who were friends, and those who were enemies."[36] They also started up a factory pro-management organization (ATEMISA), which was registered at the Ministry of Labor as an "association" rather than a union.

In an attempt to preserve its reputation, Gap Inc. replied to the letter and the protests in a written response addressed to the groups from El Salvador, informing them that Gap Inc. was canceling its current and future orders at Mandarin International. Gap Inc. also reworked its vendor code of conduct for labor practices. In it, the company states: "Workers are free to join associations of their own choosing. Factories must not interfere with workers who wish to lawfully and peacefully associate, organize or bargain collectively."[37] Despite the new language of Gap's "Code of Vendor Conduct," one leader of SETMI pointed out that it was at this same time that union support and membership dropped considerably. The cause of decreased membership can be found in the lockout of SETMI and the firing of 350 of its members while the management made sure that "those who joined ATEMISA kept their jobs and got paid, despite the fact that there was no work to be done after Gap Inc. stopped its orders at Mandarin International."[38]

According to the letter written by senior vice president Stanley Raggio, Gap Inc. would resume its production at Mandarin International on three conditions: (1) that proven violations would be corrected so that wages would be locally competitive, workers would be treated justly, and all parties would comport themselves ethically and decently; (2) that the Salvadoran government would demonstrate the ability to investigate and justly resolve labor conflicts; and (3) that Mandarin International comply with Gap Inc.'s sourcing principles and guidelines. By December 1995, security guards from Mandarin International were "persecuting those who had unionized, looking for people at their houses and threatening them by telephone."[39]

Because the campaign had come to a head in the middle of the Christmas rush, it was a considerable threat to Gap Inc.'s annual earnings. In December 1995, negotiations began in New York between Gap Inc. and the NLC, along with representatives from two Presbyterian churches in Brooklyn whose leaders were members of the NLC. A resolution was declared on December 15 that included three points: (1) Mandarin International would meet with the union representatives who had been fired to negotiate and solve their differences on the premises of the Ministry of Labor, in the presence of a representative from the Human Rights Attorney's Office, with the hope that the union leaders would be rehired; (2) Gap Inc.

would commit itself to work with religious groups and NGOs to examine the possibility of forming an independent program to survey the garment industry in El Salvador; and (3) Gap Inc. would begin working again with Mandarin International when it could be assured that its orders would result in humane and productive employment in El Salvador, and the government of El Salvador would act in good faith to resolve labor conflicts in a quick and just manner.[40] Gap Inc. would return to Mandarin International when it could be assured that the factory would conform to its "Code of Vendor Conduct."

What Happened?

The National Labor Committee and the human rights and labor groups working with it to resolve the Mandarin International situation carried out their project of witnessing on behalf of the Mandarin International workers. The NLC's press releases coincide with what I was told in various interviews with participants and observers of the Mandarin International organizing, lockouts, and firings that occurred in 1995. The chronicling of events in the form of press releases, however, poses a political dilemma. Are witnessing and documentation sufficient as a principal form of political action taken, or does battle over whose reality is portrayed become a victory only in its reconfiguration for public relations?

The NLC-Gap campaign in the United States ended with the December 1995 Brooklyn resolution. On January 25, 1996, the reform of the Ley de Zonas Francas y Recintos Fiscales was approved by the national legislative assembly. The revised law added a "social clause" to the existing law for EPZs and bonded areas and established "the obligation on the part of garment factories to conform with Salvadoran labor laws, giving the Ministry of the Economy the right to sanction those who do not conform to the law."[41]

As of February 1996, at Mandarin International, no one who had been fired in 1995 for belonging to SETMI had been rehired, and Mandarin International factory management continued to support ATEMISA.[42] The national human rights advocate and other independent human rights organizations affirmed allegations that labor violations were still happening inside the factory. The president of El Salvador, Armando Calderón Sol, denounced the human rights groups as traitors and ingrates and said that they deserved "the death penalty" for denouncing the continued violations of labor rights.[43] The leaders of SETMI reported that they were receiving anonymous death threats. As Gap Inc. again threatened to cancel orders, and Mandarin International threatened to close shop over the allegations, negotiations began in San Salvador during March 1996 between representatives from Gap Inc., Mandarin International, the Archdiocese of El Salvador and other human rights organizations, labor activists, and NGOs who had signed the original letter denouncing labor practices at Mandarin International—all of the groups involved except SETMI and ATEMISA.

Because Mandarin International did not recognize SETMI, and ATEMISA was only an "association" with no formal rights in the workplace, neither group was allowed to participate in the San Salvador negotiations. Even though they were not invited to the negotiations, both SETMI and ATEMISA signed the final accord, which provided for the following: (1) the reinstallation of the ex-leadership of SETMI and the recognition of SETMI by management; (2) the rehiring of all of the workers who had lost their jobs during the unionization attempts; and (3) the formation of an independent monitoring group, the GMIES, to assure that Salvadoran labor law and the Gap Inc. "Code of Vendor Conduct" would be enforced at Mandarin International. GMIES representatives would be allowed to enter the factory unannounced to monitor working conditions; furthermore, GMIES was allowed to talk to workers and receive reports of their working conditions and to place a suggestion box on the factory floor for complaints and suggestions with regard to working conditions.

With pressure from the GMIES and the NLC, Mandarin International promised to rehire the SETMI leadership over the period of March through October 1996. Although a few of the SETMI leadership were rehired, the factory management did not follow through with its promise to rehire the majority of fired workers and follow Gap Inc.'s "Code of Vendor Conduct."[44] In September, negotiations were reopened in San Salvador between the Mandarin International management, Gap Inc., the NLC, and the GMIES to come to an agreement about the rehiring of all fired employees. As a result, in January 1997 the factory contacted former workers by telegram and telephone, while radio, television, and newspaper announcements were made to invite those fired during the 1995 conflict to apply for reinstatement at Mandarin International. At the end, 160 workers responded to the announcements and 38 were rehired, with the idea that others would be rehired according to the needs of the factory. By the following November, a total of 75 workers had been rehired, and the monitoring group continued its factory visits and maintained contact with the factory managers, along with SETMI and ATEMISA. According to GMIES reports,[45] working conditions had improved with the implementation of the "Code of Vendor Conduct" and the presence of the monitoring group.[46]

SETMI members told me that, although they were rehired and that working conditions had improved, their lives have been made difficult since their return to the factory. One member of the union leadership complained, "The supervisors of ATEMISA have encouraged workers to make life hell for the SETMI members; we have been attacked, separated into different departments, and continually insulted. They have made our lives impossible." Another union member said, "They make fun of me, and sometimes do not give me work."[47] Others reported that they have been threatened and that their coworkers have been warned not to talk to them.

The final agreement between the NLC, the GMIES, Mandarin International, and Gap Inc. is not legally binding. Because the GMIES has been criticized by ATEMISA workers and by the factory managers for taking the side of SETMI in disputes and is afraid of being denied access to the factory, its monitors do not feel that they can intervene to a great extent in such situations, and the insults continue. Also, because SETMI has not grown in membership since its reinstatement—it has, in fact, been struggling to maintain its existence—it has remained relatively powerless in the face of growing ATEMISA membership.

The dispute at Mandarin International and the resulting negotiations and resolutions have been successful in calling attention to the situation of workers in the export-oriented garment *(maquila)* sector in El Salvador, both within the country and in the international community. Economist Francisco Lazo, a member of the board of directors at the Center for Labor Studies (CENTRA) in San Salvador, which forms part of the GMIES, has argued that the Mandarin International case has been "a good experiment in bonsai: it has not grown, but it looks good."[48] The GMIES was allowed to work only with Mandarin International, despite its attempts to work with other factories in the country's EPZs, and Carolina Quinteros, a member of the GMIES, pointed out that the country's factory owners will not open their production sites to independent monitoring without being forced to do so.[49] Without a strong, independent union on site, it is difficult to improve working conditions to any great extent; and unless SETMI can increase the number of its members, it cannot have much effect on the day-to-day running of the shop floor.[50] One SETMI member argued: "The factory and ATEMISA are the same thing. The independent monitoring group took the place of the union in negotiating with the factory, and now I feel that the factory has imposed itself on the GMIES. They have no power."[51] What then of the transnational organizing campaign and the workers at Mandarin International?

While the campaign, its resolution, and the independent monitoring project have served to assure the integrity of Gap Inc.'s brand name and have made Gap Inc. retail outlets safe once more for progressive-minded shopping, their effects on the shop floor have been either ambiguous or, in some cases, unqualifiedly negative. The GMIES worked hard to solve labor disputes and to serve the interests of the workers at Mandarin International by acting as a buffer between workers and the unfair practices of the factory managers. The GMIES often posed itself, and was supported by the NLC and North American labor groups, as the solution to the problems of old-style unionism. In its first public report, from April 1997, the GMIES stated that its fundamental mandate is "to promote the active participation of civil society in the prevention of and alternative solution to labor conflicts in the garment industry in El Salvador."[52]

The GMIES intervened at times when workers had been fired without notice or when there were minor disputes between workers and management at the plant. In other instances, the group either acted without taking into consideration national or international labor standards or reverted to support the hierarchical and patriarchal practices of traditional unionism. The continued existence of a company union on the site is a violation of ILO conventions, of which El Salvador is a signatory, and the pat-downs of women who work on the factory floor—upon entry, at lunch time, and at the end of the day—continued even after the signing of the 1996 accord.[53]

Despite the efforts of SETMI and the GMIES, women working in Mandarin International and in other garment factories continued to work long hours (voluntarily at Mandarin International, rather than by force), most in order to make 1,260 colones per month, which is the national legal minimum wage.[54] Often, at Mandarin, production quotas were set at one hundred or more pieces an hour; only by reaching daily production quotas of eight to twelve hundred pieces a day could anyone actually get paid the legal minimum wage. When these production quotas are taken into consideration, overtime is still a necessity, if not an obligation—especially with consumer prices rising by nearly 10 percent annually. According to data on real wage growth from the Inter-American Development Bank, in El Salvador real wages had decreased at the national level by 0.5 percent between 1994 and 1995, by 6.9 percent between 1995 and 1996, and by 4.5 percent between 1996 and 1997.[55]

What about the lives of those SETMI members who were fired and never rehired? I met Judith Viera, one of the garment workers featured in the 1995 NLC tour of North America, in November 1997.[56] Viera was working as a cashier at a gas station in Apopa, a town outside of San Salvador not too far from her home. She told me that when she returned from touring the United States in 1995, she was met by hecklers upon her arrival in the San Salvador airport and immediately vilified by the press as a traitor to the nation. She could not find work and felt that she was treated badly by all sides in the campaign, even though, she told me, the apparent success of the campaign and the December agreement would not have happened if she had not gone on the tour.

During the tour, Viera said, she would work for the NLC for twelve hours a day, often without eating or resting. According to Viera, she was eighteen years old while she was at Mandarin International, where she worked as a secretary, not as a garment worker. She had been chosen by the Central de Trabajadores Democráticos (CTD), the union central to which SETMI had belonged, to represent them on the NLC tour. One SETMI member said, "Judith wasn't a member of the union, nor was her sister, but they were close to the leadership of the CTD."[57] In fact, Viera herself told me that she is the niece of Amanda Villatoro, a leader of the CTD, and was willing to go on the tour of the United States. She was chosen to go, she says, as the "child symbol" of the Mandarin International/NLC-Gap campaign, and that it was her "performance" on the speaking tour that really helped the Mandarin International case.

While the NLC promised to keep her on its payroll because of the risk she had taken in going on the tour of the United States, Viera said that after her return to El Salvador she received only four monthly paychecks from the NLC, for one thousand colones each (approximately $115). The checks stopped after January 1996; she did not hear from the NLC after that, and Viera was not sure whether the checks were sent but kept by the CTD, with whom she was no longer on good terms, or whether they were simply stopped after the NLC-Gap Brooklyn resolution in December 1995. Viera told me: "My performance on the tour helped the country and brought to light the maquila situation and its problems. It also helped the groups in the United States and added to their image. I feel betrayed and left behind."

"Una Gran Zona Franca"

In light of El Salvador's, and the garment workers', dependence[58] on the garment industry as a source of needed income, the everyday practices of exploitation, domination, and patriarchy on the shop floor are difficult to combat. Then-president Armando Calderón Sol, as part of his bid to counter the allegations of the corporate campaigns and those of human rights organizations, labor activists, and unions regarding poor labor practices in the garment industry, argued that the maquilas represent El Salvador's only hope for development. In 1995, Calderón Sol promised to provide employment for hundreds of thousands more Salvadorans by turning the country into "one big export processing zone," an effort, he argued, that was being sabotaged by activist groups pushing for greater labor rights. As he told the national daily newspaper *La Prensa Gráfica:* "What we have in this country is amazing, a class of people willing to work, proud to work and aiming for efficiency and excellence. Since this is the situation, then, why don't we make the country into a single free trade zone?" In the same interview, he said, "globalization means incorporating ourselves into global commodity chains" at any cost—including giving multinational companies sway over a large sector of society in return for jobs (see Map 2).[59]

For Calderón Sol, the choice is one between labor rights and employment—a threat that has been felt by workers in all sectors. In one of the training sessions organized by Central de Trabajadores Salvadoreños (CTS) for SETMI that I attended in 1997, the union spent three hours discussing the compromise between the need for money and for work, and the doctrines and principles of unionization. In the training session, the CTS explained to the SETMI directorate the separate workings and the overlapping jurisdictions of national labor laws, the national constitution, and the

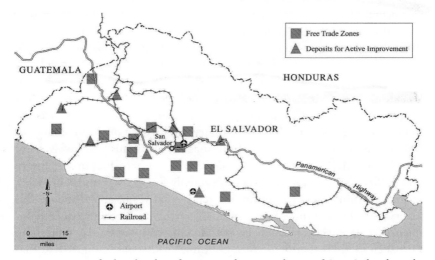

Map 2. Map of El Salvador, featuring the capital city of San Salvador, the country's free trade zones, and the deposits for active improvement where export-oriented garment manufacturing is centered. The main FTZs and deposits are located around El Salvador's transportation infrastructure (the Pan-American Highway, the main airports, and railroad lines) in order to make export easier and faster. The sheer numbers and locations of FTZs and deposits in El Salvador have transformed it into the big free trade zone promised by former president Calderón Sol. Courtesy of Rutgers Cartography.

law governing the country's EPZs. Because the jobs were needed, as was the money they brought in, their debates were focused on how to improve working conditions, fight for recognition, and draw in other members without jeopardizing their own positions or the garment factory's production orders on which those positions depended.

Military Repertoires and Postwar Paradigms

The physical manifestation of the presidential threat and promise to make El Salvador into one big EPZ is in the locked gates and armed guards that surround the EPZs. The zones are scattered around the country, with many on the outskirts of San Salvador itself, and are often difficult to reach and somewhat isolated. High walls surround the large factory buildings that often have their own armed guards to deter people from entering or leaving without permission from either or both the director of the EPZ and the director of the factory itself. Workers are not allowed to enter or leave the site until they have been fully searched—their bags and personal belongings examined as well as body searches.[60] Such guarding and surveillance ensures that people who enter do so to make clothing and do not leave except at designated hours or with prior permission. It also makes organizing or protest difficult, since people inside the factory walls do not interact with people outside except before and after work and sometimes during the lunch hour.

The director of the San Marcos EPZ is a former military colonel who had participated in the recent civil war, and the bunker-like aspect of San Marcos is evidence of his experience in designing fortified sites. It is rumored that he also served as the military intelligence officer in charge of union activities and has applied the lessons learned in his past involvement with labor activists to the running of the EPZ. Other EPZs may not have army officers as directors, but they are equally fortress-like and militaristic in their running. Activists and union representatives have had to face this reality, and they continue to rely on many of the tactics they learned fighting on the other side of the civil war and living with day-to-day repression. One such tactic is that of alliance building; in this paramilitarized situation, local and transnational alliances between labor groups, feminist organizations, academics, church groups, and the international community are both important and necessary.

Repertoires: Used and (Un)Usable

We have seen some of the tactics used in the NLC-Gap campaign in the United States and El Salvador. I now turn to analyze some local organizing tactics that were not taken up within transnational repertoires of contention. The results of the December 1995 negotiations and the subsequent negotiations in 1996 were scripted into the official narrative of the Mandarin International campaign. As told by Gap Inc., the NLC, and North American consumers, it was a protracted struggle that ended with the eventual triumph of the October 1996 rehiring of the union members. Other local organizing initiatives were left out of the Mandarin International story. El Salvador's human rights, labor, and activist communities, with the support of international solidarity organizations, have organized a number of local and transnational organizing campaigns in the garment industry.

In 1996, the Committee in Solidarity with the People of El Salvador (CISPES) sponsored a tour of the United States by Ana Maria Romero, a union member at the GABO factory in San Salvador, and Wilmer Erroa Argueta, a telephone worker and member of the Salvadoran Association of Telecommunications Workers (ASTTEL). Romero and Erroa testified before the U.S. Congress on working conditions and labor repression in El Salvador. The GABO factory, like Mandarin International, was located in the San Marcos EPZ. In 1996, GABO workers organized a union at the factory. The GABO union was subsequently destroyed through mass firings and workplace intimidation of those who joined.

During her 1996 tour, Romero gave her own testimony of life as a garment worker and talked about labor control in the garment industry in El Salvador. Romero told an audience in the United States: "The managers are above the law. . . . All foreign firms are generally able to treat the workers however they see fit. But, for all the abuses, Salvadorans do not want the companies to leave the country and take away much-needed jobs."[61] As a result of the tour and the CISPES campaign, Romero was vilified by the Calderón Sol government and in the national press as a "bad Salvadoran" who wanted to destroy the nation's economy. CISPES was targeted as a radical U.S. protectionist group whose goal was to send garment production back to the United States, thus robbing Salvadorans of their means of subsistence. In another linking of patriarchy with garment production, Calderón Sol personally told the press: "I can only call them inhuman traitors, who strike against the Salvadoran family."[62]

One effort to combat the attacks in the press and by government and business representatives was the formation of the Coordinating Group for Dignified Employment in the Maquila (COSDEMA) in 1996, after the attacks on Judith Viera, Ana Maria Romero, and the national and international organizations that supported them. COSDEMA was created by a number of Salvadoran groups that focus on labor rights, including unions, NGOs, solidarity organizations, women's groups, human rights groups, and research organizations. COSDEMA initiated a campaign in El Salvador that was called "For a Just Christmas Bonus and a Dignified Salary in the Garment Industry."

The campaign was supported internationally by CISPES, and members of the group visited the various maquilas and EPZs throughout the country to encourage workers to denounce violations of labor rights, low salaries, and the non- or underpayment of the annual Christmas bonus. COSDEMA did not last much longer than the Christmas campaign. Many have argued that its formation demonstrated the need for many organizations to work together in order to come up with a solution to the problems of maquila workers. Its demise could be attributed to the postwar atmosphere of competition that still exists among unions and labor organizations in El Salvador, a legacy of the civil war and international cold war unionism that pitted unions against one another for political reasons. The competition among union and labor organizations was fostered as part of counterinsurgency tactics and often organized and funded by the American Institute of Free Labor Development (AIFLD), AFL-CIO's international section. COSDEMA's short lifespan proved the necessity for a "strong and capable union movement to assume its role as an organized class . . . in order to coordinate the diverse organizational sectors in society" interested in promoting workers' rights.[63]

Such coordination could not be sustained for longer than the life of a particular campaign. Since any given company can simply stop production in the face of labor conflicts, COSDEMA's participants argued, protests have to be carried out at the transnational level in order to mirror transnational corporate structures. The GMIES and others also played an important part in calling the government and the factory to account over working conditions and questions of human and labor rights. According to participants and observers of the Mandarin International conflict and other labor-based campaigns aimed at the maquila industry, the presence of an international solidarity group like the NLC was important in the process of negotiating the conflict, though the outcome was not always good for workers such as Viera.

With the Mandarin International case, although the union was the subject of the negotiations, the management of the factory prohibited SETMI from taking an active part in negotiating or deciding on the resolution of the conflict. Even before the corporate campaign began, SETMI's membership had been gutted by mass firings, and most of those fired were never rehired.[64] Inside Mandarin International, the GMIES worked to ensure that there would be discussion between the management of the factory and the members of SETMI and ATEMISA. The presence of the GMIES on the shop floor meant, however, that SETMI was not able to engage in collective bargaining with the factory management. Instead, it was often the independent monitors who brought employee complaints to the notice of the managers and returned to the shop floor with the managers' response.

The relationship between the GMIES, SETMI, ATEMISA, and the Mandarin International management brings up the larger issue of the effects and efficacy of third-party monitoring programs to make factories accountable for labor violations. While Mandarin International was one of the first factories in which a program of independent monitoring was employed, it has now become the precedent for many such programs. Just as corporate codes of conduct for labor conditions have become accepted tools for specifying labor rights at various levels of the commodity chain, third-party monitors have become accepted agents to verify compliance with those codes. A number of companies have hired accounting firms to monitor their labor and environmental conditions and to produce regular reports that are similar to audits of labor conditions at the subcontracting level. Mandarin International is monitored not only by the GMIES, but also by an internal monitor for Gap Inc. who visits there and other factories in El Salvador and Guatemala that subcontract for Gap Inc. in order to take note of working conditions, complaints, or problems on the shop floor.

Three models of monitoring are practiced in the garment industry. The first, supplier certification, has suppliers applying for certification from an independent group that monitors labor standards. Once suppliers get a seal of approval, retailers can source their production from those suppliers certified by the program. For example, the U.S. policy activist group Council for Economic Priorities (CEP) developed a supplier certification program called SA8000. The second model for monitoring labor conditions is that of independent monitoring, of which the GMIES is an example. In the Netherlands, aid agencies, trade unions, and retailers' associations have coordinated to set up the Fair Trade Charter Foundation, which includes all three constituencies, to monitor the implementation of a code of conduct for the garment industry. In the third model, retail companies themselves oversee the process. Nike has established such a program, hiring the accounting firm Ernst and Young to monitor its subcontractors and provide reports to the company about labor standards in factories producing its products. Just as Gap Inc. has not released the recommendations of its own monitor in Central America, Nike has not allowed public disclosure of these reports.[65] Corporate monitoring and nondisclosure mean that retailers cannot be held accountable for working conditions in any significant way.

What are the positive effects of garment industry monitoring? Monitors are able to document the enforcement of labor standards and compliance with corporate codes of conduct at various levels of subcontracting. When monitoring is in place, factories can be made accountable to a set of standards in order to maintain orders and production ties with participating retailers. The documentation and enforcement of an agreed-on set of standards also provide concrete information about the names, locations, and conditions of particular factories as well as data about labor conditions in the industry as a whole. However, *all* monitoring—whether it happens or not, how it happens, and what is done with the monitors' reports—is optional. When monitoring reports are not made public, for example, there is no public accountability for corporations. In other words, labor standards still depend on corporate goodwill.

While public disclosure of subcontracting is a solution to the problem of accountability, monitoring programs pose a larger dilemma: if shop-floor organizing and collective bargaining are not recognized legally, or if unions are not respected, then workers have to accept monitoring in place of collective bargaining or shop-floor organizing. We saw with the GMIES at Mandarin International that unionists were resentful because the potential for them to exercise their power in organizing or collective bargaining was diminished by the very legitimacy of the monitoring group, while factory managers were resentful of what they saw as the pro-worker bias of the monitoring group.[66]

The blurring of lines between the responsibilities of monitoring and those of collective bargaining potentially leads to greater inaction on resolving conflicts than would otherwise have been without the third-party presence on the factory floor. When monitors are in day-to-day contact with factory owners, managers, union members, and other workers, they are put in an awkward position. Their very independence, in fact, is dependent on being allowed to enter the factory premises. Maintaining an attitude of objectivity in the face of daily disputes, some of which are minor and some of which constitute labor violations, is often impossible.[67]

Union-to-Union International Solidarity?

In addition to being the focus of a highly publicized corporate campaign, El Salvador was also the Central American headquarters for the reformation of the AFL-CIO's international organizing project. AIFLD, a cold war project that often employed tactics of counterinsurgency in the name of labor organizing, was reconstituted in 1996 as the Solidarity Center of the AFL-CIO.[68] The Solidarity Center's new organizing mission continued the

former focus on union-to-union solidarity without the rabid anticommunism and ties to the CIA that marked its predecessor.[69] The Solidarity Center
employed an organizing model that emphasized worker participation and
empowerment, rather than the old hierarchical structures and politics of
U.S. foreign policy that tend to ignore the everyday reality of the factory
floor, and looked to incorporate international solidarity campaigns into its
organizing efforts. For the maquila sector, it meant collaborating with the
U.S. garment union UNITE to apply corporate pressure in support of labor
organizing efforts in Central America and the Caribbean. In keeping with
this new collaborative effort, the Solidarity Center began an organizing initiative called "Group 3" in an attempt to bring together three union federations interested in organizing the maquilas.

Because of the politicization of El Salvador's union movement during
the war, and its subsequent dispersal, many of the existing union federations
are corrupt, debilitated, or still unable to reorient their politics to fit the
postwar situation.[70] Many unions depended on funding from AIFLD for
their existence and tailored their politics to such funding; other unions had
participated with the guerrillas under the umbrella of the Frente Farabundo
Martí de Liberación Nacional (FMLN) and are still living with the legacy
of wartime repression, violence, and counterinsurgent antiunionism. A
number of unions continue to look for international funding to supplement
their budgets, focusing more on networking with NGOs than on shop-
floor organizing.

Finally, postwar conditions for labor organizing are still adverse; while
unionists are not necessarily threatened by death squads, they still do not
have the backing of the nation-state or the respect of the capitalists that
would bolster national labor laws and allow them to organize export-
oriented manufacturing sectors. The Ley de Zonas Francas still exempts
free trade zones/EPZs and bonded areas/deposits of active perfection from
national labor and trade laws, so while unions have had a number of successes in organizing nationally, the maquila sector continues to represent a
serious challenge. This has led to barriers in organizing workers at the factory level; given the immense difficulty of organizing in the maquila sector,
union efforts have often been destroyed before they even began.

The other obstacle to organizing that has faced the traditional union
movement is that the majority of the maquila sector consists of urban
women between the ages of sixteen and thirty-two.[71] Of the 60,000 people
employed in the export-oriented garment industry in El Salvador, "78% . . .
were women, of which about 50% were single mothers."[72] According to
feminist activists in El Salvador, the Salvadoran union movement has been

marked not only by a top-down orientation, but also by patriarchal methods of organization. Men continue to lead the majority of unions, even those organizing in the maquila sector; women workers and those in the union leadership are often too overworked to be able to participate in organizing actions, and their double workday continues to go unrecognized by men higher in the union hierarchy. This orientation has often led union federations to ignore the interests and issues that are important to their women members and to focus on politics and fund-raising rather than shop-floor organizing.[73] Fitzsimmons and Anner argue, "[P]oliticized unions are likely to respond differently to a change in their political environment than those that focus on bread-and-butter labor issues."[74]

Only those unions that focus on "bread-and-butter" issues have attempted to address the needs of women on the shop floor and in the union meetings. It is these unions that have met with the most success in organizing the maquila sector. The three federations that make up the Group 3 each have different political leanings, with Federación de Asociaciones y Sindicatos Independientes de El Salvador (FEASIES) on the left, and the CTS and the Centro Nacional de Trabajadores Salvadoreños (CNTS) forming the center-right of the group. The federations began to meet in May 1998 to discuss methods for organizing the maquila sector, including international solidarity efforts, corporate campaigns, and a clearer focus on the gendered aspects of maquila production. At that time, there was still much work to be done on the ground before any effort could be coordinated. The CNTS had a factory organized with the SITEMSAL union, which counted more than 51 percent of the workers in its membership. Besides SETMI, it was the only garment workers' union that had organized at the level of the factory and not been annihilated.

In my discussions with garment workers and union organizers, many outlined for me how maquila-sector organizing attempts had been defeated in the past.[75] Corrupt unions would enter a labor dispute to represent workers who were on strike, locked out, or had reported abuses by the management of a particular factory. These unions would force factories to pay workers indemnities for labor violations but would take a considerable percentage of the factory's payment to the workers as a commission for representing them or would sell protesting workers' names to the factory management so that they would be blacklisted from working in the garment industry. In either case, the payments were little better than extortion from factory owners and betrayal of the workers.

Shop-floor organizing attempts have also been destroyed through the introduction of a company-supported union into the factory, as was the case with ATEMISA in Mandarin International.[76] These company unions offer extra benefits to workers, such as participation in discount buying clubs for groceries and lunch programs, in return for affiliation and the renunciation of independent organizing attempts. As we saw from the experience at Mandarin International, such methods of encouraging workers to join a company union can be combined with firing organized workers en masse and blacklisting them from future employment.

Unions and labor organizing were one of the many battlefronts of El Salvador's civil war. Because for many years unions were either active combatants or fighting for existence rather than for membership, they do not have the capacity to organize workers and to recruit membership from the factory ranks. There is a need for new coalitions of groups to fight for workers' rights in light of the peace agreements, neoliberal politics, and the privatization of most industries and services in El Salvador. This need has arisen precisely because of the progressive debilitation of the union movement over the past twenty years and the continued lack of new alternative organizing methods. It is in this situation that transnational organizing could do its best solidarity work. This is especially true given the history of people-to-people solidarity between the United States and El Salvador during its civil war, and the ability of groups in El Salvador to contribute to information politics that would educate North Americans, Europeans, and third world workers about their context and their organizing efforts. But first, North-South hierarchies that maintain organizations in the global North in positions as brokers must be reconfigured, and the focus on image making and consumption must be dismantled in order to bring forth the centrality of the politics of production and the agency of women working and organizing in the maquila sector. Such moves depend on a dismantling of race, gender, national, and class hierarchies in protest that will lead to their reconfiguration in both transnational organizing and production. These are the challenges of organizing in postwar times.

3

The Ideal of Transnational Organizing

The consumer campaign carried out against celebrity talk show host Kathie Lee Gifford and U.S.-based megaretailer Wal-Mart targeted working conditions at factories producing Wal-Mart's Kathie Lee line of clothing. The campaign was a joint effort of the NLC and UNITE, the U.S.-based Union of Needletrades, Industrial, and Textile Employees.[1] When it burst into public view in the summer of 1996, the Kathie Lee campaign seemed to be a model of transnational organizing among labor activists and garment workers whose shop-floor organizing attempts had been thwarted by the neoliberal rewriting of national and international trade laws, creating hyper-exploitative subcontracting regimes throughout the world.

The campaign focused on Kathie Lee Gifford's subject position as a white, middle-class mother and her bourgeois raced, gendered body. Through its media-focused tactics, it created a scandal that affected Gifford's reputation, media presence, and brand name, along with that of Wal-Mart. The "Kathie Lee" scandal drew attention to the effects of national and international structures of labor, trade, and health laws on workers in Honduras and New York City alike. Unlike the Bangladesh anti-child-labor campaign, to which Wal-Mart could respond by touting clothing "Made in the USA," this campaign emphasized the links between U.S. and third world production sites in ways that made nativist responses difficult to mobilize. Furthermore, the campaign was able to bring to light the connections between garment workers from Honduras and New York City, TV personalities and public relations firms, and state and national government officials in the United States and Honduras.

The resolution of the scandal was marked by Gifford's appearance on television in tears, while her husband, former football player Frank Gifford, handed out envelopes of money to garment workers in Manhattan, all orchestrated by a public relations agent hired by the couple. Despite the fact that Kathie Lee Gifford joined New York governor George Pataki in creating a statewide task force to improve garment industry conditions, the nation's media outlets covered the scandal to such an extent that the summer of 1996 was marked in New York City tabloids as the summer of the sweatshop, with immigrant workers, labor violations, and poor working conditions in New York's garment industry featured on front pages for several months.

After this, then-president Clinton convened a garment task force that introduced the much-disputed Fair Labor Agreement (FLA) to deal with working conditions in the garment industry, while student activists all over the country created the United Students Against Sweatshops (USAS) to protest the sourcing of their universities' clothing. Kathie Lee Gifford's name has since been linked periodically to the use of sweatshops in various parts of New York City and Central America.[2] The Kathie Lee campaign sparked a number of policies, organizations, and activism during that period. What were the effects of the Kathie Lee campaign on the shop floors of garment factories in the United States and Honduras and on the politics of transnational labor organizing?

In this chapter, I examine the Kathie Lee campaign in light of its historical relation to the development of the revitalized union movement in the United States, especially as part of the larger political project of building and maintaining the boundaries of the nation-state, both internally and externally.[3] Internally, it has replicated older divides of race, class, gender, and immigration status; externally, it has marked a reconstitution of the United States' national pact within the space of globalization, transnationality, and neoliberalism. As with earlier versions of the pact, some people speak, while those left out of the pact are spoken for.

Unionism, New and Old

Within the realm of the transnational, the new unionism, as marked by the Kathie Lee campaign, could be seen as a marker of U.S. foreign policy during the Clinton administration. Anticommunist, cold war labor-organizing tactics were replaced by other forms of patronage whose boundaries were at the same time flexible and exclusionary. These boundaries defined a privatized space of politics that constituted a global, yet U.S.-centric, "civil society" best exemplified in the work of Robert Putnam.[4] This privatized space is characterized by the prevalence of the NGO model and an entre-preneurial citizenship that takes up the work of the dismantled welfare state in a politics of neoliberalism.[5] The structure of the NGO model is one where private voluntary organizations not only take up the former work of the welfare state but are often organized with a top-down structure similar to corporations, frequently becoming their own public relations agents.

The Clinton-era "new unionism" was fashioned along the lines of the corporate NGO model and as such was fundamental to the reproduction of the U.S. nation-space, the delineation of it as global and transnational, and the modes of participation of people falling both within and outside its parameters. Domestically, the cold war unionism of the United States— i.e., the policies of the AFL-CIO—had been exemplified by pacts with man-agement, the "pure and simple" unionism advocated by Samuel Gompers, and exclusionary immigration politics.[6] Internationally, the AFL-CIO's projects, produced by the exceptionalist formation of the U.S. nation-state, often paralleled U.S. foreign policy in the name of humanizing production relations in lieu of labor militancy or collective bargaining. The post–cold war labor politics of transnationality, by contrast, focused on making cor-porations into global good citizens through Clintonian politics of consent rather than through legal strictures. By focusing on the good citizenship of corporations and CEOs, the politics of the market and the quest for global flexibility remained unchallenged in quests for labor rights. The other side of corporate good citizenship was the encouragement of politicized consump-tion, boycotts, and the value of the brand name as a basis for protest, and on consumers' buying power as a basis for political access and participation.

Recycling Testimony: Agency, Power, and the Problem of Transnationality

The 1996 Kathie Lee campaign began with a focus on consumer protest around a Honduran garment factory, but quickly expanded to link labor violations there with sweatshop production in New York City. The NLC-UNITE tactics borrowed from the 1995 NLC-Gap campaign and from earlier labor and solidarity campaigns; included congressional testimony, news conferences, and television spots; and featured a tour of the United States by fifteen-year-old garment worker Wendy Díaz. Díaz had worked at Global Fashions, the Choluma, Honduras, factory that subcontracted production for the Kathie Lee Plus clothing line. The National Labor Committee worked with UNITE on the cross-border campaign that in-cluded New York and Honduras. Through the sharing of information, strategy, and funds, the coordinated campaign brought to light the con-nections between sweatshops in the United States and garment production throughout the world. The campaign was coordinated around production practices and labor violations in factories making Wal-Mart's Kathie Lee label and under the explicit joining of brand name, celebrity image, and labor violations.

The Honduras segment of the campaign was based on information gathered by the NLC during research trips for its 1995 Gap campaign. Through meetings with garment workers, who provided them with Kathie Lee clothing labels, and with the help of the Committee for the Defense of Human Rights in Honduras (CODEH), NLC directors Charles Kernaghan and Barbara Briggs were able to document labor violations and worker abuse at Global Fashions.[7] Abuses included the nonpayment of wages and compulsory overtime, limited bathroom breaks, lack of potable water, and, in some cases, the employment of underage workers. When the NLC wrote letters to Gifford and to Wal-Mart to denounce working conditions at Global Fashions, Wal-Mart's first response was to cancel its orders at the factory.[8]

The NLC and other labor activists had learned from the experiences in Bangladesh and El Salvador that taking orders away from the factories in violation would not be helpful for the women and men working there because they depended on their jobs and their wages to survive. In the case of the Kathie Lee campaign, the NLC criticized Wal-Mart's cancellation of its orders. In a push for Wal-Mart and Gifford not to cancel orders at Global Fashion, NLC executive director Charles Kernaghan testified in front of the Senate's Democratic Policy Committee on April 29, 1996. In testimony, Kernaghan named Global Fashion, the Honduran subcontractor, along with Wal-Mart and Kathie Lee Gifford, saying:

> Like many assembly plants offshore, Global Fashion was and is a humiliating place to work. The women—about 80 percent of the (workers) are women, the majority of whom are very young—need to raise their hands to receive permission to use the bathrooms, which are kept locked. Bathroom privileges are limited to two visits per day, one in the morning and one in the afternoon.[9]

In his testimony, Kernaghan offered the example of fifteen-year-old Suyapa Johana Nolasco Guerra, who had worked at Global Fashion since 1994. Kernaghan portrayed Nolasco's experience as typical of conditions at the factory, where daily production goals would reach three to four thousand pieces a day. Nolasco had told Kernaghan, who, in turn, told the congressional committee: "The supervisors make us work on holidays, telling us that they are going to pay double. They even make us work on Sundays, and don't pay us double but straight time." According to Kernaghan, Nolasco, then fourteen, was fired after one year of working at Global for "writing down the day's production goal." Kernaghan concluded his synopsis of Nolasco's situation by quoting her as saying, "Other workers were similarly threatened and fired without justification."[10]

The rhetoric of Kernaghan's congressional testimony replicated previous descriptions of working conditions and labor abuse in garment factories, from child labor (as exemplified by Kernaghan's reiteration of Nolasco's age) to impossible production quotas and gross underpayment of wages. In his testimony, Kernaghan repeated details about garment production in Honduras identical to those described in the 1994 NLC video *Zoned for Slavery*:

> Charles Kernaghan . . . revealed that Kathie Lee's budget line of garments—prices run from $10 for a blouse to $40 for a blazer—had once been produced by child laborers in a seamy Honduras factory called Global Fashion. "They bring the kids to work in broken-down school buses," he says. "You'd swear you're at high school, but you're not. You're in these factories where they work 14-hour shifts."[11]

The image of children riding on a reconditioned yellow U.S. school bus to the EPZ instead of to school, in order to work long hours in a garment factory, was the central trope of the 1994 video. The facts provided by Kernaghan's testimony and the reality put forth in *Zoned for Slavery* were horrifying to congresspeople and consumers alike. The rhetorical strategies employed in both the testimony and the video are based on the assumption that U.S. consumers—and congresspeople—are central to both the perpetuation and the elimination of these horrors.

The same facts, the same working conditions, and the same pieces of clothing that are brought out to make the point of consumer complicity are displayed in each subsequent campaign. In the 1993 *Dateline NBC* piece on child labor in Bangladesh, the 1994 video *Zoned for Slavery,* the Mandarin campaign and tour of 1995, and the 1996 Kathie Lee campaign, the formula is repeated. Such rhetorical strategies, coupled with a lack of substantive change in the relations of the industry as a whole, bound the sweatshop as a site of aberrance for the normal workings of capital while at the same time leaving the garment industry and garment workers' everyday lives outside the critique. The sweatshop becomes a space outside the everyday, a space that can be taken up by the transnational. Transnational campaigns thus serve to consolidate a repertoire of working conditions that are readily identifiable as those of the global sweatshop, around which consumer mobilization can be organized. At the same time, garment workers continue to work long days, producing clothing for export to U.S. consumers; the ideal sweatshop is consolidated in the name of conscientious consumption.

Three aspects of the recycling and repetition of a particular combination of working conditions as constituting the global sweatshop are especially problematic. First, by marking certain violations as particularly abusive, as *abnormal,* other working conditions and relations inside and outside the factory are normalized, ignored, or regarded as externalities—unfortunate, inevitable, and ultimately irrelevant side effects of the production process. The normal workings of capital—as manifested in garment production— are maintained outside the narrative of the sweatshop. Those conditions include wage labor and exploitation, long hours, gendered divisions of labor and gender gaps in pay, armed guards at the entrances and exits of factories, production quotas that are often impossible to meet, and raced divisions of labor on a global scale that reserve garment work for third world women in Honduras and the United States. In the citation of a range of aspects of garment work as abnormal or offensive, not only are factory conditions outside the official narrative naturalized, they are, in effect, relegated to the structural realm, as that which is outside of political and social relations and outside of practice. While the unmentioned working conditions become globalized, and therefore outside the reach of local and transnational organizing efforts, those that are constantly cited move into the realm of typology—categories against which working conditions can be measured, quantified, and finally rationalized.

Second, the repetition of a set of typical factory conditions categorized as unacceptable, in conjunction with the use of individual women with proper names and histories as prototypical case studies, relegated women who had been working and suffering in the factories to the realm of nonsubjectivity. The individual histories of the women whose experiences were cited as typical were translated into case studies of interchangeable garment workers. They fit into the case studies as prototypical poor, third world women workers, whose participation in garment production and protest could be used to reinforce the larger point of both (U.S.) consumption practices and (U.S.) consumer activism. In the end, Suyapa Nolasco's story was no different from that of her compatriot Wendy Díaz, who was the equivalent of Lesly Rodríguez, Judith Viera, and Nazma Akhter. All of these women, through their testimonies, their experiences as producers, and their position as tellers of truth, provided performances of sweatshop conditions for the benefit of U.S. consumers and activists. Through the practice of transnationality, difference is maintained in which U.S. consumers are able to occupy the space of modernity against the women and men who make clothing in the aberrant space of the third world sweatshop. These experiences and testimonies became the raw data around which successful campaigns were built.

Nolasco, Díaz, Rodríguez, Viera, and Akhter become the rhetorical equivalents of Rosa Martínez, the garment worker touted in advertisements in *Bobbin* as exemplifying the "Quality, Industriousness and Reliability" of El Salvador's garment industry, who can be hired for 57 cents or 33 cents an hour, depending on the year.[12] Although the names change, as do the women who are witnesses to, and victims of, global garment production, both names and people serve as the building blocks for U.S.-based labor activists and consumers to construct their ideal(ized) sweatshop around which consumer constituencies can organize.

Third, because the idealized sweatshop is a space of disempowerment and the prototypical worker can only practice the agency of victimhood— despite the texturing both are given in the campaign through the repetition of key details—only U.S. consumers and transnational corporations are capable of enacting change. In the case of Kathie Lee and Global Fashions, Kathie Lee Gifford was the only one (a) held accountable for labor violations and (b) able to change and improve working conditions. This particular campaign was not organized around attempted unionization or around long-term activism by workers at Global, so organizers did not think to coordinate their actions with people working or organizing at Global Fashions. In fact, the details given about conditions at Global, and about workers' lives there, reinforced the powerlessness of people involved in the production process. Neither garment workers in the United States nor those in Honduras were granted the agency of citizens, even those who actually held U.S. citizenship status.

Gifford, however, was granted that power and was appealed to as a person who cared about children, as a potentially good celebrity-citizen who would be able to protect workers at Global Fashions. In this case, Gifford's celebrity-citizenship is a privileged site from which to act—in a consumer-driven campaign, where citizenship and buying power are linked, celebrity status is the most privileged site of all. In an ironic twist of noblesse oblige, it is Gifford's position as the host of *Live with Regis and Kathie Lee* that seems to grant her a higher level of citizenship, moral authority, and responsibility than most Americans. In this way, Gifford's lapse into sweatshop production could be chalked up to innocence: her white, upper-class womanhood, which she could then mobilize to change working conditions in both New York and Honduras. Gifford's subject position, in the end, is both the target and the solution to the campaign and to the antisweatshop activism and legislation engendered by the discovery of working conditions at Global Fashions.

By granting Kathie Lee Gifford the ultimate power to rectify labor abuse in the factories that subcontract production in her name, the Kathie Lee campaign also reinscribed U.S. sovereignty over capitalist production relations and over Central American (gendered) subjects. Thus the supremacy of the U.S. nation-state could be fixed firmly within transnationality. Through the rhetorical strategy of emphasizing isolated sweatshop conditions in a larger industry and the working conditions of particular individuals—of individual women battling over working conditions— Gifford was the one individual woman granted agency, both for herself and for garment workers producing clothing under the name of her label. Labor and trade law, rules of collective bargaining, and shop-floor organizing fell out of the debate. Instead, capitalist relations were rewritten as questions of Kathie Lee Gifford's morality and the purity of her brand and, secondarily, those of Wal-Mart. The entire debate, the entire campaign, was translated into one about whether American power, American idealism, and American democratic ideals could be redeemed. The redemption would be symbolic, and it would be embodied by Kathie Lee Gifford. Was this, in fact, a rearticulation of Manifest Destiny, with white womanhood as the new hero(ine)? The target of this rearticulation, rather than the "empty space" of the American nation-state in need of civilizing, was the aberrant space of the global sweatshop that could be civilized through the practice of transnational, redemptive white womanhood.

Kathie Lee's Response and Redemptive White Womanhood

When the NLC confronted her with Kernaghan's congressional testimony, Gifford responded on her television show, *Live with Regis and Kathie Lee*. On May 1, 1996, two days after Kernaghan's testimony, Gifford appeared on the ABC show dressed in an outfit from her Kathie Lee line of clothing. Gifford tearfully responded to the testimony, saying: "You can say I'm ugly. You can say I am not talented. But when you say that I don't care about children and that I will exploit them for some sort of monetary gain, for once, Mister, you'd better answer your phone because my attorney is calling you today. How dare you?"[13] On the show, Gifford often talked about her children by name and detailed her family life as both idyllic and "typically" American; to call into question her dedication to children was to call into question her entire credibility. The claim that her label employed child labor and sweatshop conditions also called into question, it would seem, Gifford's own beauty and talent.

That Gifford, and her brand name, would be linked to sweatshop conditions and child labor was especially damaging. The tags for Kathie Lee–branded products point out that a share of the proceeds from their sale goes to children's charities. As Gifford said in June 1996: "When I signed on [with Wal-Mart], my overriding thought was that I had found a way to provide a continuing source of funding for . . . housing and care for AIDS and crack-infected babies of New York City."[14] In 1995, Gifford earned $9 million a year from her clothing line, $1 million of which was donated to the Association to Benefit Children, which started houses (for children with AIDS or with crack addiction) named after Gifford's two children.[15]

Kathie Lee Gifford's celebrity status was combined with her love of children in positioning her subjectivity. By targeting Gifford's image of caring, white, Christian, all-American womanhood, the campaign shifted its central focus from the shop floor of Global Fashions to Gifford herself. While pushing for Gifford to take responsibility for working conditions at Global, Kernaghan, as Krupat argues, "kept asking the key question: Didn't Kathie Lee have a responsibility to see that her name was well used?"[16] Because the Kathie Lee label bore her name, alongside that of Wal-Mart, the NLC's rhetorical strategy was directed precisely at Gifford's subject position in such a way that it made possible both criticism and potential for salvation—of Gifford's persona and of her brand name.[17]

When first confronted by the NLC and Kernaghan's testimony, Gifford denied knowledge of the factory conditions, saying that when she found out about abuses at Global, she immediately called Wal-Mart and said, "'This is obscene if this is happening.' They said, 'That happened months ago; we found out about it and took care of it.'"[18] In fact, "taking care of it" meant pulling out of Honduras, blacklisting Global Fashion and moving production to Nicaragua. It should be noted that the shifting of production from Honduras to Nicaragua had been orchestrated earlier in 1996. Ostensibly, this was to take the sweatshop stigma—particularly that of child labor—away from the Wal-Mart and Kathie Lee brands, since, as Wal-Mart stated, "they found conditions were poor in Honduras." However, in discussion with the National Labor Committee, Wal-Mart argued that they could make clothing more cheaply in Nicaragua. Wages in Nicaragua's Las Mercedes free trade zone were an average of 24 cents an hour, as compared to the 31 cents an hour that was the average in Honduras.[19] In an interview with Barbara Briggs of the NLC, she told me that Nicaraguan garment workers said that a wage of 24 cents an hour would barely buy one meal a day for their families. Such conditions led to clandestine union organizing in Las Mercedes, whose labor violations were documented in a November 1997 three-part *Hard Copy* series on Nicaraguan sweatshops.[20]

While Gifford was claiming ignorance of working conditions in the factories bearing her name, Wal-Mart's solution to the sweatshop problem was to move its production sites away from media scrutiny, in this case from Honduras to Nicaragua. This media-focused cut-and-run solution is the other side of Wal-Mart's promotion of goods tagged as "Made in America" in its stores.[21] The National Labor Committee criticized Wal-Mart for cutting and running; Kernaghan's response combined political economy with morality: "You don't exploit the kids for a year and then walk away and get off scot-free. They owe these kids something."[22] What Kernaghan did not point out was that such exploitation was central to the everyday practice of neoliberal political economy.

The regime of flexible accumulation and the geographic mobility of capital are most evident in clothing and footwear production. This implies, as David Harvey argues, "relatively high levels of 'structural' (as opposed to 'frictional') unemployment, rapid destruction and reconstruction of skills, modest (if any) gains in the real wage, and the rollback of trade union power."[23] As Doreen Massey points out, "There is . . . a hierarchy of ownership, supervision and control, a hierarchy of the relations of economic ownership and possession."[24] By having already moved out of Honduras into Nicaragua, Wal-Mart was amassing more profit for itself within a regime that was created to benefit large capitalist firms like Wal-Mart through the expansion and geographical dispersal of the labor force. Not only would Wal-Mart be able to exploit a new group of workers in Nicaragua, it would be able to do so for lower wages. At the same time, Wal-Mart portrayed its cut-and-run tactics as humanitarian, thus attempting to legitimate itself and salvage its brand in the process.

What about New York?

Wal-Mart's attempt to legitimize its production practices by taking advantage of its capital and productive mobility ensured that production sites and workers—such as those in Honduras, Nicaragua, and New York City—would have to compete with each other for orders. As an added benefit to Wal-Mart, these production sites could be played off each other to promote labor quiescence, lower wages, and preservation of the company's brand-name and corporate image.[25] Wal-Mart avoided responsibility for labor violations and mistreatment of workers by moving production sites. In the same way, Kathie Lee Gifford tried to deny responsibility for conditions at Global Fashion by saying that since she was neither the retailer nor the factory owner, she could not be expected to have knowledge about worker abuse.

A central part of Wal-Mart's avoidance tactic was to tag as many of its goods "Made in America" as possible. Such strategic branding responded to public relations problems that arose in the early 1990s, when corporate downsizing and job loss had been linked directly to companies moving offshore in search of low wages and no unions; it was in this context that transnational labor organizing and the "new unionism" of the 1990s became prominent. Links between downsizing and globalization of production were central political issues for the NLC, the AFL-CIO, and UNITE, as well as for other labor and consumer activists. In 1992, the NLC report *Paying to Lose Our Jobs* made the linkage explicit:

> In 1980, 70 percent of all apparel purchased in the United States was produced domestically. Today, imports account for half of the U.S. apparel market. A National Labor Committee study found thirty U.S. apparel manufacturers operating plants in El Salvador, Honduras, and Guatemala, as well as sixty-eight other U.S. clothing manufacturers and retailers outsourcing to the "Three Jaguars." The National Labor Committee was able to determine that these same companies were involved in fifty-eight plant closings and eleven mass layoffs in the U.S. since 1990, which left 12,234 U.S. apparel workers jobless.[26]

In this explicit connection between layoffs, plant closings, and imports, U.S. activists were mirroring U.S. corporate and government agendas that used protectionist rhetoric such as the "Made in the USA" campaign to appeal to U.S. consumers. Thus, it was a short step from connecting layoffs and economic recession in the United States with globalized production to blaming third world workers for the loss of U.S. jobs. A decade later, such arguments were made with regard to the outsourcing of U.S. telemarketing and customer service work to India, the Philippines, and Mexico.[27] In the NLC literature, USAID and the U.S. government take their share of blame for promoting the Caribbean Basin Initiative (CBI) and the infrastructure for building export processing zones.[28] In the larger U.S. political context of the early 1990s, U.S. workers and media blamed not only corporations for the loss of U.S. jobs but also workers in Central America and the Caribbean for taking U.S. jobs. The restructuring of production practices under post-Fordist models fell out of this dominant narrative, and all that was left was a form of protectionism easily manipulated by U.S. corporate interests.

This early protectionism on the part of union organizers in the United States was replaced in mid-decade by an appeal to worker solidarity and the push for companies not to cut and run when their subcontractors were caught in labor violations. However, the transnationalization of workers' rights—through the linking of labor violations in the world's export processing zones with those in garment sweatshops employing immigrants in U.S. cities—still fell short of organizing for the labor rights of all workers. In fact, it promoted a new form of labor aristocracy with similar divisions; some workers' rights were defended, while others were left to fend for themselves under the auspices of transnational solidarity and the new union movement. Those left out tended to be the poorest, mostly women and mostly nonwhite immigrants, and residents of Latin America, Asia, and Africa.

While the NLC was focusing on working conditions in Honduras at Global Fashions, UNITE had discovered sweatshop violations at Seo Fashions, a New York City factory producing clothing for the Kathie Lee clothing line. For the first time, labor conditions in Central America were linked tactically to those in New York City, through tracing the subcontracting chains for clothing produced by a brand with a celebrity endorser and sold by a large U.S. retailer. For all of these reasons, the Kathie Lee brand became the perfect target for a transnational protest action. The researchers at NLC and UNITE were able to join forces tactically to push for better labor conditions in each site as part of an integrated strategy that would highlight labor violations in both sites simultaneously. Workers at Seo Fashions, in Manhattan's garment district, were owed tens of thousands of dollars in back pay. The *New York Daily News* broke the story with information gathered from UNITE, reporting that a week earlier, fifty thousand blouses made at Seo for the Kathie Lee line were shipped to Wal-Mart, to sell for $9.96 each, while Seo workers had not been paid for nearly three sixty-hour work weeks.

Seo was one of an estimated 2,000 to 2,500 "sweatshops" in New York City, according to federal labor officials. The factory was located in a building on West 38th Street that housed other garment factories—all of which, according to a U.S. Department of Labor investigator, were "riddled with safety and health violations."[29] Workers interviewed during the initial investigation said that they were forced to work six- and seven-day weeks on the fifty thousand blouses, without being paid overtime. According to Raphael, who had worked at Seo for six weeks: "The first week, I was paid $160 in cash. I sewed on the machine. I worked from 7:30 in the morning until 6:30 at night. That was from Monday through Saturday. On Saturdays, I only worked until 3 in the afternoon."[30] In describing the working environment at Seo, Lina, then an employee of Seo, said: "Everything is dirty, the trash isn't picked up, and the two bathrooms aren't fit for pigs to use. There is never any soap or toilet paper, and the plumbing doesn't always work. So imagine the smell."[31] These conditions are typical in an industry that sub-contracts along several levels, and in a country where only 800 inspectors police 22,000 garment contractors and 6 million workplaces in other U.S. industries.[32] The U.S. Department of Labor, acting quickly in response to publicity over Seo, fined Wal-Mart $22,000 for repeated violations of federal labor laws and held the company liable for more than $47,000 in back wages to the forty-five garment workers at Seo. The Department of Labor sought $29,348 in back pay for missed wages, and $18,062 for thirteen weeks of overtime.[33]

Kathie Lee Gifford and her husband Frank, a sportscaster for ABC, were hit even harder by the latest publicity. The day after the report appeared in the *Daily News,* Frank Gifford, claiming that Kathie Lee was "too devastated" to accompany him, went to Seo and handed out envelopes containing $300 to each of the garment workers in the New York factory. As he handed out the envelopes, Gifford, apparently placing himself in the position of an emissary of U.S. business interests—and American liberal morality—to the immigrants who worked at Seo, said: "I am very sorry, and I apologize for our country. God bless all of you."[34] In this way, by apologizing on behalf of "our country" and invoking God, Gifford was able to displace his wife's—and his own—complicity in maintaining sweatshop conditions onto the U.S. nation-state. In so doing, he was also drawing a firm line between himself as an American and the immigrant workers as outsiders.

Frank Gifford emphasized that the money handed out to the Seo workers "isn't salary. This is an emergency measure." Earlier that day, Kathie Lee Gifford had announced on *Live with Regis and Kathie Lee* that she was "sick to [her] stomach" to learn about conditions at Seo. Gifford went on to promise, "We're going to go down there and take care of it," wanting "the full power of the law" to be applied to Seo.[35] The quick response of both Giffords was a reflection of their embarrassment, their horror at the situation, and, especially, their desire to protect—and enhance—their name and their brand. The latter was evinced by their hiring of public relations agent Howard Rubenstein to work with the Giffords on the "handling" of the situation.[36]

With the revelation of sweatshop conditions at Seo Fashions, and the Giffords' highly publicized response, there was a general furor in the press—ranging from the *New York Times* to *People Magazine* and *Star Magazine*—over Wal-Mart, garment production, and the Giffords. While the Giffords went to the extreme of hiring their own public relations firm, all sides were battling for media attention and favor. On the same day that the Giffords were repudiating sweatshop practices on television and publicly handing out money to Seo workers, UNITE president Jay Mazur issued a press release, stating:

> Kathie Lee Gifford has been caught up in a system out of control. Millions of workers around the world, including young girls in Honduras and—as we have just discovered—immigrants in New York City, are producing clothes under sweatshop conditions that our union and many other people of good will succeeded in eliminating 50 years ago.

Mazur's points were the first to historicize the Kathie Lee scandal as part of the history of the labor movement and to link it to the larger system of garment production:

> The system is integrated in a vast global web of design, production, distribution and selling in which it is impossible to isolate any single part from the whole. To put an end to sweatshop production requires a systematic approach by corporations, labor organizations and governments.[37]

In the initial press release, Mazur contextualized the resurgence of sweatshops and the Kathie Lee Gifford scandal within garment production as a product of corporations, labor organizations, and governments. These statements back up Gifford's claim that she was scapegoated while at the same time serving as a reminder that shop-floor organizing was crucial to eliminating sweatshops earlier in the century. However, Mazur did not go so far as to detail how, if sweatshops were "eliminated 50 years ago," this "vast global web" of the garment industry—employing sweatshops, home working, labor repression, and worldwide production chains as central operating principles—was built; neither does he explore the AFL-CIO's complicity in supporting U.S. foreign policy and trade initiatives over the course of the preceding fifty years.

Such an analysis would involve detailing the participation of his union in movements of capital and governmental trade and immigration policies. The Mazur press release and the NLC-UNITE collaboration, along with the Kathie Lee scandal as a whole, could be read as a counterhegemonic moment—one that connects the production process, and the workings of capital, with the current media frenzy. However, this is not, to use Gramsci's conception, a moment of "catharsis," indicating "the passage from the purely economic (or egoistic-passional) to the ethico-political moment . . . This also means the passage from 'objective to subjective' and from 'necessity to freedom.'"[38] Specifically, by historicizing the "new sweatshop" and laying bare the connections between earlier organizing and the current period, and the connections between garment producing sites in various parts of the world, a moment of counterhegemony was opened up. However, the tumult of publicity directed at sweatshops and the subjectivity of Kathie Lee Gifford tended to reproduce hegemonic discourses around women, the third world, immigrants, workplace organization, and consumption practices. It also worked to reestablish the primacy of commercial media outlets, image making, and globalization as naturalized frameworks within which production, consumption, and protest were to be carried out.

Mazur stated the need for "new legislation . . . to assure that acceptable standards are met throughout the industry . . . [that] would mandate corporate responsibility for all domestic production and link standards for environmental and workers rights to our international trade agreements."[39] For the first time, sweatshops were at the top of the news throughout the summer of 1996. The Kathie Lee scandal now included the involvement not only of the NLC, but also that of UNITE, the Giffords, their publicists, and various media outlets, including a *New Yorker* cartoon on "Sweatshops of the Rich and Famous" (Figure 4).

On *Late Night with David Letterman,* Letterman made Kathie Lee Gifford the subject of his sarcastic top ten list, "The Top Ten New Items from the Kathie Lee Product Line," which included a new "Sweatshop Barbie" and a new workout video titled "Sweatin' in the Sweatshop."[40] Earlier, the *Washington Post* ran a cartoon in its editorial section featuring a cut-out paper doll of Kathie Lee Gifford next to a tag of her Wal-Mart Kathie Lee brand. The Kathie Lee doll was wearing a "complete low-wage wardrobe," with arrows pointing to each item of clothing the doll wore and citing the factory, the hourly salary, and working conditions. These popular culture representations of the sweatshop helped bring production practices and labor abuse into dominant images of fashion and advertising; at the same time, they reinscribed and reinforced the power of consumption and consumers, all the while trivializing the everyday lives of garment workers.

In the midst of the extensive media coverage and attempts at spin control, New York governor George Pataki and state attorney general Dennis Vacco took legal action against Seo and against sweatshop production in New York State. Within a week of the Seo Fashions revelations, Pataki proposed "hot goods" legislation that would prohibit "the sale or distribution of apparel produced in sweatshops that cheat workers of their wages."[41] The "hot goods" legislation did not specify of what the normal payment of wages would consist. Pataki argued that such legislation would "crack down on sweatshops," upholding New York's "proud history of shielding working men, women and children from exploitation and endangerment." The

"Hello, and welcome to another edition of 'Sweatshops of the Rich and Famous.'"

Figure 4. During the summer of the sweatshop in 1996, popular culture references to celebrity sweatshops were everywhere, from this New Yorker *cartoon to the David Letterman show. Copyright The New Yorker Collection 1996; Michael Maslin from cartoonbank.com; all rights reserved.*

legislation was passed the following month, with the Giffords attending the signing and committing themselves to work on its implementation.

Just as Mazur included a promotion of the "past 50 years" of sweatshop eradication, Pataki placed himself in a larger "proud history" of New York State, positing New York as central to the larger history of unionism. This rhetorical linking to a (mythical) past served to emphasize the irregularity of Seo Fashions, "exploitation and endangerment" in the garment industry, and the phenomenon of sweatshop production. Normalcy consisted of Pataki's "working men, women and children," "shielded" by Mazur's "people of good will," defined, as Pataki went on to say, by "legitimate businesses that pay fair wages, provide a safe working environment, and contribute to the economic and social health of New York and the nation."[42] Mazur and Pataki placed themselves in the position of defending workers against sweatshop conditions while they pointed to an earlier period, or to a larger industry, where such conditions did not exist. By linking themselves to the larger history of production and to the industry as a whole, where sweatshops were supposedly an aberration, Pataki, Mazur, the NLC, and the Giffords were able to posit the hope of salvation for themselves, their organizations, and the production process as a socioeconomic whole. Overall, the Kathie Lee campaign neatly brought together histories of unionism, clearing of consumer consciences, and othering garment workers in New York City factories and third world EPZs. What about the power formations that go into these discourses of transnationality?

Kathie Lee Meets Wendy Díaz

The Kathie Lee campaign was the most highly publicized battle over sweatshops in recent history, with its myriad press releases and television appearances and its strange coalitions. The National Labor Committee accelerated the level of coverage, bringing fifteen-year-old Wendy Díaz, a garment worker from Global Fashion, to tour the United States in June 1996 and to speak about working conditions. Díaz became the star witness for the abuses by Wal-Mart and Kathie Lee Gifford in Honduras, talking with activists, students, and religious groups and testifying in front of the U.S. House of Representatives Subcommittee on International Operations and Human Rights. Díaz's testimony in front of the congressional subcommittee detailed conditions at the factory: "At Global Fashion, there are about 100 minors like me—thirteen, fourteen years old—some even twelve. On the Kathie Lee pants, we were forced to work almost every day from 8:00 [a.m.] to 9:00 p.m. . . . Sometimes they kept us all night long, working."[43] Díaz's first publicized appearance in the United States was organized by the NLC and UNITE, where she met Kathie Lee Gifford on June 6, 1996, at the residence of John Cardinal O'Connor in Manhattan. This was symbolically important, since Cardinal O'Connor had been a known advocate of workers' rights throughout his tenure as archbishop of New York.

Earlier protagonists in the Kathie Lee campaign—including Kernaghan, Mazur, Esperanza Reyes of the Committee for the Defense of Human Rights in Honduras, and the Reverend David Dyson of the People of Faith Coalition—attended the meeting and witnessed the discussion between Díaz and Gifford. Appropriately enough, since the meeting was held at the archbishop's residence, everyone involved offered apologies and forgiveness, and all promised to do their part to end sweatshop abuses in the garment industry. Díaz said to Gifford, "I hope you can help us put an end to all this maltreatment. In that way we can have better treatment, better wages, and I would like you to permit independent monitoring of the factory."[44] Díaz was asking Gifford directly to change the working conditions that she had experienced at Global Fashions, publicly claiming a voice in order to ask for a program of independent monitoring similar to the one in place at Mandarin International in El Salvador.

With this request to Gifford, Díaz shifted the terms of the debate back to Honduras and to Global Fashions. Gifford's response was both an exoneration of herself and the recognition of the morality of Díaz's request. In part, Gifford said: "I believe all children are God's children. I had no idea what was happening, but now that I know, I will do everything I can to help you."[45] In her statement, not only did Gifford affirm the rectitude of Díaz's cause, but she recalled her own dedication to children—as God's—and emphasized her own innocence. Though Gifford promised to help Díaz, she did not specify how. The discussion was not about industry conditions or large-scale solutions; it was about Gifford's individual morality and her personal pledge to Díaz. *talk but no action*

Díaz and Gifford set the stage for other apologies and other moral commitments, which took the form of resolutions. Although Wendy Díaz took the courageous stand, brought her experiences to the United States, and confronted Kathie Lee Gifford, other participants in the conference focused on Gifford's subject position. In this way, relations of class, race, and empire were reinscribed through dominant gender formations that concentrated on the morality of the white middle-class celebrity rather than on the courage of the Honduran garment worker. Celebrating Gifford as a prime ally and shifting from Global Fashions to the global garment industry, UNITE president Jay Mazur said: "The struggle against sweatshops at home and abroad has won a powerful ally in Kathie Lee Gifford. Let us hope that Wal-Mart and other large retailers will now assume their corporate responsibility to help clean up this industry.[46] Charles Kernaghan continued to center on Gifford's subject position, in the form of an accolade:

> Kathie Lee Gifford deserves tremendous credit and support for the major step she has taken to defend worker and human rights by calling upon Wal-Mart to return to the Global Fashion plant in Honduras and establish independent monitoring. The minute Global abides by the standards of decency in the workplace, Wal-Mart's return will be a watershed moment setting new human rights' standards for the entire industry.[47]

After the accolade came Kernaghan's apology to Gifford: "In our efforts to defend the rights of children and women working in the assembly plants of Central America, we never intended to hurt anyone personally and are truly sorry for any pain caused to Kathie Lee Gifford and her family by this work."[48] Although Díaz's and Kernaghan's congressional testimonies about Global, the complaints of Seo workers, and the conditions at each factory were the material of the campaign, the final battle was over the salvation of Kathie Lee Gifford and, secondarily, of Wal-Mart. The congressional testimonies Kernaghan and Díaz provided after the meeting at the arch-bishop's residence were, in many respects, the denouement of the story.

In this campaign, two women's bodies were pitted symbolically against one another—in the press, at the meeting in the archbishop's residence—by the campaign's organizers. To have a fifteen-year-old Honduran girl travel to New York City to say that the clothes with Kathie Lee Gifford's name and the brand name of Wal-Mart were made under inhuman working con-ditions was a difficult blow—to Gifford's name and to her credibility as a symbolic mother and a television icon.

Although at the beginning of the campaign, when confronted with working conditions at Global Fashions, Gifford had claimed that she did not know about the factory conditions and, being neither the owner nor the manager of the factory, could not be held responsible for the labor condi-tions there, by the end she had become a prime weapon for activists in this particular sweatshop battle. Gifford shifted the blame for conditions at Seo and Global from herself and Wal-Mart to American consumers, manufac-turers, and citizens. In this way, Gifford rhetorically was not only able to salvage her (brand) name, but was also able to place herself at the center of an American moral salvation narrative whose target was women and child garment workers throughout the world. After meeting Díaz, Gifford stated:

> Wendy Díaz has a message that compels every American consumer, every American manufacturer and every American citizen to ask, "Under what conditions are the products we buy being manufactured?" Her courage is to be admired while her personal call to action is nothing less than critical for the entire garment industry. Ms. Díaz needs to be heard by everyone with a conscience.[49]

Interestingly, not only were the "facts" presented in the U.S. Congress sec-ondary to this meeting between Gifford and Díaz, but the garment indus-try, the working conditions, the garment workers, and the sites in San Pedro Sula and Manhattan had, by the end of the campaign, dropped out of the media(ted) battle.[50]

A Bonanza All Around?

These two cases of labor violations forced Gifford and her husband to hand out money to workers in New York City and pushed Wal-Mart to accept independent monitoring in Honduras. Gifford had stated that she would employ independent monitors for working conditions at all factories pro-ducing clothing for her brand, but an independent monitoring system was never put in place for the Kathie Lee line or for any of Wal-Mart's clothing lines. According to Wal-Mart policy:

> Wal-Mart, not Kathie Lee or her company, chooses the suppliers that produce the Kathie Lee merchandise. The suppliers then select the factories, which are inspected and must be certified before production begins. If the factory fails in the certification, no merchandise is allowed to be produced in the factory. Wal-Mart and its suppliers ensure that all inspections are completed before any Kathie Lee merchandise is produced.[51]

But after the promises were made and Gifford's name brand was restored, the press did not cover the follow-up, so the Wal-Mart policy never became part of the official record of the Kathie Lee campaign.

The official record was made on the day of the June 6 meeting between Díaz and Gifford. After the meeting in the archbishop's residence, the attendees issued a joint communiqué, whose ostensible subject was the garment industry as a whole. The communiqué stated that the group had agreed to the following:

> The challenge of eliminating sweatshops can only be met when corporations, governments, unions and concerned citizens assume their responsibilities. By acknowledging the reality of labor abuse in the apparel industry and speaking out against it, Kathie Lee Gifford has admirably met her responsibilities.
>
> Workers, like those in the Global Fashions factory in Honduras, who insist on exercising their legal and moral rights, should not be punished by losing their jobs. . . . Kathie Lee Gifford believes an independent monitoring program . . . should be implemented so that abuses can end and jobs can be protected.
>
> Kathie Lee Gifford agreed that she would encourage Wal-Mart to return garment manufacturing to the Global Fashions factory providing that conditions at the plant consistently meet standards that protect labor and human rights and that conditions are monitored by independent organizations such as the Committee for the Defense of Human Rights in Honduras.[52]

It is telling that the communiqué focused mostly on Kathie Lee Gifford. It did not address the efficacy of independent monitoring. Rather, each point included a reference to Gifford, to her agency and her moral authority; Kathie Lee's humanity was privileged over that of the people who worked in the garment factories supposedly at the center of the campaign.

After the June meeting, Díaz continued her NLC-sponsored tour of the United States. During that period, Díaz, Gifford, Kernaghan, representatives from the U.S. Department of Labor, Honduran apparel manufacturers, child labor activist Craig Kielburger, and others testified in front of the U.S. House of Representatives. Later that summer, Gifford and her husband "pledged at a press conference with Labor Secretary Robert Reich to lead a star-studded campaign against child labor and sweatshop conditions the world over."[53]

The summer of sweatshops educated U.S. consumers, retailers, legislators, and television watchers about garment factories, sweatshop production, and the possibility for hope, as embodied by Gifford and Díaz. Krupat pointed out:

> By the P. T. Barnum standard of name recognition, the publicity was a bonanza all around. On the level of survival skills, these adversaries were well matched. The Giffords had fame, money, and an adoring public on their side; NLC had the moral authority of teenaged Wendy Díaz. Under the circumstances, Kernaghan didn't care too much about being villainized. "We fight to win," he says.[54]

The publicity bonanza continued and drew in celebrities, CEOs, politicians, and numerous media. On August 2, 1996, U.S. president Bill Clinton and U.S. secretary of labor Robert Reich issued a joint statement at a White House meeting attended by Phil Knight of Nike, Kathie Lee Gifford, Senator Tom Harkin, and Representative George Miller. Clinton began the meeting by lauding the fact that "our economy produced nearly 200,000 more new jobs [in the United States] in July." He went on to say that "we now have the economic equivalent of our dream team: strong growth, millions of jobs, low inflation, low unemployment and growing incomes."[55]

Clinton's opening statement at the White House meeting was planned for the one-year anniversary of the discovery of the El Monte, California, sweatshop.[56] The presidential statement echoed the self-congratulatory tone of those attending the June meeting at Cardinal O'Connor's residence while at the same time celebrating Clinton's own accomplishments. In fact, Clinton's speech framed the current meeting as part of the larger success of the booming U.S. economy. Like the participants in the June meeting, Clinton congratulated Kathie Lee Gifford: "When Kathie Lee Gifford learned that some of the garments with her name on them were being produced under terrible working conditions, she didn't bury her head in the sand. Instead she reacted quickly, decisively and responsibly. That is what the rest of us must do as well." Couching his statements by invoking

U.S. history and notions of American character and saying, "Our nation has always stood for human dignity and the fundamental rights of working people," Clinton outlined the program that was to begin with that White House meeting. Clinton stated that the group of politicians, CEOs, union and labor activists, and celebrities he had convened had agreed to do two things: "First, they will take additional steps to ensure that the products they make and sell are manufactured under decent and humane working conditions. Second, they will develop options to inform consumers that the products they buy are not produced under those exploitative conditions." In this statement, Clinton did not rule out exploitative working conditions— he just promised to find ways to inform consumers of products that were free of such conditions. Again, Clinton relegated working conditions to another option for consumer choice.

Clinton was quick to emphasize that "human and labor rights are not brand names. They are the most basic products of our democracy." However, he went on to cite the companies participating in the initiative, including Phillips Van Heusen, L.L.Bean, Patagonia, Nicole Miller, Warnaco, Tweeds, Frank and Kathie Lee Gifford, Liz Claiborne, and Nike. These companies, Clinton said, "have pledged to live up to their responsibilities." Now termed the White House Apparel Initiative, the meeting, along with the statement on fair labor practices, was the culmination of the Kathie Lee campaign. With the initiative came the final triumph of the campaign, celebrating the integrity of (particular) brand names, of American democracy, and, as Clinton concluded, of "our free enterprise system." Clinton's free enterprise system was populated by corporate good citizens, who "make America the place that it ought to be, and set a standard for the entire world." Central to Clintonian corporate good citizenship are policies of neoliberal restructuring, post-Fordist flexible accumulation, and a reconfiguration of the welfare and national-developmentalist states.[57]

After the Campaign

In Honduras, the independent monitoring project was never implemented at Global Fashions, and it was declared a failure by unionists and activists at the Kimi factory, where it was put into practice, for very much the same reasons that I discuss in chapter 2 on the monitoring experiences at Mandarin International in El Salvador.[58] In Manhattan, Bonewco Fashions, who had subcontracted the Kathie Lee goods to the now-closed Seo Fashions, paid $19,623 in back wages to forty-five former employees of Seo, along with the $22,000 in civil money penalties that had been assessed for the "repeat and willful" violations.[59] Seo Fashions was shut down, the workers were paid some of their back wages, and Kathie Lee became an example for other celebrities whose names were involved in garment production.

Working conditions in New York City's garment industry, however, remained abysmal. According to one activist with the Chinese Staff and Workers Association (CSWA), "In [Flushing, Queens,] Manhattan's Chinatown, and Brooklyn's Sunset Park, there are garment factories operating in basements, in garages and in people's homes. These are Latino, Chinese, African-American workers, 40 to 50 percent of whom have noticeable health problems" (Map 3).[60] The conditions remain the same, and thousands of people have been left out of the Kathie Lee campaign and its success story. Even in its transnationality, the campaign continued to focus on branding and corporate citizenship, and in the end it left the garment workers to fend for themselves in an industry that had been changed very little despite the media frenzy surrounding the summer of the sweatshop.

Back to New York City?

After the Kathie Lee campaign, the problem of sweatshop production in New York City and Honduras was not solved. In New York City, in particular, the light shed on the industry, along with Governor Pataki's "hot goods" legislation, caused unforeseen complications. As Peter Kwong points out:

> In August 1996 . . . Brooklyn District Attorney Charles Hynes conducted his own raids on sweatshops in [Brooklyn's] Sunset Park in coordination with the New York State Labor Department, the New York State Department of Finance, and the New York City Fire Department. Dozens of officers, wearing bulletproof vests and armed with semiautomatic weapons, smashed into the sweatshops, ordering everyone to freeze, place their hands on the table, and keep silent.[61]

Kwong documents that during the Sunset Park raids government agents broke into employers' offices to search through records. A number of factory owners were arrested and taken into custody for "violating minimum wage laws, flouting the tax code, and breaking factory fire and safety regulations." These actions, in and of themselves, were greatly needed, and completely within the purview of New York State labor and fire regulations. However, Kwong points out, "Workers were permitted to leave the factories only after they were questioned, photographed, and their files reviewed."[62]

This well-intentioned move by government agencies to improve working conditions and contribute to the eradication of sweatshops in New York City reinforced immigrants' own fears about their legal status, work permits, and residency. In written testimony, one undocumented worker stated that

Map 3. Map of New York City, featuring the garment districts of Manhattan, Flushing, Queens, and Sunset Park, Brooklyn. These neighborhoods have the highest concentration of garment factories and are also home to large Chinese and Latino immigrant communities, the source of much of the labor force for these factories. Courtesy of Rutgers Cartography.

the police never explained that the raids were targeting the employers of the factory, who were violating labor, fire, and tax laws.[63] An unintended consequence of the campaigns was that immigrant garment workers in New York City were left without jobs, and more were afraid to speak out about working conditions because of their fear of U.S. Immigration and Naturalization Service (INS) interventions that would deprive them of jobs.

The "hot goods" Brooklyn raids were carried out at the same time as a series of INS raids on New York factories. In 1996, over two thousand people were arrested in New York City for not possessing the correct government documents allowing them to work in the United States. One woman, Mara, who was interviewed after an INS raid on a Manhattan sweatshop, described being handcuffed and arrested, after which she was taken to a jail in eastern Pennsylvania and asked to pay $2,000 for her release or face deportation within two weeks. The overcrowded factory in which she worked—there was no room for even one more sewing machine—was cited for several health violations, including no ventilation, unusable toilets, no drinking water, and no emergency exits.

However, INS commissioner Doris Meissner, who had been confronted by UNITE about the practice of arresting workers for lack of papers while ignoring labor and health violations, laid the blame for sweatshops on the workers. Meissner said: "We're not going to permit this exploitation, but workers have to speak up and tell us about these abuses. . . . The reason why we're having these raids is to make sure that every day there are less undocumented workers, and although the process may last a long time, the ultimate goal is deportation." Neatly targeting garment workers rather than the managers and owners of factories, Meissner reasoned that INS raids were, in fact, helping to get rid of sweatshops, since without undocumented workers, there would be no labor abuses in the garment industry.[64]

Because the Sunset Park raids by New York State under the "hot goods" legislation were mistaken by workers as INS raids, the response to them in the Sunset Park community was marked by unforeseen class alliances. According to Kwong, while no factory owners contested the charges that they violated the minimum wage, nor did they dispute the fact that their factory conditions were those of sweatshops, they accused the district attorney's office of racism for targeting only Chinese-owned factories. The owners spread the rumor throughout the community that the raids were, in fact, to target and arrest undocumented workers. Although the raids ostensibly had been carried out to protect workers and improve working conditions, the next week saw a demonstration in Sunset Park of fifteen thousand Chinese workers carrying banners with slogans such as: "Garment Factory Is the Heart of Chinatown's Economy," "Against Arbitrary Arrest," and "We Need Our Jobs." Kwong argued that the workers had no choice but to march, since their employers closed the factories for a couple of hours that day and paid workers to show up for the protest. The factory owners threatened that employees would be fired if they did not attend. To observers, however, this seemed to be a show of ethnic solidarity that proved that "Chinese workers really did not mind working under sweatshop conditions."[65]

The Kathie Lee campaign was portrayed as a story of successful trans-national organizing, but it is important to point out the gender, race, class, and citizenship hierarchies that produced the success. Kathie Lee Gifford was transformed from a sweatshop sinner to a white woman savior of brown women and children garment workers throughout the world, while George Pataki was able to pass "hot goods" legislation that could promote New York as a past and present defender of working men, women, and children. Bill Clinton appointed a group of prominent retailers and labor activists to come up with the FLA, while the corporations participating in the FLA were touted as good citizens and the garment industry was symbolically purified of the taint of sweatshops. Even Wal-Mart's profits grew. According to John Lupo, Wal-Mart's senior vice president and general merchandise manager for apparel, "We had the best numbers ever in May [1996], so there was no impact at all [from the Kathie Lee protests]." At the same time, Lee Scott, Wal-Mart's executive vice president for merchandise, announced a new line of Kathie Lee curling irons and hair dryers. The only anomalies were Global Fashion in Honduras, where independent monitoring was never implemented, and Sunset Park, Brooklyn, where garment workers protested the "hot goods" actions and asked to keep their jobs.

Spin, Globalization, and the Nation-State

Wal-Mart came out of its sweatshop scandal of 1996 with more credibility than it had before, as did the NLC, while Kathie Lee Gifford has been able to remake herself into a champion for children's and workers' rights.[66] The consequences of these campaigns, however, are messier than one would expect. What of the central anomalies to the success story? Why was Global Fashions not placed under the auspices of independent monitoring—why, in fact, was the production for the Kathie Lee line moved from Global Fashions to Nicaragua? Why were "hot goods" raids carried out in Sunset Park without communicating that working conditions were the target rather than the workers' immigration status? Why did Chinese garment workers and employers take to the streets of Sunset Park to protest the raids?

When globalization is viewed as both the principal frame for action and an (overarching) actor, the stage of action becomes global. Because Honduras, Sunset Park, Seo, and Global Fashions were seen as aberrations of globalization, they could be overlooked in their particularities even as they remained at the center of protest. The global refers to, Jessop argues, "a complex, chaotic, and overdetermined outcome of a multiscalar, multitemporal, and multicentric series of processes operating in specific structural contexts."[67] These contexts are elided in the protest against the sweatshop. In the case of the Kathie Lee campaign, activists saw themselves as fighting against global entities: NLC director Charles Kernaghan pointed out, "U.S. corporations want an open field for their globetrotting in search of misery and low wages; the two always go hand in hand."[68]

Neither globalized capital nor the sweatshop is as self-contained as they are made to appear. Companies, in what Kernaghan called their "celebrity endorsements and slick marketing campaigns,"[69] rely on national, regional, and local structures of law, territorial boundaries, citizenship structures, ethnic and racial exclusions, gender relations, and notions of community— as do transnational, or globalized, protest campaigns. The subject position of Kathie Lee Gifford was essential for both the production and protest of sweated labor. Gifford served as the face of Wal-Mart and as the new, salvaged face of the antisweatshop movement. In this way, both capital and protest employed standard U.S. notions of gender, class, race, and motherhood as part of a global/transnational vocabulary. Gifford also was the main protagonist in a quintessentially (neo)liberal story of individual struggle and achievement. In this particular story, Kathie Lee Gifford fought against the assaults to her name, was exposed to suffering, and then, through her honesty and hardheadedness, won the day and the resulting capital profits.

The Honduran factory workers were embodied by Wendy Díaz, who also embodied hierarchical U.S. notions of citizenship, race, gender, class, and age. Díaz was a young, brown Central American woman who worked in a sweatshop, therefore the perfect foil and perfect adversary for Gifford. As Kernaghan pointed out:

> When Kathie Lee Gifford came face to face with 15-year-old Wendy Díaz and heard what it was like for her and other 12, 13 and 14-year-olds to work for 13-hour days sewing Kathie Lee pants for Wal-Mart in a Honduran factory—under armed guard, being screamed at to work faster and earning only 31 cents an hour—Gifford responded as all decent Americans would.[70]

Díaz, upon meeting Gifford, confronting her, and, finally, taking part in her forgiveness, also participated in her exculpation. In a parallel to garment production, once Díaz's work is done, Global Fashions is easily forgotten in the celebration of Gifford and the day-to-day profit making of Wal-Mart.

George Pataki and Bill Clinton participated in attempts to reconcile corporate imperatives with American morality and the structure of U.S. laws. The actions of the U.S. nation-state appear as background—through legislation, congressional committee meetings, presidential task forces, trade laws, and, finally, raids on garment factories. These raids, and the community responses to them, rested on racist, exclusionary, and hierarchical formations of the U.S. nation-building process as part of Manifest Destiny; the gendered, classed, and raced geography and community relations of New York City; the politics of immigration, citizenship, and national origin; and notions of the paternalistic state.

These formations exclude immigrants, conflate class with race, and rely on law enforcement to maintain boundaries. The ultimate recourse to force—in the guise of the law—can be seen in both the district attorney's raids looking for sweatshops and the INS raids looking for illegal workers. It is also in this context that the march in Sunset Park was organized. In this way, the ethnic, racial, and class boundaries of the nation-state were maintained and reconfigured within New York City and between the United States and Honduras. With the vindication of Kathie Lee Gifford, neoliberal politics, and capitalist production relations, Global Fashions, Seo Fashions, and poor brown women working in garment factories in Sunset Park and Nicaragua could be safely set aside in the name of triumph during 1996's summer of sweatshops.

unintended, neg. impact

4

Disciplining Bodies

The notion that the global economy is both the site and the object of post-Fordist labor regulation mobilizes a spatial and conceptual shift from the terrain of the national to that of the transnational. This shift produces transnational discipline as an erasure of all that has come before; the project of making the new global worker is fundamentally different from earlier Fordist disciplinary projects that produced national forms of subjectivity. In this chapter, I move away from notions of the erasure, replacement, or supplanting of disciplinary forms to engage with site-specific practices of regulation and discipline both within the global productive processes of the garment industry and within the politics of transnational protest. Are there particular transnational practices of labor regulation and discipline?[1]

The previous chapters offered critiques of globalized production and transnational protest and the strategic and theoretical position of the shop floor within these formations. Central to the critique offered in this chapter is an examination of how the categories of gender, class, nation, race, and history are deployed in the practices of transnational protest campaigns and in the literature on social movements, globalization, and the new international division of labor. In my examination of the geography and production practices of the garment industry and the specific relations of the shop floor, processes that are apparently transnational in nature depend on local histories, geographies, laws, and projects of nation-state building.

The second part of my analysis involves the circulation and reproduction of brands, corporate and celebrity names, and the ways in which signs, symbols, and representations of advertising reproduce—and add value to—

capital. Once particular sets of abuses, disciplinary functions, and laboring subjectivities are documented, how does such documentation manifest itself at the level of the retail outlet, the corporation, the nation-state, or the international arena? What is the position of the shop floor in relation to public relations and advertising? How is the social reproduced within this doubled process of added value: on the shop floor and in the retail outlet, board room, advertising agency, and transnational protest campaign?

One effect of transnational labor protest and of the agendas set forth by the groups organizing them is that workers' rights are discussed in limited ways. Bringing production processes into the purview of consumption and advertising foreclose possibilities for understanding everyday practices of discipline and subject formation on particular shop floors located in particular sites of nation-states, sociolegal formations, and transnationality. How are the phenomena of EPZs and the militarization of work spaces—with body searches of workers upon entering and leaving the workplace and armed guards at factory entrances—addressed in the campaigns? How, for example, are the disciplinary functions of the informal schools set up in Bangladesh and the "learn to earn" programs for former child garment workers related to advertising campaigns for Levi Strauss and Wal-Mart?

Abuse and the Global Sweatshop

The campaigns that I examine document a number of labor abuses and production practices that mark current garment industry formations. Through protest, the practice of witnessing, and the use of testimony—by people who work in garment factories and by sympathetic "experts" such as development practitioners, union organizers, and academics like myself specializing in labor relations—labor activists constantly redeploy a particular repertoire of workplace abuses as defining the new global sweatshop. This process of documentation is carried out, for the most part, through media-centered campaigns and the utilization of images in practices such as culture jamming, which seek to debunk the power of corporate media practices and representations through alternative critical advertising campaigns.[2] Antisweatshop activists have carried out culture jamming on a large scale through an explicit linking of corporate reputation and brand names with production in sweatshops worldwide.

One example of the often-cited violations that are mobilized in campaign after campaign is in the National Labor Committee's description of the Beximco Factory in Bangladesh's Savar export processing zone outside of Dhaka. Beximco workers faced conditions such as "forced overtime, 12½ hours [a day], seven days a week, 80-hour work week . . . Paid less than ⅓ of the legal overtime rate. Not uncommon to be forced to remain in the factory beyond 8:00 p.m., working a 24-hour shift right through the night. Days off are very rare."[3] Outside that repertoire are, for example, the militarization and geographical isolation of most export processing zones and the high-tech ways in which control, discipline, and limited access are maintained inside and outside the zones. The Sarvar export processing zone, like the San Marcos free trade zone outside San Salvador discussed in chapter 2, is located an hour outside of the city by bus, in the middle of large fields, and is surrounded by fences, locked gates, and an elaborate system of armed guards to restrict access to those without "legitimate business" within the zone.

Because such militarization and isolation are structural factors central to the everyday running of the EPZ, they cannot be cited as part of the repertoire of the sweatshop; they are boundaries that frame the exceptional space of the sweatshop in order to maintain it as outside the normalized circuits of globalization. In this way, EPZs throughout the world depend on the geographical and legal boundaries and contexts of the nation-states in which they are situated in order to be part of globalized circuits of power.

Within the United States the boundaries of the new sweatshop are drawn through the notion of force as an exception. The 1995 discovery of the virtual enslavement of seventy-two Thai garment workers in an El Monte, California, garment factory became definitive of the new U.S. sweatshop. Julie Su, an attorney with the Asian Pacific American Legal Center, described the conditions discovered at El Monte on August 2, 1995:

> [A]bout 70 garment workers were found sewing for some of the nation's top manufacturers and retailers behind barbed wire with armed guards and the threat of harm to their lives. They were being paid less than 60 cents an hour and were not permitted to leave. . . . They lived in crowded conditions where they sewed in one room and then slept in another room.[4]

Other conditions, cited in workers' testimonies, videos, and activist media spots, included the nonpayment of wages, scheduled and restricted bathroom visits, and mandatory pregnancy tests and enforced birth control. These conditions reflect earlier sweatshop conditions in the United States, such as that of the Triangle Shirtwaist Factory, where on March 25, 1911, 146 of 500 employees, mostly young, low-paid, women immigrant workers, died when a fire broke out in the factory, which had insufficient safety precautions and no fire escapes. As a result, "the International Ladies' Garment Workers Union (ILGWU), the union to which some of the Triangle workers belonged, stepped up its organizing efforts and fought to improve working conditions for garment workers."[5] The narrative of U.S. exceptionalism within normalization of the global is troubled through a focus on the past and present existence of sweatshops such as Triangle and El Monte in the United States that employed women immigrant workers under oppressive conditions.

This distinction between global and local sweatshop conditions reproduces the United States as the definitive site of both exception and globalization. Labor abuses that are left out of most sweatshop narratives include factory fires and deaths of garment workers in Dhaka, documented in an Asian-American Free Labor Institute (AAFLI) informational flyer on workplace hazards:

> The Sharaka Industries, Ltd., garment factory in a Dhaka suburb was a fire trap. As usual, the main door was locked. The stairwells were too narrow. So it wasn't surprising that, once ignited, the December 27, 1990, fire quickly engulfed the workplace. The toll: twenty-five dead and about one hundred others injured. Most of the dead and injured were women and children.

The same flyer also highlighted a fire in a toy factory in Bangkok in which 188 people died and a series of fires and explosions in Taiwan and China. All the examples pointed to locked doors, barred windows, and blocked passageways as contributing to the death tolls.[6] In Bangladesh, fires break out in dozens of garment factories every year, killing hundreds of workers because of locked doors and lack of fire escapes.[7] Other commonplace hazards that are documented but not often well publicized include respiratory problems from airborne dust and threads due to the lack of proper ventilation, and repetitive stress injuries of arms, shoulders, and hands from working long hours at a sewing machine.[8] Recent campaigns also revealed the lack of a living wage among garment workers throughout the world—an important subject, given the fact that in El Salvador, for example, most garment workers are not even paid the legal minimum wage for the hours they work.[9]

El Monte's horrific conditions, the fire hazards at factories in Bangkok, Bangladesh, and China, the lack of a living wage in Central America, and Beximco's hyperexploitation of its workers are all examples of extreme force in the process of labor extraction, superseding and supplementing everyday disciplinary practices such as militarization, production quotas, and geographic isolation. They also serve to mark an apparent return to an earlier age of sweated labor. The conditions cited as abusive are violations of international labor and human rights law and are therefore compelling to both activists and consumers. The very enormity of these abuses marks them as media worthy; their shock value serves to affect the profitability of name brands and logos for corporations and consumers. For this reason, such egregious abuses are often cited within the repertoire of the global sweatshop.

Recognition of regimes of torture, abuse, and control in globalized production sites of the garment industry is an essential first step to their rectification. At the same time, these examples of extreme abuse are both grounded in and reproduce a larger political economy of production, consumption, and image making. In the conception of the new global sweatshop, the figure of the post-Fordist garment worker, who—for purposes of production *and* consumption—has been portrayed as both a throwback to an earlier period of sweatshops and as the new subject of globalization, is the crucial subject of sweated labor. It is clear that by citing such conditions—and subjects—as exceptions to the global, they can be relegated to the realm of the excessive outside of normalized globalization.

Such regimes are neither simply a throwback to earlier moments nor something completely new. The division of production practices into Fordist and post-Fordist temporalities posits a continuist interpretation of labor history in capital and, at the same time, obfuscates the ways in which local histories, practices, and relations are brought into regimes of discipline and reproduction. Body searches carried out at Mandarin International in El Salvador, for example, although a common feature of garment factories throughout the world, also mirror the tactics of anti-insurgency campaigns during the recent war, thus mixing post-Fordist labor control with the practice of wartime repression.[10] These regimes of force and Foucauldian disciplinary practices are products of everyday struggle, Fordist regulation, Keynesianism, inequalities of income and access to media and retail outlets, and empire, war, capital, public relations, and nation-building.

Sweatshop Abuse and Globalized Rectification

One form of global rectification of sweatshop abuse has been the institution of corporate codes of conduct for labor conditions in garment industry sourcing. I return to codes of conduct here to discuss their prevalence throughout the industry and the awareness of these codes by retailers and factory managers alike. In a 1996 U.S. Department of Labor survey of leading U.S. manufacturers and retailers, thirty-seven of the forty-eight companies surveyed provided copies of their codes of conduct.[11] Conditions covered by codes of conduct included the general Family Dollar Stores statement: "We are committed to legal compliance and ethical business practices in all our operations." Some codes of conduct were more specific, prohibiting the use of forced or child labor, prohibiting corporal punishment or sexual abuse of employees, and requiring compliance with fire safety regulations.[12] In order to ensure their competitiveness, especially in the face of the 2005 implementation of the Multifiber Agreement under the WTO that signaled the end of quotas, individual factories in various countries have responded with improvements of specific working conditions, such as the provision of purified water, ventilation fans, and clearly marked fire exits.

One factory manager of Brothers Fashions in Dhaka said that such improvements—including forbidding the employment of children under the age of fourteen—are implemented to attract orders from what he called "first-class" companies like Tommy Hilfiger and Calvin Klein, although neither of these has instituted codes of conduct.[13] At Brothers Fashions, the management made sure that people did not work for longer than ten hours a day. Brothers' managers also said that they planned to provide a medical program, higher salary, and shared company ownership to the employees to minimize the turnover rate and help the factory attract more lucrative production contracts. The same general manager pointed out that such improvements in health and safety conditions are essential because "everyone is conscious of political disturbances" that drive away the first-class companies.

But other factories have continued to operate even after having been caught in severe violations of labor standards. In April 1996, a fire broke out at Tri Mode France, Ltd., a garment factory occupying the second, third, and fourth floors of a six-story complex in Mirpur, Dhaka. The fire spread from Tri Mode to Suntex Fashions, a factory that produced sweat suits, occupying the fifth and sixth floors of the building (Figure 5). According to witnesses, the factory gates had been kept locked for the month before the fire while new stairways were being built. When the fire broke out at lunchtime, the few people who remained in the factory were trapped, and twelve Suntex workers died.[14] When I visited the factory three months later, although Suntex had not reopened, Tri Mode was again producing sweaters in the burned-out shells of its third and fourth floors (Figure 6). The factory space contained new knitting and sewing machines, supplies of yarn, and people working in assembly lines. Tri Mode employees were working to produce a shipment of sweaters for France in a charred building with exposed wires and beams, water dripping from pipes, blocked stairwells, and entire walls—formerly made of glass—that had been blown away and were only gaping holes facing the outside of the building.

Labor violations and their rectification have naturalized the "science" of Taylorist production regimes, often in the midst of fire, health, and safety violations and severe repression and exploitation of workers. While the latter are a central part of antisweatshop activism, the former—scientific

Figure 5. Outside the Tri Mode/Suntex factory complex in Dhaka, three months after the fire. Jute cloths have been placed in the window frames in lieu of windows. Even though the floors are burned out, work continues inside.

Taylorism—contributed in a significant way to the process of corporate and retail marketing. When Frederick Taylor wrote his *Principles of Scientific Management* in 1911, his objective was "To point out . . . the great loss which the whole country is suffering through inefficiency in almost all our daily acts. . . . [T]he remedy for this inefficiency lies in systematic management."[15] In the case of Suntex and Tri Mode, Taylorist management techniques—including the necessity of getting orders out on time—were being carried out within the burned-out shell of a building. Retailers depend on subcontractors' implementing Taylorist "principles of scientific management" and use computerized tracking of production and design in order to maintain the high turnaround rate for clothing timed for changing seasons, fashions, and marketing strategies. Whereas the anticorporate campaigns of image making rely on depictions of the "worst" abuses for success, corporate image making and branding regimes rely on the high turnaround and centralized styling that computerized Taylorist regimes provide.

Taylor's science assumes that people who work in factories lack basic intelligence, "either through lack of education or through insufficient mental capacity," who then require "scientific management," where "fully one-half of the problem is 'up to the management.'"[16] Taylorist principles combine standardization of production practices, the breakup of work into assembly

Figure 6. Garment workers produce sweaters bound for France in the burned-out Tri Mode/Suntex factory complex, Dhaka.

lines (each person doing one part of assembling the product over and over again in short intervals), and strict hierarchies with close shop-floor supervision. Taylor describes his system of management:

> By having a man . . . who understood this law [of scientific management], stand over [a factory worker] and direct his work, day after day, until he acquired the habit of resting at proper intervals, he was able to work at an even gait all day long without unduly tiring himself. . . . The writer trusts that it is now clear that even in the case of the most elementary form of labor that is known, there is a science.[17]

The application of "science" to production practices would not only increase output, but also make "labor troubles of any kind, or a strike, impossible."[18] Taylor summarized his science of management as follows:

> Harmony, not discord.
> Cooperation, not individualism.
> Maximum output, in place of restricted output.
> The development of each man to his greatest efficiency and prosperity.[19]

Taylorism has continued to dominate productive practices through the current period. Figures 7–12 show the gendered divisions of labor that go along with Taylorist organization: men work as material cutters, finishers, inspectors, and packers, all of which are better-paying jobs; women work as sewing machine operators, trimmers, and helpers. All of the managers in Bangladesh with whom I talked about gender divisions on the shop floor cited the cliché of women's nimble fingers and told me that women were "settled" and "passive" and could sit still at a sewing machine for hours on end without complaining or even feeling it, while men were "active" and "had" to work in jobs where they could move around and take breaks for tea, cigarettes, and walking outside.[20]

Labor on the factory floors is divided not only by gender and class but also by age and experience. The youngest and oldest workers on the floor—those without enough experience to operate the sewing machines and those whose eyes and coordination are not as sharp after years of repetitive sewing—are employed as helpers who trim and cut loose threads on finished garments and bring more material for the machine operators to sew. These multiple hierarchies are at work in all levels of production—from home-based work subcontracted from small factories to larger factories, buying houses, and retailers—and such hierarchies are maintained in the name of transnational efficiency and flexible production practices. Global production practices have, in fact, intensified Taylorism; divisions of labor in

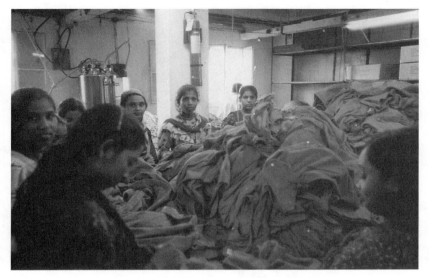

Figure 7. Helpers, mostly young women who are apprentice sewing-machine operators, trim excess thread from finished clothes in a garment factory, Dhaka.

Figure 8. Women working as machine operators and helpers in the production line of a garment factory, Dhaka.

Figure 9. Women work through lunch to meet quota as others take a midday break, Dhaka.

Figure 10. Men use jigsaws to cut cloth from patterns, Dhaka. They wear cloths over their noses and mouths to protect their lungs from the fibers and dust that permeate the factory.

Figure 11. Man supervising women garment workers, Dhaka. Production goals are posted on the blackboard at the front of the factory. As the machine operators sew, they can look at the board and see the hourly production goals and to what extent these are being met. Supervisors move around the factory, observing work, telling operators to work harder, correcting their work, and making sure they are keeping up with individual production quotas over the course of the day.

Figure 12. In Dhaka, women making baseball caps for the U.S. market. This factory, run by a former Oxfam employee, was considered a model in Dhaka: it provided regular lunch hours, a day care room (which was never used), and a less stringent production quota than other factories.

production are now not confined to the factory floors but implemented in commodity chains and multiple, transnational levels of subcontracting that render labor organizing on a large scale complex and difficult to carry out.

Discipline and Transnational Domination?

The Lenor garment factory, a *recinto fiscal*[21] in Santa Elena, a town just outside of San Salvador, combines Taylorism with piece-rate payment, anti-unionization tactics, and computerized production. Every week, the factory bulletin board posts the top ten workers—those who produced the most pieces during the week—and the bottom five *ineficientes*—those with the least output. According to the owner of Lenor, Arturo Carías, an engineer by training, there is a high turnover rate at the factory because he tries to "keep the good ones and get rid of the bad ones" on a regular basis. In another layer of labor discipline, the workers at Lenor are squeezed because, Carías argued, he himself is being squeezed by the quota system that restricts the number and type of items and the number of vendors that have access to the U.S. market. The quota system is the everyday term for the Multi-Fiber Agreement of 1974, a piece of U.S. legislation that delineated the number and types of clothing imports into the United States.[22] The agreement was adopted globally by industrialized countries in the 1980s. This agreement detailed the number and type of garments that could be exported to the United States and Europe from any given country over the course of a year. It was replaced on January 1, 2005, with the Multifiber Agreement, which ended national quotas and allowed any country to export any amount and type of clothing and textiles as long as there was demand in the receiving country. Before 2005, the quota allowances, according to Carías, would go to those companies that were part of the export *pandilla* (gang), who networked with and supported each other and maintained connections to U.S.-based retailers.[23]

I spent a day at the Youngone Fashions factory, located just across the road from the Beximco factory, inside Bangladesh's Savar EPZ on the outskirts of Dhaka. In a parallel to Lenor's posting of *ineficientes,* the Youngone factory posted, at each workstation and assembly line, large, color-coordinated tally sheets on poles to monitor production levels. The tally sheets are stationed above the people seated at sewing machines and in finishing areas, at the eye level of managers, buyers, and others who walk around the factory observing production processes. Each color code signifies overall production levels, the level of coordination among people working on a particular line, and how well individual workers are doing relative to the daily production goal.[24] Whenever an individual worker, or an entire line, is behind the daily production goal set by management, people are required to stay extra hours to complete the goal. Since the production goals at Youngone, like those in every factory I have entered, are usually impossible to meet in an eight-hour day, people are forced to work overtime without compensation in order to keep their jobs. Payment by the piece is one way that garment manufacturers—such as Seo Fashions in New York City—are able to avoid paying minimum wage. With production goals ostensibly aimed at an eight-hour day, overtime is considered making up for inefficiency, and people are paid only for that set number of pieces, no matter how long it takes to produce them. Piecework is part of a system of disciplinary functions—tally sheets, quotas, management surveillance, and the posting of the names of inefficient workers—that are part of the repertoire of conditions in the ideal sweatshop; they are all central to the everyday production of garments throughout the world.

Youngone Fashions, a South Korea–based company and the largest garment-manufacturing company working in Bangladesh, employs 5,200 people at the Dhaka site and another 13,400 employees in Chittagong. The Dhaka building, owned by Youngone, is an enormous red brick edifice. Its six floors contain eighty-five production lines; a water treatment plant; a facility that designs, produces, and dyes synthetic materials; and its own computerized design area. The design area houses industrial engineers, computer-generated cutting and pattern planning, silkscreen, and embroidery. Youngone seems to be an ideal Taylorist, (post-)Fordist production site; it maintains daily disciplinary functions on a large scale and produces for retailers in the United States, Europe, and throughout East Asia. Youngone also has an on-site health clinic for workers and their families, a cafeteria that provides its employees with lunch—consisting of rice, lentils, and sometimes vegetables, meat, eggs, or fish on the side—and, for those working overtime, an evening tiffin (lunchbox) with tea and bananas. Because the majority of Youngone's orders come from Nike, for which it produces athletic clothing and outerwear in Dhaka and shoes in Chittagong, the Nike code of conduct for labor practices is posted on a large board inside the factory entrance in both Bangla and English. However, in the Bangla version, the line guaranteeing the "rights of free association and collective bargaining" is missing.[25] Managers at Youngone justified the omission because the EPZ bylaws forbid unionization. Instead, the factory assigned counselors to the workers, and eventually an in-house union would be created to "discuss grievances and know about and deal with disgruntled workers."[26]

It is impossible to enter the Youngone factory without prior permission.

One has to pass through a guarded gate at the EPZ entrance and then through the Youngone factory's own guards and checkpoints. Entering the site with official permission is to participate in a particular form of Mitchell's concept of "enframing" of factory life.[27]

The factory and its inhabitants were presented to me as a bounded site, and I was the objective observer. Everything in the factory was laid out, presented, for my viewing and consumption. I was able to enter through the connections offered to me by fictive kinship—a complex network of relationships, acquaintances, and an elision of Bengali relationship ties—as the sister-in-law of the factory's Bangladeshi assistant manager, whom I had never before met. In fact, I was not aware of the existence of the assistant manager until the day before my visit, when a nephew of my aunt told me that he had made arrangements for me to visit the factory on the following day. The executive vice president of the factory, Don Hamilton, was a British man who took my relationship to the assistant manager—of brother/sister-in-law—at face value. Everyone knew that I was writing a book on the garment industry that looked at gender and labor practices, and they allowed me inside despite this and because of my ostensible kinship with the assistant manager. In this way, Hamilton assumed formal family ties rather than the tenuous, fictive, recent—and, in fact, momentary—relationship that it was.

Don Hamilton had worked for forty years in garment manufacturing as a buyer in Hong Kong and a factory manager in Nicaragua, El Salvador, Guatemala, Costa Rica, and, most recently, Jamaica. Although willing to meet visitors, Hamilton was suspicious of my intentions. After providing an accounting of production levels, the number of employees, and worldwide export data, along with a history of Youngone in Bangladesh, Hamilton asked, "Are you one of those rabble-rousing bluestockings, come around to destroy our livelihoods?" He went on to say that if I were a do-good union organizer or an undercover reporter, he would make sure that, if I were to expose Youngone, the assistant manager—my fictive brother-in-law—would be fired. At this point, nearly ten years later, the situation on the ground has shifted to such an extent that I can finally discuss Youngone in a public medium. If the gates of Sarvar and Youngone were a physical manifestation of production discipline, Hamilton's accusatory performance and his attempt to link my family ties with my ethical stance added another, more personal layer to the disciplinary structure at Youngone.

During the initial meeting, before allowing entry into the factory, Hamilton provided me with a copy of an article from the February 5, 1998, Asia edition of *Time* magazine that documented sweatshop abuses in the

U.S. protectorate of Saipan, in the Northern Mariana Islands. Hamilton told me that most people allowed their preconceptions to rule over judgment when dealing with labor conditions, and since clothing made in Saipan was labeled "Made in USA," it was easy for companies to hide abusive working conditions. Hamilton went on to argue that while clothing made in Bangladesh was of higher quality and working conditions were much better, the "Made in Bangladesh" label was, in effect, bad publicity for clothing makers that had to be countered by higher than average workplace standards. The stigma of the "Made in Bangladesh" label was compounded, he argued, by the problems of protecting intellectual property and building up infrastructure for shipping and transportation and the refusal of the "United States and European public . . . to pay for clothes; they want [everything] cheaper."

My tour of the factory site was already being constructed through Hamilton's discussion of the industry and of his own and Youngone's position as part of the industry. Hamilton went on to say that there was no time to work on "cultural traditions, [such as] yelling and screaming at underlings. [Even though] foreign bosses try to cure it, it will take hundreds of years to get rid of the cultural thing." Hamilton used racism and colonialist notions of culture to pathologize working conditions at Youngone, placing the blame for abuse on Bangladeshi culture rather than on production imperatives. This echoes debates in El Salvador, where factory owners, government representatives, and the media blame Taiwanese and Korean managers of maquilas for worker abuse—despite the fact that physical abuse and daily disciplinary functions are common in factories owned by Taiwanese, Korean, Salvadoran, and U.S. companies—in an attempt to displace abuse onto racist notions of culture and backwardness. In another racist attempt at cultural pathology, this time combined with Foucauldian surveillance practices, Hamilton added that besides monitoring the workforce to look for signs of unhappiness among Youngone workers—a clear reference to union-busting practices—there were counselors available who would "patrol the dining hall to make sure [the employees] use spoons to avoid staining the garments." Since most Bangladeshis eat with their hands, this was an attempt to single out eating practices, unionization attempts, and verbal abuse as distinctly Bangladeshi and particularly "cultural," ills that Hamilton insisted could be cured through (his own British) foreign intervention.

Hamilton and the assistant managers went on to enumerate the various features of the factory that put it ahead of its competitors with regard to working conditions. Within the factory, which makes outerwear for Nike, Tommy Hilfiger, L.L. Bean, Elan, Land's End, and EMS, there is a facility to produce padding, down processing, and dye processing and a water treatment plant with its own electrical generator, separate from the generator used for the rest of the factory. Since the materials used in outerwear are flammable, there are two people on every floor who are trained in fire emergencies, and fire drills ensure that 5,200 people can take off their shoes and exit the six-story building in less than five minutes.

The Youngone factory was close to the Taylorist ideal, right down to the management's conviction that if it is aware of unhappy employees and is able to monitor shop-floor relations at all times, then it can avoid unionization of the workforce. Hamilton said, "Well-managed companies will work with unions and with workers, and there will be no labor problems. Without the [on-site] counselors, who patrol the factory throughout the day to determine [whether] people [are] sitting around, there would be labor unrest." Hamilton maintained that it was his forty years of experience in the garment industry that enabled the Youngone factory to work to production capacity, systematically and with high quality control. Hamilton clearly posited himself as a Taylorist hero, where his management style, combined with constant surveillance and other disciplinary practices, served to keep workers on target. Employees are happy, Hamilton said, because of the services provided by the company and because of amenities such as Hindi film music that is piped in through the intercoms to the shop floors and the buses that transport people to and from work on a daily basis.

Youngone is publicly listed on the South Korean stock exchange, but none of its work is done in Korea. Nike has a liaison office in Bangkok from which they subcontract work to factories like Youngone. Hamilton pointed out that Youngone has employed fifteen Bangladeshi college-graduate women to help with orders, design, and merchandising. The industry, Hamilton argued, "is run by women because they are more dedicated to work and have a feel for the industry. We have women [sewing machine] operators and men [pattern] cutters." The new international division of labor, with its gender, race, and classed hierarchies, is made clear by Hamilton, who said, "The company is run by Bengalis," without noting his own position as the British executive vice president and the majority of stockholders who are South Korean. He concluded: "The garment industry is notorious for chasing around the world for the lowest wages, milking it dry, and moving on for lower wages. Youngone is not like that; we have invested in this country for better or for worse."

This notion of "for better or for worse," a reference to Christian marriage vows, shows the heterosexist underpinnings of the NIDL: women work in low-paying jobs supposedly to supplement the earnings of the male breadwinners in their households, and Youngone is married to Bangladesh in order to produce garments and reproduce capital. The story of Youngone's investment in Bangladesh "for better or for worse" was repeated to me over and over throughout the day. During my time at the factory, I was given lunch and countless cups of tea, and I was told that I could talk to whomever I liked and could ask as many questions as I wanted about any subject. It is important to note that throughout my visit to Youngone I was accompanied by several managers who commented on and discussed what I saw on the factory floor, in Bengali and English. With Hamilton we exclusively spoke in English, and with the women working on the floor we spoke consistently in Bengali. All the while, Hamilton's warning about the potential consequences of my use of the information provided about the factory was reverberating in the back of my mind.

The management presented Youngone as the ideal work site. Even when I asked them questions about the Harkin Bill, child labor, or working conditions at the factory, managers were quick to say that Youngone was not guilty of the violations that were part of the industry as a whole. Hamilton first mentioned "labor unrest" when we were touring the cafeteria site. As he was telling me about the food provided and the structure of the lunch period, Hamilton said that there had been a protest by the workers over the type of lentils (dal) they were given with their rice at lunch. He said that one of the cooks hired by Youngone had been from Chittagong and had made dal according to a Chittagong recipe. Hamilton told me, "Since most of the Youngone employees are from the Dhaka area, when the cook from Chittagong made dal in the Chittagong style, the recipe wasn't up to the workers' par. We had a bit of labor unrest over the issue of Chittagong dal." Hamilton went on to assure me that the "unrest" was settled by the ubiquitous counselors, who encouraged him to eventually fire the Chittagong cook. Over the course of the day, various Youngone managers brought up the question of labor unrest again and again, always blaming it on the Chittagong-style dal.

Later, after the factory floors had closed and thousands of employees had left for the day, the managers told me that in 1997 Youngone had not continued its annual tradition of giving employees new calendars for Eid ul-Milad, the Muslim holiday celebrating the Prophet Muhammad's birthday. Because there were no calendars that year, there was more unrest: they told me that hundreds of workers stormed the main office and locked several managers inside to protest the lack of calendars. Hamilton corrected the account, saying that it was not Youngone workers who locked the management in the office; rather, it was the work of "outside agitators, looking to stir up trouble among Youngone employees." While recounting the story of calendars, locked-up management, and outside agitators, Hamilton darkly attributed the outside agitation to the Beximco factory just across the street from Youngone. He said that since working conditions at Youngone were so much better than those at Beximco, the Beximco management wanted to make Youngone look bad to buyers—hence, the calendar protest. Clearly, there was more to the story of labor unrest than dal or calendars; the very fact that everyone was so willing to talk about it at such length and constantly cite dal recipes was a clue that I needed to find out what was going on.

The combination of the end of the working day and Hamilton's broaching of labor unrest opened up discussion by the managers around the question of outside agitators. Hamilton repeated his praise of the on-site "counselors," a term he used interchangeably with factory "social workers," clearly part of the widespread system of surveillance instituted at the factory and connected to the deletion of the right to organize from the code of conduct posted at the factory's entrance. Without the presence of the counselors, Hamilton told me, the outside agitators would have fomented labor unrest. In the midst of this discussion, during which I mostly listened to the managers talking to each other—performing for me as their sole audience—one of them left the room and came back with a blue winter jacket with a big Nike logo "swoosh" on the back. He offered the jacket to me, saying "Bhabi [sister-in-law], we want to present this to you as a gift, so that you will remember us after you leave the factory and Bangladesh." I refused the jacket, thanking them and saying that I could not accept a gift from them since I had been at the factory as an observer, for research purposes; it would not be right for me to accept the jacket.

Following a thirteen-hour tour of Youngone, the managers wanted to take me out to dinner to continue our conversation and describe the labor unrest that had erupted, they said, over the "small" matters of Chittagong dal and Eid calendars. Hamilton explained, "Youngone workers have the best conditions in Bangladesh, and because we spoil them so much—with free cafeteria food, social workers, a factory health clinic, bus system, and a formal wage scale—they take advantage by complaining about the small things." The daylong presentation of Youngone by its executive vice president and numerous managers, assistant managers, and counselors showed clearly the structures and practices of discipline, surveillance, and modes of protest that were part of the everyday workings of the factory. My discussions with the management of Youngone also brought to the fore questions of symbolic violence, disciplining, and my own intellectual, moral, and political compromise.

Symbolic Violence, Discipline, and Field Research

Bourdieu defines symbolic violence as one of "the elementary forms of domination, in other words, the direct domination of one person by another," which are employed when a "social machine . . . has not yet developed the power of self-perpetuation." In this situation, Bourdieu argues, the "dominant class" has to "work directly, daily, personally, to produce and reproduce conditions of domination which are even then never entirely trustworthy." Bourdieu goes on to say:

> Thus the system contains only two ways (and they prove in the end to be just one way) of getting and keeping a lasting hold over someone: gifts or debts, the overtly economic obligations of debt, or the "moral," "affective" obligations created and maintained by exchange, in short, overt (physical or economic) violence, or symbolic violence—*censored, euphemized,* i.e., unrecognizable, socially recognized violence.[28]

Since this symbolic violence is domination exercised in its "*elementary form,* i.e., directly between one person and another, it cannot take place overtly and must be disguised under the veil of enchanted relationships."[29] My encounter with the Youngone management was marked by multiple forms of discipline and symbolic violence. Symbolic violence was played out through the fiction of kinship ties, my eating food provided by them, and their offering me the gift of a jacket. We can see the same relations on the factory floor, through the cafeteria and provision of lunch for the Youngone workers, and even in the Eid ul-Milad calendars, which is why, I would argue, the managers focused so much on these in our discussions. The jacket, as a gift and as a commodity, was marked by capitalist relations of production and consumption. It was the product of Youngone workers' labor and was branded with the Nike logo. Their very treatment of me as both researcher and guest was part of the process of disciplining me and the narrative I would build upon leaving the building.

This localized mode of discipline—among individuals—was at the same time transnational. During my dinner with the managers, their discussion of labor unrest opened up—beyond dal and calendars—and became more explicit, including a lockout of the Youngone workers by the management, the use of paramilitary forces to beat up workers, and the imprisonment of those who led a unionization drive. This is part of what Bourdieu describes as the "intelligible relation—not a contradiction—between these two forms of violence [overt (physical or economic) violence and symbolic violence], which coexist in the same relationship."[30]

While the managers were joking over dinner about the summer of 1997 and the labor unrest, I interrupted and asked if there was, in fact, more to the story than what they had told so far. Hamilton, laughing, asked, "You really don't know what happened last July, do you?" I asked them to tell me what happened, and all of them started laughing, finally deferring to Hamilton, who told me about the six thousand workers who were locked out of the factory and the workers who were beaten up by local security guards and police forces.

Bourdieu argues that there is an intelligible relation between overt violence and symbolic, censored, euphemized violence. He argues,

> Hence, the *censorship* to which the overt manifestation of violence, especially in its naked economic form, is subjected by the logic characteristic of an economy in which interests can only be satisfied on condition that they be disguised in and by the strategies aiming to satisfy them.[31]

In this case, Youngone management's veiled allusions to unrest and the joking way in which the story of the lockout was told were part of a structure disguising relations of domination. Earlier in the day, the managers had told me about discrete moments of unrest, caused by insignificant things like the spices used in food or the giving of calendars. Later, at dinner, they went on to say that the summer before had seen a massive lockout of six thousand Youngone workers after they had barricaded the management in their offices for hours on end and presented a list of demands about wages, forced overtime, bathroom access, and the unreachable daily production quotas—not about calendars and dal recipes. The managers told me that none of the problems would have happened if security and employee screening had been tighter because the problems had been caused by a few troublemakers who had "infiltrated" the Youngone factory in the guise of "legitimate" employees. They said that the factory was under investigation by the Nike headquarters because the union organizers had reported the incident to European activists who had then complained to Nike.

When I asked what specifically Nike was investigating, Hamilton told me that police and paramilitary forces had been called in to suppress the "riots" that resulted from the lockout. Several people were held in detention by the local police after being beaten up by the paramilitary forces called in to take control of the situation; nine of them were still being held—more than six months later. In fact, according to a July 14, 1997, article in the Dhaka newspaper *Independent,* more than three hundred Youngone workers had been injured in attacks by police armed with long sticks, and fifty workers had to be admitted to local clinics for injuries. The nine workers still in detention the following January were held under the Special Powers Act, which enables the government to detain people on the grounds of mere suspicion. It was this hidden story of workplace repression that the managers were trying to finesse by inviting me to the factory, calling me sister-in-law, giving me tours, lunch, dinner, and offering me a jacket as a parting gift.

Bourdieu points to such symbolic violence as part of the precapitalist economy. I disagree with his progressivist narrative that pits the "modern" against "pre-capitalist"; such mechanisms of domination are central to power formations in all sites. It is useful, all the same, to theorize the ways in which Foucault's arguments about discipline, surveillance, and governmentality are accompanied by Bourdieu's analysis of symbolic violence. Bourdieu points out,

> Because the pre-capitalist economy cannot count on the implacable, hidden violence of objective mechanisms, it resorts *simultaneously* to forms of domination which may strike the modern observer as more brutal, more primitive, more barbarous, or at the same time, as gentler, more humane, more respectful of persons.[32]

Youngone, both in its everyday practice and in the course of my visit to the factory, manifests this combination of symbolic violence and governmentality.

Hamilton told me that there would be no more problems of "labor unrest" at Youngone since they had "gotten rid of" all of the "troublemakers" after the lockout. According to the European activist organization Clean Clothes Campaign, who wrote a letter in favor of the detained Youngone workers, Hamilton confirmed the "termination" of ninety-seven workers while "complacently [referring] to certain facilities provided to workers at Youngone Hi-Tech, such as transportation and a subsidized lunch."[33] The Youngone lockout and firing of its workers and the use of paramilitary forces against the protesting Youngone employees were much more carefully documented outside Bangladesh than inside the country, and the memory of the 1997 lockout was preserved by European activists. Why has such a large conflict been suppressed or forgotten by both Bangladeshi working women and more generally within Bangladesh? I think it has precisely to do with the combination of symbolic violence, outright force, and Foucauldian discipline that I experienced during my time at the factory—added to which is the national dependence on the garment industry and the positioning of garments as the national development model I discussed in chapter 1.

When I left the managers at Youngone after the dinner, they pushed the

Nike jacket into my hands. In the end, I accepted it and then gave it away immediately afterward. The gift of the jacket and the threat of firing my fictive brother-in-law were supposed to mask, be other than and be outside of, the relations of physical violence and economic extraction that marked Youngone—the Nike swoosh would seal the pact. Within Bangladesh, the story of Youngone did not receive much attention because of the same process of masking physical or direct domination. It was not widely covered by the national media, nor was it discussed in the communities of garment workers with whom I talked. Youngone is Bangladesh's number-one foreign investor. As the Clean Clothes Campaign points out:

> [Youngone] operates nine factories in two export processing zones, one near Dhaka and one near the port of Chittagong. Moreover, as a national weekly recently reported, Youngone is the principal sponsor of an export-processing zone (the KEPZ) yet to be built. "More than 1.2 billion dollars would be invested at the KEPZ over 10 years in 130 factory units by investors from across the world." . . . This KEPZ is scheduled to employ more than a hundred thousand workers.[34]

Relations of domination, in the form of structures of capital, the imperatives of the developmentalist state, and the need for employment, won the day against potential public outrage over the treatment of the five thousand workers at Youngone.

Discipline and the Legacies of Counterinsurgency

In the case of El Salvador, the larger structures of capital, the imperatives of the developmentalist state, and the need for employment combine with the particular legacy of the civil war and the U.S.-sponsored counterinsurgency campaigns in the country, which I discussed in chapter 2. During the Salvadoran civil war, the U.S. government, under the Reagan administration, in conjunction with the USAID and the AIFLD, carried out a number of development and labor organizing projects that have shaped political-economic relations in present-day El Salvador. These projects, in addition to combating the FMLN insurgency in El Salvador over the course of the 1980s, set up the legal framework for free trade zones and bonded areas and for postwar labor repression. The legacy and practical effects of U.S. counterinsurgency policy are part of parallel projects of neoliberal restructuring that took place in other parts of the world.

EPZs and FTZs throughout the world grant corporations tax incentives, a guarantee of nonunionized labor, transport subsidies, and other promotional policies to attract companies to set up production facilities.

Union movements worldwide have been destroyed through corruption, dependence on particular political parties, and on the regional counterparts of AIFLD, e.g., the Free Trade Union Institute (FTUI), the African-American Labor Center (AALC), and AAFLI. In El Salvador, particularly, these projects exemplified the convergence of "low-intensity warfare"—the U.S.-supported proxy wars throughout Central America in the 1980s—and neoliberal political economy. Hugh Byrne points out that U.S. strategy in Central America combined "military assistance to stop and ultimately defeat the Salvadoran insurgents [and] the diplomatic track" with "political and economic reforms in El Salvador and elsewhere [and] the Caribbean Basin Initiative to win congressional backing and the support of regional leaders."[35]

In El Salvador the labor movement was both a central battleground and a key player in the civil war. Fitzsimmons and Anner argue that the political polarization that occurred during the civil war in El Salvador affected all aspects of civil society.[36] In the case of labor organizing, the unions that were most politicized during the war, with links either to the leftist guerrilla group FMLN or to the U.S.-sponsored counterinsurgency project funded by AIFLD, had the most difficulty shifting their organizing agendas. Only those unions and nongovernmental organizations that were either politically unaffiliated during the war or more independent by the war's end were well able to carry out organizing projects in a number of industries. This weakening of large sectors of organized labor, combined with the move to export-oriented garment production—through the proliferation of *zonas francas* and *recintos fiscales*—throughout the country, led to serious barriers to organizing. It is in the face of these barriers that the transnational labor campaigns were organized in El Salvador's garment export-processing (maquila) sector.

As of 1997, there were seven EPZs in El Salvador, six of which were built after 1992.[37] According to 1996 statistics from the Vice Ministry of Industry and Commerce, the 208 factories within the seven EPZs produced $765 million in exports, up from $90 million in 1990. Vice minister Rolando Alvarenga Argueta estimated that, besides the direct employment of 30,000 people, the maquila sector in 1996 generated approximately 60,000 indirect jobs on which 200,000 Salvadorans depended.[38] This 750 percent growth in maquila exports between 1990 and 1996 was an essential part of the postwar reconstruction process, where job creation and infrastructure building were highlighted by the Salvadoran and U.S. governments as a crucial part of the project of rebuilding.

San Bartolo, El Salvador's first EPZ, was built in 1974 with funding from and under the direction of USAID, but the construction of other zones was halted by the war. At the end of the 1980s, USAID showed renewed interest in promoting the construction of EPZs in the country as a way of generating nontraditional exports and providing large-scale employment.[39] This resurgence of interest in maquila production in El Salvador was the long-delayed manifestation of earlier U.S. policies toward the country during the war. In the wake of failed agrarian reform policies supported by the U.S. government during the war, AIFLD and the Salvadoran oligarchy supported centrist unions, arguing that they would stabilize the country and provide an alternative to both the left and the right.

FUSADES, the Spanish acronym for the Salvadoran Foundation for Economic and Social Development, was created in 1983 with funding from USAID in order to revitalize traditional agricultural exports and to promote export growth under the Caribbean Basin Initiative.[40] At the beginning of the 1980s, "external nonmerchandise flows—mainly in the form of aid grants from the United States and, to a lesser extent, from money sent back by Salvadorans living abroad—replaced coffee as the principal source of foreign currency in El Salvador's economy."[41] FUSADES was founded by Salvadoran elites as a nonprofit association whose purpose was to revitalize private enterprise in the country. To that end, FUSADES received over $100 million from USAID to promote "nontraditional" exports between 1984 and 1992.[42]

At the end of the war and after, FUSADES became the country's main promoter of maquila production, exports to the United States, and building more EPZs in El Salvador. Its wartime mission of export promotion was easily translated into one of postwar reconstruction through private investment. In its funding agreement for 1991, USAID instructed FUSADES to "aggressively promote El Salvador abroad, seeking direct foreign investment, co-investment, and long-term subcontracting opportunities through the use of overseas promoters." In 1991, FUSADES established offices in Miami and New York City, and at the 1991 Bobbin Apparel Show the FUSADES exhibit drew about one hundred people interested in outsourcing or investing in El Salvador.[43] As the FUSADES 1991 report indicated, it then had more than 250 people working "under the same roof." In that same year, with USAID funding, FUSADES built offices in Santa Elena, an elite enclave outside San Salvador, next to the newly constructed U.S. Embassy compound.[44]

The FUSADES-promoted infrastructure of EPZs, clustered between San Salvador and the port city of Acajutla, and the mirrored-glass offices of FUSADES next to the U.S. Embassy compound mark El Salvador and its economic recovery as central to global/postwar disciplinary practices. The country—with the help of USAID—made every effort to create the "big free trade zone" promised by former president Armando Calderón Sol in 1995.[45] The five EPZs built between 1992 and 1994 (ranging in size from the smallest, El Progreso, at 225,000 square feet, to the largest, San Bartolo, at 5,106,250 square feet) have provided jobs for both generals and people displaced by the war and have proven to be fruitful ground for the application of disciplinary practices learned in counterinsurgency.

The *zonas francas* have provided foreign reserves for the country and an outlet for USAID projects—as well as a limited extension of FUSADES's mission. To foreign investors, El Salvador's EPZs provide "industrial energy, industrial waste collection and disposal, plenty of potable industrial water, telephone, fax, telex, water sewage treatment, maintenance, cleaning and security for common areas, customs office and international communications lines."[46] The law that governs the country's EPZs provides for total exemptions from income taxes, municipal taxes on assets and patrimony, import duties, taxes on dividends and value-added taxes, and supplies limited options to sell products in the local market.[47] As one investment brochure points out: "In order to operate an efficient and profitable business in a Free Zone a large labor force to pool from is a necessity. El Salvador offers just that. A skilled and semi-skilled labor force numbering in the hundreds of thousands. Companies from around the world have commented favorably on the work ethic and productivity of the Salvadoran worker."[48] The "work ethic and productivity of the Salvadoran worker" for a "total hourly cost" of 85 cents came with the EPZ management's concentrated effort to prohibit unionization and labor activism within the zones in a manner similar to Youngone's.

From the middle of 1994 through the end of 1995, at least four thousand garment workers were fired from factories in El Salvador's EPZs, mostly because of pregnancy or union organizing.[49] During that same period, mass firings were part of a larger climate of conflict throughout the Salvadoran maquila sector. Although the Mandarin International conflict in 1995 was the most highly publicized, it was not the only instance of attempted unionization, mass firing, and lockout of workers. In the San Marcos EPZ, one thousand workers were locked out after the organization of the SETMI union at the Mandarin factory and "security guards had hit Mandarin employee and union affiliate Christina Domínguez Hernández in the face with a club, making her nose bleed."[50] The year after the Mandarin conflict, four hundred workers at the GABO factory in San Marcos were fired after organizing a union at the site, and the factory eventually shut down. Two years earlier, in 1994, a GABO employee died after the manager of the factory refused to give her permission to go to the doctor. Former GABO workers, who were fired for attempting to assist their colleague, said: "Julia Esperanza Quintanilla, 24 years old, suffered from strong stomach pains and asked permission to get medical treatment at the ISSS (the Salvadoran Social Security Institute). . . . [T]he permission was denied by the person in charge at the time . . . and Quintanilla died the next day."[51]

The situation in San Marcos was similar to those at other EPZs and *recintos fiscales* in the country. Between 1994 and 1998, there were thirty-six initially successful attempts at union organizing in El Salvador's maquila sector. By 1998, only three of those unionization projects remained, and only two of them were still active to a greater or lesser degree.[52]

Since 1994, there has been significant press coverage—nationally and internationally—of the maquila industry and mistreatment of workers, the majority of them young women. The press coverage and reports of the Human Rights Commission cited the following violations as common:

> A probationary period of two weeks without the benefit of salary to "qualify" for a position; forced overtime and unpaid vacations; illegal salary deductions for sick days; illegal salary deductions for arriving late to work; firings for being pregnant; firings for trying to form or joining a union; keeping "black lists" of alleged unionists; unjustified firings; firings without severance pay; sexual harassment or assault of workers; physical and verbal mistreatment of workers; hiring of minors, and other violations.[53]

These documented violations, and the high level of national and international publicity around them, resulted in the mass firings of garment workers and denunciations of the violations and firings by unions and NGOs within El Salvador and internationally. According to a 1998 survey by the Salvadoran Human Rights Commission, *Procuraduría General de la Defensa de Derechos Humanos,* accusations persisted that some factories abused their workers and that some women were not hired because they were pregnant. The report presented the following survey results:

> 37.7 percent of the workers surveyed stated that they had been mistreated, 37.7 percent had been threatened, 3.2 percent had been harassed sexually by bosses, and 3 percent had been harassed sexually by other workers. . . . 7.8 percent of workers in its survey sample were not paid legally required extra pay for working beyond the normal 44-hour workweek, a strong indication of forced overtime.[54]

After all the coverage of abuses, especially in the mid-1990s, many of the same conditions persisted. A 1995 study by CENTRA, a think tank that documents working conditions and labor rights, cited four reasons why abuses persisted, despite having been documented and denounced:

> (1) Lack of respect for human and labor rights: . . . FUSADES and our government omit informing foreign investors of the constitutional mandate to comply with labor law when they are promoting the competitive advantages of El Salvador. (2) The non-working Ministry of Labor: . . . the labor conflicts in the maquilas have demonstrated the urgent necessity of restructuring, reorganization . . . and modernization of this institution. . . . (3) Legal loopholes; and (4) Internal limitations of the union movement.[55]

The continued documentation of abuses and the lack of recourse for improving working conditions were aspects of the overdetermined nature of the industry in El Salvador where political economy, international relations, postwar rebuilding, structural adjustment, and elections to office manifested themselves. One woman I interviewed, who wished to remain anonymous, said: "They are selling the poverty of the country. The factory owners do it, as do the unionists, NGO people, and academics, too."[56]

In the wake of the twelve-year civil war, the union movement, especially, was decimated. Ruíz and García argue:

> the labor and union movement, after having expended its energies during the 12 years of struggling for the political and social rights in the armed conflict that our country suffered, lacks direction and familiarization with the very work of unionism. The level of qualification that the present moment demands is very high, and in the case of the maquila, clearly we have seen its limitations.[57]

Marina Ríos, a feminist organizer of garment workers with the Movimiento de Mujeres Mélida Anaya Montes (MAM), pointed out: "Maquila work is difficult, and it is difficult to make contact with the women who work in the factories. Women are scattered throughout the factories, and the work day is long." Ríos went on to say that "the union movement in El Salvador is broken and exhausted," and that it was time to find "a different model, one that takes into consideration the point of view of women."[58]

El Salvador's unions often competed with each other for international legitimacy and funding. "If the Unión Nacional Obrero Campesino (UNOC) says that it has 200,000 members, the Unión Nacional de Trabajadores Salvadoreños (UNTS) says that it has 250,000. All of a sudden, the UNOC announces that it has 300,000."[59] This competition is both a sign of the difficult challenges facing unions in the current period and a legacy of the war and counterinsurgency politics. Ruíz and García argue that "the union movement, in its current difficult state, needs to confront an enemy that has new and better advantages compared to traditional bosses. . . . The current enemy has an unusual level of impunity to violate the labor code, and the unions need a high level of organization, coordination, solidarity, [and] astuteness" in order to carry out shop-floor organizing or address labor violations.[60]

The legacy of the civil war on the union movement, and that of AIFLD, USAID, and the U.S. State Department, has been especially debilitating.[61] Upon its reentry into El Salvador in the early 1980s, AIFLD, in conjunction with then U.S. State Department policy, "set out to help build a 'democratic center' . . . by creating a base of support for the Christian Democratic Party among rural and urban unions."[62] To that effect, AIFLD gave organizational guidance and funding to form the Popular Democratic Unity (UPD), supporting Reagan's strategy of "democratization" in El Salvador. According to Barry and Preusch, UPD members went door to door in 1984 to encourage people to support civilian José Napoleón Duarte's candidacy for president in the middle of the civil war. Organizers for the UPD were often flown to Washington to tell the U.S. Congress that there was strong popular support for agrarian reform, the electoral process, and the Christian Democratic Party. When later in 1984 AIFLD saw that one sector of the UPD—the UCS (the Salvadoran Communal Union)—was becoming critical of the Duarte administration, they demanded that the UCS leave the UPD and join another federation. AIFLD warned the UCS and others "not to 'push Duarte to the left' . . . [and] AIFLD's brass-knuckle tactics ultimately split the UPD and caused great bitterness towards the AFL-CIO."[63]

Two years later, AIFLD supported the Salvadoran and U.S. governments in their efforts to discredit a left-leaning labor union in El Salvador, the Unión Nacional de Trabajadores Salvadoreños (UNTS). AIFLD went so far as to hold a press conference in order to "release documents allegedly captured from the FMLN that AIFLD said revealed a secret guerrilla plan to manipulate the union movement . . . [saying that] Marxist-Leninist guerrillas had infiltrated the union movement to foment discord between labor and the Duarte government."[64] The divisiveness fostered by AIFLD's involvement in El Salvador's labor movement was carried through to the period of maquila organizing. Many groups wanted to claim to be doing the "real" organizing and accused others of concentrating on fund-raising and self-promotion.

In 1996, a group of NGOs, unions, human rights groups, and others came together under the name COSDEMA. COSDEMA published its mission in the national newspapers, accusing governmental and business sectors in the country of carrying out a campaign "to intimidate garment workers so that they will not demand the defense of those rights that support them as both workers and as human beings, under the unspoken threat of losing their jobs." The group went on to "make a call to all garment workers, as well as national and international institutions, governmental or nongovernmental, to . . . give dignity to the employment of garment workers and, in this way, to guarantee employment and labor stability for themselves."[65] The group worked together for several months, and, Marina Ríos pointed out:

> COSDEMA continues to be important [as a model for activism]. But the problem of different types of interests remains—questions of hegemony, finances, who will lead, since there are those who would like to take control over the rest. What we need is a specific cause around which we can work in order to have agreement within the group. We have to see ourselves as complementing each other.[66]

One of the big challenges to labor organizing under the system of transnational subcontracting and the rewriting of trade and labor laws in EPZs has been that of sustaining the work over time: factory owners and managers are able to move transnationally, and workers are often in the factories for up to twenty hours a day. Disciplinary formations have become transnational even as they depend on local histories of war, nation-building, colonialism, race, class, gender, and sexuality.

Discipline and Difference

Many of the protests and much of the press coverage of abuses focused on those factories owned by Asian capital, and critiques of the garment industry have often been overlaid with racism on the part of press outlets, government officials, and unions. During the Mandarin strike, Juan José Huezos, leader of the union federation FENASTRAS, arrived at San Marcos and shouted to the workers, who were not then affiliated with FENASTRAS, through a megaphone. Huezos declared: "We are telling you that FENASTRAS has already sat down to negotiate with the Chinese, and the first thing we have achieved is that nobody will get less than full severance pay. Do you disagree with this, compañeras?"[67] The emphasis on the ethnicity or nationality of owners and workers, often combined with gendered notions of difference, was a central part of El Salvador's national labor rights discourse. While questions of gender relations and difference on the shop floors are brought into the discourse of global labor rights, the use of racist and nativist rhetoric by local capitalists and workers alike often went unmentioned.

The notion that abuses of workers by managers and factory owners is a problem of cultural difference, for example, a problem of Chinese managers not knowing how to treat Salvadoran workers, is often repeated by the managers themselves. In this context, "Chinese" was used to refer to Taiwanese and Korean managers alike. Mr. Jhon, owner of the GABO factory, argued for the need for better training of the managers on treatment of workers:

> Before, we had problems with some companies that were not accustomed to the ways of Salvadorans. It was a problem also recognized by our government. Now, if a Korean company wants to open a factory, it has to be approved by the government of Korea, a process that means training and education about cultural norms, so as not to create problems for other companies or reflect badly upon the Korean people.[68]

The language of cultural difference, along with the raced, gendered bodies of the GABO factory's owners and its workers, stood in as a marker of the highly contested realm of relations of power, money, class, race, and gender. This, in turn, was intertwined with the realm of capital accumulation and social reproduction.[69] Gender and race, along with immigration status, serve as markers of discipline both nationally and globally. Within Central American orientalist discourses, Asian bodies are marked as "culturally other" capitalists, while in New York City, their bodies and legal status mark them as both "culturally other" and objects of capital.

The Production and Consumption of the Global Worker

I have examined the global worker as a gendered, raced, classed, and national subject of activism, production, and consumption. This figure of a quintessential globalized worker adds another layer to the larger project of capitalist discipline. A focus on a particular type of worker and a particular set of abuses, in the consumer-oriented transnational campaigns for labor rights, is part of the search for resistance against global corporate domination. In the search for resistance, hope, and authenticity within the framework of globalization, labor activists have managed to leave aside other structures of domination, other histories, and exclusions into which the attempts at resistance fall.[70]

By citing the worst abuses of production, the ultimate forms of domination, and extraction as exceptional to normalized production, consumer action can become the ultimate form of resistance and the ideal manner in which to save working bodies from the machine of capital. This is the perfect combination of Taylorist discipline and sweated labor with advertising image and the marketing imperatives of corporate research and development. Consumer-based activism becomes a quintessentially "new" solution to the "old" problem of sweatshops. By maintaining the idea that the Taylorist science of production, as Harvey and others have argued, has given way to flexible production systems as part of a post-Fordist regime of "flexible accumulation," activists and corporate heads alike are able to cite consumption as the only alternative. According to Harvey,

> Turnover time—always one of the keys to capitalist profitability—stood to be reduced dramatically by deployment of the new technologies in production (automation, robots) and new organizational forms (such as the "just-in-time" inventory-flows delivery system, which cuts down radically on stocks required to keep production flow going). *But accelerating turnover time in production would have been useless unless the turnover time in consumption was reduced.*[71]

Consumers are depended on, in this new formation, both to keep the engine of flexible accumulation running smoothly and to become the political conscience of this system of accumulation. Consumer protests against the global sweatshop romanticize the Fordist factory, post-Fordist production practices, and the Keynesian welfare state. While post-Fordist production rests on Taylorist theories of regulation and on uneven development patterns worldwide, consumer-centered activism elides this into a focus on the global. It also depends on projects of bodily abuse that can be traced to anticommunist counterinsurgency tactics, early twentieth-century sweatshop production practices, and consumers who are willing to maintain their levels of consumption as part of acting on their political convictions. The practice of consumption, then, is reconciled with the very forms of discipline that consumer activists are attempting to document and protest.

5

Women First?

On a summer day in June 1995, Judith Viera stepped up to the podium in Miami at the founding convention of UNITE, the Union of Needletrades, Industrial, and Textile Employees, to tell her story. Viera described her co-workers' struggles to form a union at a factory in El Salvador. Armed guards denied entry to anyone without an identification card and, Viera said, carried out full body searches of those they did allow to enter, the majority of whom were women between the ages of fifteen and thirty years old. Viera described the regimen of severely limited bathroom visits and forced birth control at Mandarin International, a factory producing clothing for the U.S. market, subcontracted by companies such as Gap Inc., JCPenney, and Eddie Bauer. She also talked about the mass firing of more than three hundred Mandarin workers and a lockout of over five thousand garment workers at the free trade zone when, after many attempts, they were able to form a union that was recognized by the Salvadoran Ministry of Labor. In chapter 2, I discussed the conditions at Mandarin International and Viera's participation in the NLC-Gap campaign; in this chapter, I return to Viera in order to address questions of gendered agency in transnational labor organizing.

Viera's testimony in Miami about unionization struggles at Mandarin was timed strategically to coincide with the founding convention of UNITE. Viera's testimony also launched the tour of the United States and Canada by Viera and Claudia Molina, a Honduran garment worker, and caught the attention of both labor activists and the U.S. consuming public. Viera had been brought to the United States by the NLC, and her participation in the tour and in the founding of UNITE signaled the reinvigoration of garment workers' organizing and a renewed commitment to immigrants and third world women in the United States and throughout the world. UNITE was created through the merger of the ACTWU and the International Ladies' Garment Workers Union (ILGWU) at a time when they faced severely dwindling membership and criticism for their brand of "business unionism" and lack of shop-floor organizing. UNITE became one of the first sites of the "new unionism" that marked the union movement in the United States over the course of the 1990s. The testimonies were part of a larger campaign to push the U.S.-based retailer Gap Inc. to take responsibility for labor violations in Central American factories producing clothing under its brand names. Viera's and Molina's testimonies about garment work, workplace abuse, their own position as young women of color in the new international division of labor, and the widespread activism that occurred as a result of their efforts, jump-started the Mandarin campaign. The transnational protest campaign connected factories in Honduras and El Salvador with retail outlets in the United States, ending in the agreement between the National Labor Committee and Gap Inc. on December 15, 1995, at a church in Brooklyn Heights.

As discussed in chapter 2, the Brooklyn agreement called for a reinstatement of the fired Mandarin workers, company recognition of the union and the right to organize, and an independent monitoring group made up of nongovernmental organizations and local human rights and religious groups. The independent monitoring group was set up to observe the Mandarin factory and was to have unlimited access to inspect the factory, verify compliance with the national labor code, and guarantee union recognition by the management.

The Double Edge of Transnational Labor Protest

The NLC-Gap agreement and the transnational labor rights campaign that featured Viera and Molina were seen as proverbial success stories and thus were replicated in subsequent labor rights campaigns and subsequent tours of the United States by young women garment workers from throughout the third world. In this chapter I examine the ways in which women are mobilized, defined, and deployed as a category in various contexts of transnational organizing: What are the positions of women in transnational labor organizing? To what extent do transnational labor politics complicate agency in garment factories employing women throughout the third world?

Transnational labor organizers take up categories of gender, race, class, and nation in ways that are monolithic, misogynist, and difficult to contest. The space of the "new sweatshop" as a site of national and discursive production is both central to and in excess of the global imaginary. First, in garment production sites such as Mandarin in El Salvador, Seo Fashions in New York City, and Samrana Fashions in Bangladesh, local patriarchal and gendered practices are deployed in producing clothing for the world's retail outlets.[1] Second, in transnational protest campaigns against labor violations of women workers in the global garment industry, these categories and practices appear to be challenged in sophisticated ways by spokespeople like Viera on behalf of her coworkers at Mandarin. Third, in corporate advertising and retail consumption practices, gendered, raced, classed, and national hierarchies are redeployed in the name of difference in order to maintain the circulation of capital for the benefit of U.S. retailers.

The speaking tours of the United States by garment workers find their roots in the abolitionist movement, when former slaves would provide testimony about their experiences in order to educate the (white, nonslaveholding) public. Paul Gilroy, in *The Black Atlantic,* argues that the writings of Frederick Douglass and others are "notable for marking out the process whereby the division of intellectual labour within the abolitionist movement was transformed. The philosophical material for the abolitionist cause was no longer to be exclusively generated by white commentators who articulated the metaphysical core of simple, factual slave narratives."[2]

Given their roots in the abolitionist movement and their focus on the raced, classed, and gendered experiences of women workers in the United States and throughout the third world, transnational protests against the new sweatshop would appear to be an example of what Lisa Lowe, in her work on Asian-American women's activism in the garment industry, calls "the complex encounters between transnational capital and women within patriarchal gender structures, [where] the very processes that produce a racialized feminized proletariat both displace traditional and national patriarchies and their defining regulations of gender, space and work, and racialize the women in relation to other racialized groups." According to Lowe, this challenge has the potential to produce "new possibilities precisely because they have led to a breakdown and reformulation of the categories of nation, race, class, and gender, and in so doing have prompted a reconceptualization of the oppositional narratives of nationalism, Marxism, and feminism." Lowe goes on to say that the shift toward "the transnationalization of capital is not exclusively manifested in the 'denationalization' of corporate power or the nation-state." She argues that, perhaps more important, "it is expressed in the reorganization of oppositional interventions against capital that articulate themselves in terms and relations other than the singular 'national,' 'class,' or 'female' subject."[3]

The antisweatshop campaigns, however, reconsolidate configurations of nation, race, class, and gender at the transnational and local levels and are evidence of the double-edged effect of transnational organizing. Gilroy's discussion of the role of testimony in the abolitionist movement can help to theorize the current antisweatshop movement, showing how Lowe's notion of the "reorganization" of capital, corporate power, and the nation-state— and oppositional interventions—can also mean retrenchment alongside the opening up of possibilities for activism on the part of the "racialized, femininized proletariat." This particular combination of retrenchment and possibility point toward the need to interrogate more closely the ways in which these very reorganizations depend on the maintenance of the boundaries of the nation-state and "singular" identities.

Questions of representation are especially important if we consider the crosscutting relationship among image making, production, and protest within the garment industry and the antisweatshop movement. Campaigns against labor abuse in garment manufacturing, with its production regimes based on the (cross-border) migration of people and capital and its intrinsic ties to consumption, style, and the fashion industry, by implication have to rely both on crossing borders and on making (counter-)images. Within these border crossings and battles over image and branding, it is important to trace and define the workings of gender, class, and race in the tours of the United States, in the activist campaigns, and on the shop floor.

It is my contention that what we see is not so new; rather, it is a replication of globalization from above but framed as a new globalization from below. Within these discourses of globalization, activists, consumers, producers, and retailers alike use the bodies and subjectivities of third world and immigrant women in their production regimes of clothing and images. It is only when scholars and activists do not take into consideration the ways in which the new internationalism employs raced and gendered agency in its image-making battles that the new transnational politics can be deemed successful in its contentions.

The problematic of the new international division of labor shows the garment industry to be part of a feminized labor process. In the literature on production processes and global labor formations, the shop floor often has been shown as either a feminine site or a masculine site, or as a previously masculine site that has become feminized.[4] In scholarly and organizing literature, production practices have traditionally been carried out by mostly men workers who serve as the male breadwinners; conversely, consumption has been theorized as practiced by mostly women shoppers. Consumer-oriented transnational labor campaigns have worked to connect the two sites and to show that they are not separate realms; in fact, practices carried out in each site are intrinsically connected to practices in the other. What are the class-based, race-based, and nation-based implications of transnational labor protest? How do gender categories get taken up or, alternately, not taken up within the labor campaigns and in the factory sites? Finally, what do we risk by emphasizing the feminization of the shop floor or of the (globalized) labor process, and what do we gain?

Gender and "Collective Psychosis" at DINDEX

Traditional unionism has often addressed gender issues on the shop floor and in union centers by ignoring questions of gender identity in favor of organizing its membership as workers first and foremost. The garment industry has been traditionally a site of women's work, and, in the United States, women have been at the forefront of organizing and building the union movement, but the labor aristocracy has traditionally consisted of white men in its highest positions. Because of this hierarchy, women's participation in labor activism has often been muted in favor of that of the (white American) "working man." Often, the deployment of particular gender categories at the workplace and within the union movement reinforces disciplinary relations within factories. It also mediates relations between people who work in the factories and those who organize the labor rights campaigns, while not necessarily addressing everyday relations that negotiate questions of gender, sexuality, and age. The deployment of these categories does not address the specific concerns of the (exploited) women who make up the majority of workers in most of the world's garment factories.

In this section, I will identify how specific concerns of workers are addressed within national and transnational discourses around garment production, the new sweatshop, and working conditions through a discussion of an episode of mass fainting in a garment factory in El Salvador that was picked up by national and international labor activists and media outlets. In November 1997, at the DINDEX factory in San Salvador, a *recinto fiscal* (a bonded area of an individual export-oriented factory falling under the same trade and labor laws that govern export processing zones in El Salvador) that produced clothing for local and international markets, more than two hundred women were taken to the hospital after suffering from fainting spells, dizziness, nausea, and convulsions. The women were apparently poisoned by the synthetic materials they worked with, their drinking water supply, or carbon monoxide expelled into the air by machines inside the factory.[5] At the beginning of the DINDEX work day, around 7:30 in the morning, two women fainted and were taken to the hospital. Over the course of the morning, more people passed out or experienced nausea until, around 10:30, women were falling onto the factory floor "one after the other."[6] Those showing symptoms of poisoning were taken to area hospitals in ten ambulances provided by the Red Cross and the National Civil Police, while others left the factory in fear of being poisoned.

I was in the neighborhood of DINDEX around lunchtime on that day. The streets around the factory were filled with ambulances, and I saw women running in all directions away from the factory. When I asked some of them what was happening, they said that everyone needed to get away from the factory because of contaminated water or air inside the factory. Most were quick to mention that several of those affected were pregnant, and that some people had passed out over the course of the two weeks before that day's factory-wide poisoning. All of those with whom I spoke were heading for their homes in outlying areas of the city, hoping that they would not be affected.[7] Unlike the factories that are inside the walls of El Salvador's various EPZs, DINDEX is located in the center of the city in a neighborhood dotted with several *recintos fiscales*. Therefore, the women running away did not have to pass through gates or armed guards to leave the area.

The DINDEX factory's windows had been bricked over during the civil war, and there was no ventilation or air circulation within the factory where 450 people made clothing during workdays that lasted between eight and ten hours and sometimes longer.[8] The women who stopped to talk to me said that they were making underwear for Salvadoran and Central American markets, although at other times they made clothing for U.S. and European markets. In the midst of the poisoning, employees found out that the DINDEX managers, who had been deducting from their paychecks social security charges that were supposed to cover medical visits, emergencies, and hospitalization, had never sent the money to the Instituto Salvadoreño de Seguridad Social (ISSS), El Salvador's national social security administration.

Therefore, the women at DINDEX did not have insurance coverage for their hospitalization and subsequent treatment, despite the fact that their illnesses occurred on factory grounds and were most likely caused by hazardous working conditions.[9] Those apparently most affected by the poisoning—and the first to faint and have convulsions and nausea—were pregnant women who worked at DINDEX and needed to remain under observation for longer periods of time. According to news reports, employees had been asking about their insurance coverage for some time. The DINDEX management told its employees that they would receive their updated insurance cards as soon as the social security administration sent them. The women who worked at DINDEX waited for weeks and months to receive insurance cards that had never been paid for by the factory.[10]

Despite the lack of insurance coverage, DINDEX employees were taken by ambulance and treated at public hospitals and clinics while El Salvador's minister of health, Eduardo Interiano, threatened legal action against DINDEX in order to make the factory pay for its employees' medical treatment.[11] Interiano called for the intervention of the Ministry of Labor, and the head of the Salvadoran Red Cross said, "the problem had been detected a week earlier, but when it arose there had been no interest on the part of the management to solve it."[12] While the management was being criticized for its inaction, the police cordoned off the DINDEX factory on the afternoon of the poisoning so that the Ministry of Health could carry out tests to determine its causes and decide who should be charged with criminal negligence.[13]

DINDEX's owner, Américo Martínez, said that there was nothing wrong with the factory and that he had always paid for the social security benefits of his employees; the problem was that the cards had not yet arrived. Martínez added that he regularly drank water from the cistern, "Here I am now, along with everyone from the administrative area [of the factory], and until this moment nobody has had any symptoms. The way I see it, more than anything, it was panic, a shock of nerves [among the employees]."[14] The water in the cistern appeared dirty, and it contained "lead, arsenic, chromium, organochlorides and phosphorus [and also] dead insects and other debris."[15] The filter used to clean the cistern was too small to do the job, and the Ministry of Health first suspected that it was the cause of the workers' illnesses. When the test results of DINDEX's water came back from the Ministry of Health, and the water was declared safe enough to drink, there was intense speculation about the cause of the accident. Public health technicians inspected the site. They found a lack of ventilation and "only ten toilets in the factory, five for [the 504] women [who work in the factory] and five for [the 54] men, in disgusting, unhealthful conditions. The ideal would be one toilet for every 25 people."[16] The gender disparities in the provision of sanitary facilities among men and women—there was approximately one toilet for every eleven men, as opposed to one for every one hundred women—was not mentioned in the inspection report.

Katia de Ramírez, an ISSS doctor who treated the DINDEX workers, said: "Probably the victims inhaled carbon monoxide and approximately five people were poisoned at a low level. The rest can be explained by a convulsive neurosis, that is to say, they took on the symptoms of their co-workers."[17] What Ramírez called "a convulsive neurosis" received more attention than the possible inhalation of carbon monoxide or the unhealthful conditions of the factory. Health authorities claimed that the poisoning was most likely due to carbon monoxide, but because there was no way to determine conclusively what caused the poisoning, DINDEX managers and the national media framed a public debate about DINDEX that began to focus more closely on the notion of "mass psychosis" among the workers.[18] Health minister Interiano said that there was no doubt that some DINDEX workers had been affected by something that poisoned them, but that many others had "a neurotic attitude" at the factory.[19] Before the tests came back from the laboratories indicating the cause of the fainting, Interiano stated, "It is normal that, seeing their coworkers fainting, they would feel the same . . . but there was a bit of an exaggeration."[20] The "exaggeration," coinciding with what Interiano called the "neurotic attitude" of the women at DINDEX, echoed the factory owner Martínez's judgment that the women had suffered from a generalized panic on the shop floor.

In *Spirits of Resistance and Capitalist Discipline,* Aihwa Ong argues that the rash of spirit possessions and mass hysteria that happened among garment workers in Malaysian free trade zones was a way of negotiating factory disciplinary regimes and carrying out localized struggles against male domination. Ong argues: "The eruption of spirit possession episodes in transnational companies disclosed the anguish, resistance, and cultural struggle of some neophyte female workers. . . . Spirit attacks were indirect retaliations against coercion and demands for justice in personal terms within the industrial milieu" (220). In the case of the more than two hundred women at DINDEX who fainted that November morning, their symptoms cannot be categorized simply as a performance of resistance—either to male domination or to factory discipline—but Ong's research certainly opens up that possibility. Descriptions of the fainting at DINDEX reproduced gendered difference in the use of the feminine forms of "workers" *(trabajadoras),* "coworkers" *(compañeras),* and "employees" *(empleadas).* The feminine form was used by the women I interviewed who were running from the factory that morning as well as by official sources in the press, the Ministries of Health and Labor, and the factory owner to describe those who had fainted.

Every media outlet, government official, and labor organization that covered the DINDEX poisoning said that those most severely affected by the poisoning were pregnant women working in the factory. This pointed to both the particular vulnerability of mothers and mothers-to-be to the rigors of factory work and to the heteronormativity of gender relations on the shop floor and in labor organizing practices. As one leading news report on the DINDEX poisoning said:

> Sources at the Salvadoran Social Security Institute [ISSS, the public hospital system] stated that . . . between 10:00 in the morning and noon . . . they saw 87 employees that were in various states of illness. Three of them were pregnant and were taken to the [maternity hospital] where it was determined that despite being in serious condition, [they] were not at risk.[21]

Other press outlets and government officials were quick to reassure the public that the pregnant workers were not in jeopardy. The women I interviewed during the evacuation of the factory were most worried about their pregnant coworkers, saying that the pregnant women were particularly undeserving of the illnesses they had experienced on the DINDEX factory floor.

The day of mass fainting and illness drew the attention of labor activists and the media to the poor working conditions inside the factory. As many people pointed out, various women at the factory had previously passed out within the two weeks before that day, and people had complained of headaches and numbness that accompanied a strange odor inside the factory. One DINDEX employee, Susana Sánchez, who was being treated at a local hospital, said: "Since last November 3, many of my coworkers had been experiencing fainting spells. We did not think it was too important, although a few of them went for consultations at the [hospital], but nobody gave them a medical reason for their suffering."[22] It was not until the majority of women in the factory began to have spells of fainting and nausea on the morning of the November 11 that any attention was paid to the situation. The media coverage focused on the spectacle of women fainting and being carried away in ambulances, all of which was depicted in full-page color spreads in the newspapers and extensive television reports. The press coverage, while sensationalized, served to draw attention to working conditions inside the factory and in the industry as a whole.

The national human rights advocate Marina de Avilés, upon being notified of the emergency at DINDEX, immediately demanded that the Ministry of Labor pay more attention to export-oriented factories, since often they do not follow Salvadoran laws. De Avilés stated, "We [the Procaduría General de Derechos Humanos] have a study that we will soon make public that documents the number of violations suffered by these workers, that makes a mockery of their labor rights, which arises as a consequence of their arduous work." The Ministry of Labor said that the DINDEX situation was "a wake-up call for the authorities, that it is their job to carry out inspections of working conditions in these places, in this case, the Ministry of Labor, in order to take advantage of the services offered them."[23]

A number of labor violations were brought to light at DINDEX as a result of the attention on the mass poisoning. First, the episodes of fainting, both before and on November 11, exposed workplace health and safety violations. The levels of water pollution were not high enough to have caused the illnesses exhibited among the workers, but air pollution and lack of ventilation were cited as the most probable causes of fainting at DINDEX—clear violations of Salvadoran health and workplace safety codes. Second, DINDEX employees needed medical attention. Because the on-site illnesses were experienced by so many, their uninsured status was brought to public attention. Although the DINDEX management had been deducting the social security charge from the employees' paychecks according to national labor laws, the money was never paid to the ISSS to provide DINDEX workers with guaranteed public health insurance.[24]

Significantly, however, because so many women were taken ill that morning, they were on the front pages of the national newspapers for several days, and the country's highest authorities paid attention to them, their lives, and their work at DINDEX in an unprecedented way. In this way, the faintings at DINDEX parallel the spirit possessions explored by Ong.[25] However, it is unclear whether there was any substantive change in conditions at DINDEX or at the other factories put under the spotlight.

The day after the mass fainting, only three workers remained hospitalized. The rest of the women showed up to work at DINDEX and were met with locked doors and nobody to tell them what would happen next. I went to the factory site with a group of researchers and labor activists after we were told that the DINDEX management was planning to close the factory and leave the site without notice. When we arrived at the factory at 7:00 that morning, there were hundreds of people filling the street outside the factory gates. Rumors were spreading that the owners were planning to move production to another country. Some people said that the owners were, at that moment, packing up the sewing machines to ship to another site and that nobody would get paid for the previous two weeks of work. Several people in the group claimed to have spotted various owners and managers sneaking out of the side or back of the factory. One woman told a reporter in the crowd: "We have children to feed and our work is ending. We have already met the production goals for the clothing that they asked us to sew, and we want to be paid for that."[26] The woman's statement pointed to her own and her coworkers' vulnerability and dependence on the biweekly paycheck and revealed a violation of Salvadoran labor law: the system of daily production quotas that indirectly proved payment by piece rate rather than by hours worked.

As with the Malaysian women documented by Ong who were possessed by spirits on the factory floors, the women who fainted at DINDEX and those who camped outside the factory the next day waiting for their jobs and their paychecks were, in essence, contesting the everyday conditions of their working lives. The authorities called for widespread factory inspections and respect for labor rights in El Salvador's garment industry, but the day after the poisoning most of the DINDEX employees were faced with the loss of their jobs. Many women had no idea where to go for answers to their questions. Some colleagues and I stayed with the hundreds of DINDEX workers as they waited outside the DINDEX gates the following day to collect the pay they were owed. We asked them if they would go to the Ministry of Labor, local labor unions, or the public defender for human rights to denounce DINDEX's intentions to cut and run; most people did not think that they could approach any of these entities for help or advice. Many women we talked with had no idea that they had a legal right to their paycheck or to their jobs, nor did they know how to contact public offices or labor unions. Some were wary of contacting unions because they were worried about being fired or blacklisted and therefore unable to find other jobs. Others continued to be suspicious of unions because of those groups' perceived linkage to the politics of the recent civil war. There were few alternatives for women working at DINDEX to contest the politics of the workplace.

The women had worked for months without receiving insurance cards to grant them access to health care and medical examinations, with no potable water or proper ventilation, and grossly inadequate sanitary facilities. Only after half the women in the factory passed out was their subjectivity—and rights as citizens—recognized; they were seen, for once, as having a particular set of needs and rights.

The women waited outside the factory and talked among themselves about whether they would get paid and whether they would be able to keep their jobs. At midday, dozens of women from DINDEX took buses to the Ministry of Labor to file formal complaints about factory conditions, social security deductions, and the possibility of the factory closing down without paying its employees. Others in the group went to meet with union representatives and the MAM women's group to discuss alternatives for organizing. MAM had been an active part of the FMLN insurgency during the war and was at that point carrying out women-focused shop-floor organizing in the maquila sector. The women depended on DINDEX for both their health and livelihood, and the fainting episode made them more vulnerable in both aspects while at the same time opening up new spaces for debate and gendered agency that were not available to them before.

The DINDEX workers' illness and the environmental conditions in the factory were covered extensively in the national news, though they received increasingly less newspaper coverage as the week passed. After being threatened with legal action, DINDEX's owner agreed to pay the workers for the weeks worked and did not close the factory. While his employees were filing their complaints with the Ministry of Labor and meeting unions and women's groups, the factory owner, Américo Martínez, issued a press statement, "Tomorrow afternoon, they can pick up their paychecks corresponding to the first two weeks of November."[27] At the same time, the Salvadoran Garment Industry Association (ASIC) expressed its "solidarity with the affected workers." The legislative branch of the FMLN made an official statement asking that an in-depth inquiry be carried out about the massive poisoning of the DINDEX workers and that the factory not be closed. The turnaround happened because of the women's efforts in contacting MAM and the Ministry of Labor and because of all of the press coverage over the faintings and their aftermath.

Once women from DINDEX informed MAM about their situation, MAM sent a request to the U.S.-based CISPES for international solidarity action on behalf of the DINDEX workers. Within a few weeks, the news of DINDEX spread among U.S. solidarity groups. CISPES, with support from the Campaign for Labor Rights (CLR), organized a letter-writing campaign that called for a "full investigation of violations of labor, and health and safety standards at DINDEX" and insisted that the Ministry of Labor "enforce the laws to ensure that this tragedy is never repeated."[28] CISPES's "action alert" began by detailing the worker poisoning at DINDEX and pointed out that there were "several pregnant women" who were among those taken ill. The alert said that many of the workers required "artificial respiration and cardiac massage" and two weeks after the DINDEX poisoning "at least 3 workers remained hospitalized."[29]

The campaign encouraged activists to send letters to the Apparel Industry Partnership (AIP) denouncing "this gross violation of garment workers' human rights." The letters were to tell the AIP that "their global anti-sweatshop code must include the right to organize and truly independent monitoring carried out by local human rights, labor, and religious groups, following the successful model in the Mandarin factory in El Salvador."[30]

Judith Viera's role in the Gap campaign and her tour of the United

States sparked the Brooklyn Heights agreement regarding Gap Inc.'s production practices at Mandarin. One outcome of that agreement was the creation of the GMIES. For the U.S.-based activists protesting in solidarity with the DINDEX workers who were poisoned, the GMIES was a key part of the model for a successful resolution to transnational labor organizing. The call for independent monitoring and the institution of corporate codes of conduct for working conditions connected Viera with those poisoned at DINDEX and was seen in the United States as a way to defend the interests of the women who worked in the export-oriented garment industry, in places where local and international labor laws and their guarantees of the right to organize were not carried out in practice.

Back to Mandarin?

The narrative of the successful labor rights campaign, seen through the prism of various shop floors in El Salvador and Bangladesh, is disrupted by an examination of everyday gender relations in the factories, communities, and the campaigns themselves. My analysis takes into consideration the circulation of bodies, capital, and performance in garment production and in the transnational labor campaign. The NLC-Gap campaign, the institution of independent monitoring at Mandarin, and their position as models failed in a number of ways. What happened at Mandarin after the apparent success of the 1995 campaign?

Members of the all-woman union directorate of Mandarin told me in 1997 that although 35 of them were rehired and that working conditions improved, their lives had been made difficult since they returned to the factory. They also repeatedly brought up the fact that 315 of their co-unionists were *never* rehired—that they were completely left out of the negotiations, the agreement, and its success story. U.S.-based activists along with representatives from Gap Inc.—all white North American men—made the decisions that resulted in the Brooklyn agreement, which was then implemented by Salvadoran compradors and subcontractors. Women were no longer forced to take birth control pills but neither were they allowed to wear makeup on the factory floor because they were told it might damage the clothing they produced.

The Mandarin transnational success story brought together U.S.-based consumer activists, under the banner of Viera's testimonies, to pressure Gap Inc. to change its production subcontracting policies. In the end, however, although some working conditions improved, the very women who worked at Mandarin and took the risk of forming a union on the site have been left out of the story. From the 315 workers never rehired to the 35 who continue to struggle as unionists at Mandarin, isolated and ridiculed, all are forgotten casualties of this model transnational labor organizing project. In my discussions with Viera, she told me that she was completely aware of the ways that the success of the Mandarin campaign relied on her performance and her agency during the tour of the United States.

The NLC-Gap campaign in El Salvador is an example of how transnational protest has relied on gendered, racialized exclusions and of how the oppositional politics that is employed parallels the very relations that are being contested. The choice of Viera to tour the United States was determined by the same set of assumptions that guide corporations to subcontract production and employ her coworkers at Mandarin. These assumptions about women of color from the third world and from immigrant areas of U.S. cities, about what they are capable of doing and how they are useful, are central to my analysis of the workings of race, class, gender, sexuality, and nation on the shop floors and in the transnational circuits of garment worker tours.

Through their testimonies on the 1995 tour, garment workers themselves were attempting to address and redress problems on the shop floor and in their daily lives and contesting the ways that femininity as a category was implemented in the production process. The tour itself was nearly immune from criticism because it was framed as a means of contesting power. In order to analyze the effects of the tours and the practices of transnationality, it is necessary to move between localities—between the tour and the shop floor and between sites of activism and sites of production. Without an eye to all sites of transnational protest, we cannot recognize the ways in which Viera was no less central to the Gap campaign in 1995 than were her coworkers to daily production at Mandarin, women who were fired and replaced by hundreds more needing jobs to support their families. The same assumptions about women, race, and class that determined conditions on the shop floors of Mandarin and DINDEX determined Viera's position on the tour.

Gender and Transnationality on the Shop Floor

The point at which a local incident becomes transnational connotes a shift in both the relations of the (formerly) local incident and a widening of those relations to include other actors, other histories, and other circulations of meaning. In the case of DINDEX and Mandarin, the transnationalization of the campaign to support the garment workers takes up localized relations and structures of gender, race, class, and capital. At the same time, national and transnational contexts and histories—often without being recognized as such—worked to both supplement and destabilize the relations and structures of the particular locality. In this instance, given the widespread notion of the Mandarin-Gap campaign as a successful resolution of transnational labor organizing, there was the hope that Mandarin could serve as a replicable model for future campaigns. This hope manifested itself in an unspoken conviction that women working in export-oriented industries could be best defended by local human rights and religious organizations and the solidarity of transnational labor activists. In El Salvador, for instance, the Ministry of Labor has been lax in carrying out inspections, defending labor rights, and supporting unionization claims in the country's free trade zones and bonded areas. Transnational organizing worked to take the place of local factory owners, government officials, and transnational corporations who were unwilling to follow local and international labor laws.

Relations of gender, sex, class, and position on the shop floor are fraught with local meanings and context and overlaid with people's positions and relationships within the larger society. The export-oriented factories are often run through the maintenance of family-like, patriarchal relationships on the shop floor, and working lives are wrapped up in personal histories, gender and sexual formations, and societal conventions. The stories from El Salvador and New York City differ from, even as they are similar to, stories from Bangladesh and Jamaica. A number of Bangladeshi garment factory managers I interviewed, for example, repeatedly cited the quiescence and nimble fingers of their female workers as the reason for having women work as sewing machine operators. This "nimble fingers" argument circulates transnationally, even as it manifests itself differently from site to site. One factory owner in Bangladesh, who hired employees mostly from his home village, told me: "We have 450 workers and 75 percent are women. The other jobs call for big physical labor, so women concentrate on sewing and the helpers trim threads and carry clothing to and from the workstations." The manager went on to say that newer employees work as helpers and "pick up the sewing techniques needed to become skilled operators. With more efficiency comes more salary. Always, someone comes to our door needing a job, and we try to help out by giving jobs."[31]

The idea of efficiency on the factory floor was mediated by convictions of gender difference that were at once particularly Bangladeshi and at the same time part of transnational circuits. Factory floor efficiency was further mediated by questions of age: in that factory and in many others, older women (over fifty) would often work alongside younger girls (under sixteen) as trimmers and helpers, while men and boys of all ages worked as pattern cutters, finishers, and pressers. The jobs men performed were more highly paid. Men often received double the pay of the sewing machine operators and four times that of the helpers. In the estimation of several managers I interviewed, those jobs require more strength and physical exertion. One manager said, "Men are stronger, more active, and therefore better suited to the active jobs, which, naturally, are better paid with better conditions."[32] One factory owner—a woman and self-proclaimed feminist—told me that 75 percent of her employees are women who concentrate on sewing; men are cutters, finishers, and supervisors because these jobs require education, and educated women will not work in garment factories.[33]

In their study of industrial women workers in Bangladesh, Hossain, Jahan, and Sobhan argued that while in many industries men and women do the same or similar work, "women generally are not assigned to heavy machines." In a survey of salary levels broken down by gender, Hossain and her colleagues found that one-third of women workers surveyed earned less than 500 taka a month. In the same survey, only 15 percent of the men surveyed earned below 500 taka, and the majority of industrial workers in Bangladesh "earn less than Tk 900 which is not likely to meet even basic needs." Hossain, Jahan, and Sobhan argued:

> [Women] are given work, which, while considered as light, nevertheless entails manual dexterity and concentration to detail. However, management's conventional attitude leads them to reward male strength more readily than female dexterity. Through no fault of the women this sort of assignment often results in an appreciable difference in mobility, in opportunities of skill formation and ultimately in the scale of salary.[34]

A 1994 study on occupational mobility among women garment workers in Bangladesh by Pratima Paul-Majumder and Sharifa Begum of the Bangladesh Institute for Development Studies found that most of the jobs in the garment industry were based on gendered divisions of labor. Sewing sections are reserved for women; the cutting and finishing sections are reserved for men. In another study, they found that "there is further segmentation within the gender segregated jobs." They point out: "It has been found that most of the top rank jobs in sewing . . . are held by male workers. Mobility of the female workers from lower segments to the higher ones is very limited while it is not so for male workers."[35]

In most garment factories, security guards are men, although in some cases women security guards carry out the body searches of women entering and leaving the premises. At Mandarin, men carried out the body searches, guarded the locked doors, and policed the factory floor, monitoring the workers. At Samrana Fashions, and in most other Bangladeshi garment factories, older men worked as security guards and gatekeepers, and women carried out the body searches at the entrance to the factory floor. One Bangladeshi manager I interviewed told me that it was important to maintain (locked) boundaries between the ordered factory floor and the disorder outside. He argued, "Dhaka's streets are unsafe, and women enter in large groups that are difficult to monitor, [so] everyone is searched at the entrance."[36]

The situation at Samrana paralleled a Salvadoran manager's explanation: the searches were carried out in order to prevent sabotage by unhappy employees, to prevent people from stealing the clothes they made, and to keep the clothes clean of food and makeup stains.[37] In this case, barbed wire, guns, and body searches were utilized to guard working women's bodies, with the excuse of protecting the clothing from theft and stains and the machinery from damage.

In an interview with a woman factory owner in Dhaka, she told me that she made sure that her employees were taking birth control pills. "Most women have not gone to school; we have to teach them to sign their names. We also have to teach them to take birth control, because there is a lot of migration and a high turnover rate of employees. Marriage usually ends work, so they have to be taught to be more conscious." The boundaries between work lives and home lives of women, as in this case, are often fluid—or at times deliberately broken down. In the same interview, the factory owner told me: "One woman who worked in this factory had a husband who took a second wife. So I told her, "'You have to divorce your husband.' She did, and now, to support themselves, she and her three children work here."[38] The factory owner defended herself by saying that what she had done had saved the family and that it was necessary to teach the women in the factory to be feminists. Another Dhaka factory owner, who provides day care and extra holiday time for the employees, told me it was important to avoid attempts at union organizing: "One has to take care of these women, since unions, by law, have to be allowed. That does not happen—not in this factory."[39]

While gendered divisions of labor mark shop floors in the garment industry worldwide, they take on different forms depending on local contexts. In Naila Kabeer's account of women and the Bangladeshi garment industry, she discusses the representation of factory space by women workers as marked by fictive kinship relations similar to that of an extended family. Kabeer argues that this representation is used to counter any threats to reputation that women encounter when working in the garment factories and to reconfigure the "male-female proximity" that is part of production relations in Bangladesh's export-oriented factories:

> A very common metaphor employed in this context was the familial one. This creation of fictive kinship is by no means unique to factory life; it

is employed in a variety of circumstances in Bengali society to permit forms of cross-gender interactions between non-related people which both de-sexualise the encounter and also, through choice of kinship terms, acknowledge the hierarchy of age and gender. In the factory context, it clearly played an important role in defining acceptable forms of relationships between women and men who were, by and large, strangers to each other but spent a significant portion of the day in close proximity to each other.[40]

My own experiences in garment factories in Dhaka show this to be the case. Often, factory workers knew about each other's family lives and called each other brother and sister. As Kabeer points out, "female supervisors were referred to as Apa (older sister) while male supervisors were addressed as Bhai (older brother), while older men (the gatekeeper, the master tailor) were called Chacha (uncle)" (151). In Bangladesh, the same fictive kinship relations are used among friends and acquaintances in everyday life outside of the garment factory; the factory floor, in turn, layers fictive kinship onto gendered and classed divisions of labor and production hierarchies.

Sometimes workers and managers alike use fictive kinship in order to deflect sexuality; at other times sexual relations and sexuality on the shop floor are emphasized. This happens especially when a worker wants to underline his or her own virtuous position as a woman, man, or worker. One of Kabeer's interviewees said: "Some men and women like to flirt. Men who are married, but go after other women and behave like lovers should not work here; nor should such women. But women like myself, who have come to work, not to flirt, will have no problems working in garments. They will regard men like brothers, or fathers, or uncles."[41]

In El Salvador, where fictive kinship is not a cultural convention and is not used on the factory floor, sexuality was still part of the worker-to-worker disciplinary formation. A group of garment workers I interviewed gossiped about one of their colleagues, saying that she had become pregnant while having sexual relations with one of the managers. She had married the manager and had subsequently moved into a higher position in the production line. When I expressed surprise and disbelief, everyone laughed, and one said: "There are always people who want to marry owners and managers to get ahead. Flirting and other things can always move you up in the hierarchy."[42] The women contrasted such actions with those of unionists, who were interested in working and defending their working rights rather than in flirting with the managers. Such local deployments of sexuality on the shop floors, in New York, Dhaka, and San Salvador, have not been picked up by transnational campaigns—even though, once translated into U.S.

and European legal-cultural contexts, they could be discussed within the frame of sexual harassment in the workplace.

The New International Division of Labor in Context

How does this complexity of relations, contestations, negotiations, failures, and contingencies bear on labor organizing? How are such local relations and contestations understood within the dynamics of transnational protest? What work did Viera's presence and her story do for U.S. activists and consumers and for the success and failure of organizing efforts at Mandarin?

In all of the campaigns I discuss, from activism against child labor in Bangladesh to the Kathie Lee and Gap-Mandarin campaigns and the implementation of independent monitoring in El Salvador and Honduras, to the national and transnational attention received by the mass fainting at DINDEX and protests of the lockout at Youngone, activists relied on the circulation of stories of abuses, visions of factories, and representations of women's bodies. The founding convention of UNITE, which merged two U.S. unions with long histories and tainted reputations, featured Viera and Molina. Viera and Molina—both as individuals and as representatives of their coworkers and co-unionists—were deployed tactically as signifiers of UNITE's new commitments to shop-floor organizing and to international solidarity, instead of corporate-labor pacts and cold war support for U.S. foreign policy. When Viera addressed the assembled unionists, her raced, national, and gendered body stood as a solution to the fifty-year history of U.S. nativism and national protectionism, gender discrimination within the labor movement, and a legacy of racial exclusion in the U.S. labor movement.

The tours of the United States made by Viera and Molina and other garment workers parallel the tours of former slaves in the United States and England for the cause of the abolition of slavery. Gilroy points out that with the work of Douglass and others, "a new discursive economy emerges with the refusal to subordinate the particularity of the slave experience to the totalising power of universal reason held exclusively by white hands, pens, or publishing houses."[43] The mobilization of particularity, in this case of individual garment workers working in specific factories, has been employed in the antisweatshop movement as a way both of positing abuses as particular aberrances in normalized global flows and of educating consumers about the means of production of each of their clothing items. The garment workers and the factories they come from serve as particular localities of globalized capital. Each instance, each worker—nonwhite, women, exploited, and living outside the centers of consumption, advertising, and retail decision making—becomes yet another example of what mostly white, consuming activists, living in centers of consumption and retail decision making have to fight. The shop floor is mobilized as the locality of globalization and women workers as the (gendered, raced, classed) citizens of particular nation-states working on particular shop floors. Viera and Molina, standing on the podium at UNITE's founding convention, are living proof of globalization and of the triumph of capital. Their presence, their words, and their experiences are circulated within the antisweatshop movement and are essential both for the success of the individual campaigns and for reminding consumers and activists alike why the existence of UNITE is necessary, despite the weight of its troubled history.

On the other side of the circulation of images and of bodies on the tours of the United States is the white, upper-class celebrity Kathie Lee Gifford whose subjectivity has been utilized both as an example of the evils of globalization and, once rehabilitated, as a paragon of caring womanhood. Kathie Lee Gifford's white, American, caring femininity, especially when taken as a foil to her husband, Frank, whose sportscaster and ex-football-player image is emblematic of American upper-class, white, strong masculinity, makes her easily vilified and especially salvageable. Gifford was a symbol of how ties to capital can corrupt an otherwise good person.

Kathie Lee Gifford's race, nationality, and gender position also serve to make her stand in for well-meaning consumers caught buying clothes from sweatshops despite their best intentions. Both Gifford and U.S. consumers are guilty, it would seem, because they did not know how the clothing was made, and it is this very innocence that makes it possible for them to be saved by the simple act of changing their purchasing—or subcontracting— habits. Because agency, in the case of Viera and Molina, Gifford, and the consumers and activists, is subsumed in the totality of the global, a victim-model dichotomy—and salvation story—is possible. Gifford and U.S. consumers are just as much victims of corporate greed as Viera or the DINDEX workers. Over and over again, in the circuits of transnationality, women are cast in the role of either victims or models in relation to capitalist production and consumption regimes.

Is agency reclaimed in the transnational quest for labor rights, whether under ILO conventions, national labor law, human rights, or women's rights? Wendy Brown points out the double-edged nature of rights-based claims and pushes us to consider the universalistic idiom of rights, as opposed to their local effects. She argues: "I want to acknowledge the diverse, inconstant, even contradictory ways that rights operate across various histories, cultures, and social strata. . . . Thus, while a measure of their political efficacy requires a high degree of historical and social specificity, rights operate as a political discourse of the general, the generic, and universal." Brown's conceptualization of rights discourse as paradox between universal idiom and local effects points to some of the problematics of carrying out transnational protest, especially when there is an intellectual and material division of labor between the work being done in one site and that being done in another. Brown continues:

> This paradox between the universal idiom and the local effect of rights itself transpires on both a temporal and spatial level. On the temporal level: While rights may operate as an indisputable force of emancipation at one moment in history—the American Civil Rights movement, or the struggle for rights by subjects of colonial domination such as black South Africans or Palestinians—they may become at another time a regulatory discourse, a means of obstructing or co-opting more radical political demands, or simply the most hollow of empty promises.[44]

In the case of DINDEX, many of the women affected by the poisoning and by the threat of losing their jobs were doing a number of things to contest their situation. At the same time, in the global (read U.S.) arena, a system of independent monitoring at the factory was being demanded in the name of their labor rights. In this way, particularly U.S. forms of liberalism circulate as transnational without recognizing the local and national significance of DINDEX workers appealing to Salvadoran labor and health laws to rectify their situations. Because independent monitoring was seen as a successful resolution to an earlier (similar) problem, it was resuscitated as the solution to another example of abuse. Both examples of sweatshop conditions, at Mandarin International and DINDEX, have become particular localities within the universalistic idiom of globalization.

Many stories of successful transnational campaigns against sweatshops and the globalized system of subcontracting reinforce the totality of globalization; in fact, they make local efforts and local effects almost impossible to recognize. Most of the DINDEX workers left MAM after the fainting incident, Youngone went back to business as usual, and, when I met Viera, she was working at a gasoline station and not in a garment factory or union office. However, their images continue to circulate in the antisweatshop movement as victims of globalization and exploitation and as models of successful resistance against corporate domination. They have become part of a circulation of signs and symbols, of virtual factories and perpetual incidents, among activists, consumers, and academicians alike.

The (Im)Possibilities of Transnational Organizing

Does this mean that transnational organizing cannot happen? That it is impossible to forge transnational coalitions? Not necessarily. But how can we challenge the politics of globalization in ways that are not hegemonic and that do not replicate and utilize current categories of gender, race, nation, or class? There are places where women are reframing their own subjectivity in the new international division of labor as actors and as agents, as in the example of the women's group UBINIG.

UBINIG is a feminist activist and research group based in Dhaka that carries out transnational alliances but refuses to allow international solidarity organizations to define either its community work or its agency. UBINIG is located in Shyamoli in the Mohamedpur section of Dhaka— a neighborhood full of garment factories and bamboo *bastis* (slum areas). It offers programs that include primary schooling for women and for neighborhood children in areas of Dhaka as well as in Chittagong, cities with a high concentration of garment factories. UBINIG's schooling program combines reading, writing, and mathematics with what UBINIG organizer Sheema Das Shimu called in an interview an "anti-patriarchal, pro-environmental, school and living program." UBINIG members have also set up a neighborhood women's library and tea house called Adda (Bengali for "gossip") and a cooperative store that sells books, clothing, paper, and jewelry made by members.

UBINIG's members publish a critical activist journal, *Chinta* (Bengali for "worry"), which they distribute to members, sell in the bookstore, and use in their women's literacy classes as a base text. Along with their schooling and community programs, UBINIG runs Shramo Bikash Kendra, the Trade Union Education Center, and holds classes on labor law, discharge policies, overtime, and striking. They also take on court cases for garment workers and sex workers who have been denied pay, sexually harassed, or abused. As Shimu pointed out in one of our discussions: "Many women don't know their rights, and they need to know. It isn't necessary to become a member, but they do need to know." UBINIG's members worked to organize Dhaka's garment factories but were often met with harassment, firing, and blacklisting (Figure 13).

UBINIG participates in transnational solidarity and carries out exchanges with similar groups in other parts of Asia, Europe, and Canada. According to UBINIG members, those groups with whom they work respect their feminist model of community organizing and allow members to determine their own participation. Some international organizations provide what Shimu calls "solidarity funds" with no strings attached. In the communities in which the workers live, UBINIG representatives visit people's homes, provide them with classes and the bookstore-cooperative– tea house, and organize protests in the streets. Members write critical articles

Figure 13. Former garment workers in Dhaka affiliated with UBINIG who were fired for trying to organize garment factories, in the home of one of the UBINIG activists.

in *Chinta* and in international publications and work with transnational activist groups such as the Inter-Church Action for Development, Relief, and Justice (ICA) and the Canadian International Development Agency. In short, theirs is an example of how international solidarity can be helpful if there is respect for localities and local conditions on the part of transnational activists in the North and the South. In many ways, the UBINIG experience points to the possibilities of a transnationality that takes local conditions seriously.

Women First?

I now return to the gendered raced and classed categories that are critical to the performance politics carried out on the NLC-Viera tour of the United States. Transnational campaigns such as this have been held up as models for global, woman- and-worker-centered activism, while they actually have reinforced the categories of nation, race, class, and gender, often reproducing the new international division of labor within the movements themselves. Women (of color, third world, working, immigrant, Latina, Asian, African) are included, but in terms of spectacle, image making, and marketing. The campaigns I study would not have succeeded without relying on the testimony, the body, and the performance of Viera, Molina, or Gifford.

Gender, race, nation, and class—and the garment workers themselves—do the work that holds the process of transnational protest together while fields of local agency are channeled into a politics of performance.

Transnational organizing, as it has been carried out in model campaigns that seem to place women first, actually continues to rely on gendered and racialized hierarchies. Some women consume while others produce; some participate and act, and others are portrayed as victims of forces out of their control. This image making is parallel to advertising images and to images from earlier anthropological and developmentalist discourse, cleaned up and made attractive and consumable. Even when women's participation seems open and obvious, analyses of gender—and how it works with race and nation—remain submerged. Certain women's bodies are used to market jeans, and others are used for protesting. Still others are used to produce the jeans and to produce the narrative of victim/model for the benefit of U.S.-based leftists.

In fact, the successes of transnational labor organizing over the past few years have not led to a breakdown and reformulation of the categories of nation, race, class, and gender. Their very success has relied on the maintenance and reproduction of these categories both in the campaigns and on the shop floor. My examination of transnational campaigns for labor rights and the coalitions that they engender raises further questions about the possibilities of global civil society and of creating transnational social movements able to negotiate gendered, raced, classed, and nation-based difference within and among participants in transnational efforts to widen citizenship.

It is the local that matters and on which the transnational depends. Without a consideration for local meanings, organizing efforts, and contestations, transnational organizing will continue to replicate the global-local split and reinforce the new international division of labor—both within the campaigns and on the factory floors of the garment industry.

6

Living Proof

Can living proof be the basis on which we claim transnational subjectivity? If a person provides living proof of her existence, can she then claim citizenship? In this chapter, I address the questions of subjectivity and agency that have run throughout the preceding chapters by focusing on the living proof provided by women's everyday experiences as garment workers. "Living proof," in this instance, is what I am calling the offering of life stories, subjectivities, bodily materialities, and practices by women as acts of courage and political claim staking. By theorizing the living proof offered by garment workers in production and protest, I analyze transnational organizing through a closer attention to subjectivity, citizenship, and capital (re)production, on the one hand, and the practice of testimony, on the other. I hope to shed light on circuits of subjectivity as they travel transnationally and the practice of agency by women within the production of modernity.

I begin with the stories of three Bangladeshi garment workers I met during my first fieldwork trip to Dhaka in 1996. They shared their experiences as women, as workers, and as union members, knowing that I was doing a research project on garment workers' lives and experiences in neighborhoods and shop floors throughout Dhaka. I write about them now in order to think through the conundrum of living proof and what happens to such proof once it is given. I am aware that I am also reproducing them as surplus value, that their stories are entering into my own practices of extraction and production of surplus value even as I attempt to disrupt those circuits.

I met two of the women while I was attending organizing and training meetings for garment workers and talking to women who came to the union offices of BIGUF (Bangladesh Independent Garment Union Federation) in the upper-class Dhaka neighborhood of Gulshan. BIGUF is a union supported by AAFLI, later called the Solidarity Center. I first came into contact with them through garment worker union leaders who toured the United States earlier in 1996. I met the third woman while I was carrying out participant-observation with the ILO inspection team during their tours of Dhaka garment factories and schools following the signing of the memorandum of understanding in 1995.

I want to lay bare the networks that I entered into as I carried out discussions, interviews, and participant-observations with garment workers in Dhaka in 1996 and 1998 in order to contextualize my later discussion of the networks through which testimony, subjectivity, and agency circulate and citizenship practice can be carried out. I also want to make clear my own position on, and complicity with, these networks regarding not only labor organizing but also capital and the creation of surplus value and state power, U.S. foreign policy, anticommunism, and the national-developmentalist state and neoliberalism. I have drawn on the privileges of whiteness, gender, and class that I garnered by dint of a series of postcolonial, transnational, heterosexual family ties while living in Dhaka as a white, U.S.-born woman who wears saris and speaks Bengali, who is also a Bangladeshi *bohu* (daughter-in-law) and *bhabi* (sister-in-law), and who, because of accent and skin color, sometimes passes for Pakistani.

While in Dhaka doing fieldwork I worked through these networks, circuits, and subject positions. These were the only possibilities through which I was able to talk with women working in garment factories, in union offices, and in the garment worker schools; to carry out interviews with factory managers, representatives from NGOs, government agencies, and UN organizations; and to enter factories and people's homes as both outsider and kin. I write of my experiences in a book that is published by a U.S.-based university press and can be purchased in U.S. dollars and will enhance my position as an assistant professor in a U.S. research university. Even as I provide a critique of capitalism, the state, and the disciplining of women's bodies through structures of race, class, heterosexuality, and gender relations, I cannot help but both depend on and reproduce these hierarchies in my work. Spivak, in a discussion about strategic essentialism, says, "The strategic use of an essence as a mobilizing slogan or masterword like *woman* or *worker* or the name of a nation is, ideally, self-conscious for all mobilized." In my critique of hierarchical structures of race, class, heterosexism, and gender, I mobilize these very hierarchies; they are, as Spivak goes on to say about strategic essentialism, "something that one cannot not use."[1] Garment workers, in their provision of living proof—even as this living proof disrupts the everyday production of surplus value, of what Marx calls "M'"—take up such "necessary errors" of strategic essentialism discussed by Spivak. This very preliminary admission of my subject position as it resonates with my fieldwork in Bangladesh should be taken as the grounding on which I base my discussion of Dhaka garment workers' testimonies and the ways in which they serve (or not) as living proof.

Stories, Reason(s), Proof

Paril Akhtar has worked in various factories in the garment industry for six years as a finisher. In one of our discussions, Akhtar said, "It is always the same; they don't give holidays and they never give money [to the garment workers]—they say they will give [you] six [taka], but you only get three."[2] Akhtar went on to say that the factories give no support for medical issues and none for housing, which is why she joined the BIGU. She has worked in factories where unions have tried to organize, but the attempts always ended in problems. Akhtar told me that even in a factory with 615 of 1,200 workers organized, the movement still collapsed. She asked, "Where is Bangladesh labor law? I like garment work, but garment work doesn't work."[3] Akhtar said a helper on the factory floor is legally supposed to be paid 900 taka a month but usually receives only 500 taka a month in practice.

I approached another woman, Rokeya, who had come to the health clinic that is part of the BIGU office in Dhanmondi. She told me "I can't eat" since she had come to Dhaka several months ago from her village in Rajshahi. "I can only eat one banana a day. When I do garment work, my stomach gets upset."[4] I asked her if it was because she didn't have enough money for food; Rokeya told me no, she had money for food and some to send back to her family, but she was not able to force food down. She missed her village and her family; everything in Dhaka was dirty and rushed. She was doing garment work because her family needed the income, but she wanted to go back to her village and be with her family. However, she said, "I will stay in Dhaka if my family needs me to stay."[5]

The third story is that of a twelve-year-old girl whom I met while visiting the nonformal schools set up for children garment workers after the signing of the MOU. Wahida had worked in a garment factory for two years before entering the garment workers' school. On the day of my visit to her school, Wahida and her schoolmates sang and danced to a song about their lives as garment workers and their bright futures now that they were able to go to school. The teacher told me that singing was central to the curriculum and that students had written their own songs and had learned songs about the 1971 Bangladeshi war of liberation and by Bengali nationalist poet Rabindranath Tagore as well as popular Hindi film songs. Because of the MOU, Wahida earned a stipend of 300 taka a month for being in school. Wahida told me that she hoped to be a teacher or a doctor so that she could help others when she grew up and that she would never go back to garment work.

These stories reflect some of the pains, injustices, bodily experiences, joys, and hopes experienced by the women and girls who talked to me in my position as a woman, a scholar, a sister(-in-law), niece, foreigner, and as someone who simply listened to what they had to say. In his book *Contentious Lives,* Javier Auyero talks about his experiences interviewing participants in an uprising in the Argentine city of Santiago del Estero. He points out that, in an ethnographic interview, people often want to talk and to be heard: "This desire to talk, to relive episodes of their lives, was also present in almost all of my interviewees. They wanted to talk to me about the uprisings; they wanted to share with me their experiences and thoughts." Drawing from Bourdieu and Sudhir Kakar, he argues that "the secret of a good ethnography is the respect accorded to others and the will to learn from others' lives."[6] I agree with Auyero, but I wonder about the circulation of my informants' testimonies, of their talks with me, as I share what I have learned from them in this book, in my public lectures, and in my scholarly articles. How do such confidences, and my interlocutors' confidence in me, travel through time and space? Can the confidence placed in me by the women be sustained as I share their stories with others? Where is confidence placed once life stories—living proof—circulate? Is confidence—*confianza,* in Spanish—translatable?

Living Proof and the Shop Floor

Proof, as such, can be seen in scars, in subject positions—and in women's testimonies to their experience. In protests against sweatshops, as in those against war, it is a political act to offer one's story and one's body as living proof. Drawing from Jelisaveta Blagojevic's work on love, in which she discusses the possibilities of offering love in philosophy as disrupting the maintenance of difference, I argue that women's testimony, women's witnessing, and women's telling of their histories are acts of love that disrupt the maintenance of difference.[7] Living proof is distinct from evidence or empiricism in that the latter are already framed by discourses and methodologies of political economy and the production of difference. Living proof is the product of and productive of affect; it is evidence of and contributes to emotions that are part of the offering of love. Even as living proof is given and received, it cannot be possessed or circulated. As Sara Ahmed states in *The Cultural Politics of Emotion,* "If emotions are not possessions, then the terrain of (in)justice cannot be a question of 'having' or 'not having' an emotion."[8]

Witnessing and the offering of living proof disrupt the production of knowledge and trouble the boundaries of self and other that are central to maintaining difference. Witnessing, both in its giving and receiving, entails a radical respect for difference that Lila Abu-Lughod has called for, even as difference is disrupted.[9] What happens when these acts of witnessing, testimony, and love become living proof? How does such proof travel through time and space? What becomes of the gendered bodies that provide the proof? What becomes of their subjectivity?

In order to think through such questions, it is useful to explore the uses of living proof in contestations over rights and claims to citizenship. Here, I will focus on the use of testimony as living proof for rights claims in the garment industry. Meg McLagan points to the relation between human rights testimonies and transnational publicity, arguing, "human rights testimonies can be understood as a form of political communication, as a means through which ethical arguments or claims are made and collectivities hailed and potentially persuaded or mobilized."[10] Drawing from the tactics of the human rights and Central American solidarity movements, transnational labor organizing has depended on personal testimonies to provide evidence for labor violations and worker abuse in factories worldwide. Such testimony has also been used in U.S. congressional hearings on export-oriented production facilities, labor violations, and the use of child labor in global garment production;[11] in tours of the United States by labor activists and workers in export-oriented industries; and in documentary films and videos that are used to raise the consciousness of consumers and activists in the United States and Europe.

In the National Labor Committee video *The Hidden Face of Globalization,* which focuses on labor abuses in Bangladesh's export-oriented garment industry, the testimonies of young women garment workers provide evidence for labor violations and worker abuse in Bangladeshi factories that subcontract production for Wal-Mart. The testimonies featured in the video, framed with commentary by U.S.-based labor activists Charles Kernaghan and Barbara Briggs, are used to show people in the United States that "We have the power to call upon our President and Congress to pass laws that will protect the rights of the worker and human being at least as much as the product is protected."[12] The women and men featured in the video include garment workers Mahamuda and Mapia; labor organizers Sheik Nazma of the Bangladesh Center for Worker Solidarity and Amirul Haque Amin, the National Garment Workers Federation (NGWF) general secretary; and NLC staffers Kernaghan and Briggs, all of whom tell their stories and give analyses of working conditions in the industry in savvy, political ways that tell of the participants' experiences in union and workplace organizing. The video frames the speakers, who are speaking Bangla with an English translator's voice-over, as garment workers and labor organizers but without giving the viewers a sense of their class backgrounds, their experiences as union members and organizers, or the position of garment factories in Dhaka's infrastructure and economy or to Bangladesh and U.S. nation-states.

The garment workers featured in the video, and in the 2004 tour of U.S. universities, schools and unions, share with U.S. audiences their pains and struggles while working in the garment industry, the forced overtime and abuse they are subject to on a daily basis, and their continuing efforts to keep up with hourly and daily production quotas so as not to lose the jobs on which they and their families depend. The two garment workers featured in the tour, whose testimonies are available on the NLC Web site, are Robina Akhter and Maksuda/Masuma (she is called Maksuda in most of the documentation of the tour, but in her testimony she gives her name as Masuma).[13] Their testimonies are detailed and quite painful; they include stories from the women's lives about their working conditions and hours, what and how they eat, sleep, brush their teeth, and live their lives. Their stories are verified by Sheik Nazma, a former child garment worker who now is the president of the Bangladesh Center for Worker Solidarity. On the NLC Web site there is a slide show of the worker tour that shows the participants at each of their tour stops, interacting with the audiences and smiling as their photos are taken. There is also a photo of Maksuda/Masuma crying on stage and another of Robina Akhter holding khaki pants in the air, showing the audience how her supervisor had beaten her with the very Wal-Mart pants she sewed.[14] Both the testimonies and the photos are testaments to the courage and generosity of these women who came to the United States to share their stories, their lives, and their struggles. They provide the U.S. audience with living proof of abusive working conditions that go into making the clothes we wear. This living proof is in the stories told and also in the raced, classed, gendered, abused, productive bodies that have traveled such distances to show proof of life and work in a politics of claiming subjectivity.

In Robina Akhter's testimony, she begins with her name and her

е age, then describes her experiences as a garment worker and
у life inside and outside the garment factory:

ix months I became a junior sewing operator. My job was to sew
th.. .ps on the back pockets of these pants. I had to sew 120 pieces an
hour. It was difficult to reach. If you made any mistakes or fell behind
on your goal, they beat you. They slapped you and lashed you hard on
the face with the pants. This happens very often. They hit you hard. It is
no joke.[15]

Akhter talks about working shifts of twenty hours or more when shipments
are due to go out and the extra burdens that are placed on the younger
garment workers. She says that the workers are not allowed to drink water,
go to the bathroom more than two or three times a day, talk, or stretch:
"You are not allowed to talk . . . if you even stand up or stretch, they cut
your overtime pay." Akhter describes the filthy bathroom conditions, the
frequent cuts in overtime pay, women being fired when they reach thirty
to thirty-five years of age, the lack of maternity pay or benefits, and the oppressive heat inside the factory: "The factory is very hot, and some days my
whole dress is wet with sweat."[16]

Akhter tells the audience that she owns nothing, only the three dresses
she wears, and that she lives in a room with eight people, among them a
couple, she says, "which makes me feel very shy," and she goes on to say,
"I clean my teeth with my finger, using ash. I can't afford a toothbrush or
toothpaste. Lots of other garment workers are like me." Akhter walks to
work, even in the rain, and eats mostly rice, vegetables, and lentils, and
drinks only water. She says:

I have never been to a cinema hall. I have never ridden a bike, and I
cannot afford a TV or radio. I have no relaxation in my life. No fun or
amusement. I never go out with my friends. We live only to work. Even
living like this, I still have to borrow 400 taka a month to survive. If I
could get one day off a week, I could rest with a deep slumber.

Akhter talks about being fired from her job after protesting because she
was absent one day, made up the missed day, and then was docked two
days' pay. When she asked why she was being docked, the supervisor told
her, "'Is this factory owned by your father?' Then he fired me, cursing very
filthy words at me." Finally, she ends her testimony by saying that she never
knew where the clothes she made were going and that she never thought
she would be in the United States. Akhter tells the audience that, when she
went into a Wal-Mart store in the United States, she found the clothes that

she and her coworkers had sewed. Akhter's final sentence is a plea for the audience: "Please help us win our rights."[17]

Maksuda's/Masuma's testimony complements that of Robina Akhter. She begins by saying, "My name is Masuma." Maksuda/Masuma goes on to say:

> I had to go to work in the garment factories when I was 11 years old. I started as a helper. The sound of the machines was so loud and the factory was so crowded with people that it made me feel dizzy and frightened and so sick that I vomited a lot at the beginning. It is very punishing to work so early, and I felt very hurt, but I had no choice, because my family is very poor. I never had a chance to go to school. . . . At the beginning, I earned 250 taka a month [$4.25].[18]

Maksuda/Masuma describes getting pregnant and feeling sick on the factory floor. Her supervisor told her that she could not rest and told her that if she did not want to work, she should leave the factory. She then goes on to say:

> I was sitting at the side of my machine. The supervisor was standing over me. Then he violently kicked me, hard, in the stomach and I fell to the floor. I fainted. My coworkers picked me up. I was crying. My coworkers went to the production manager and told him what had happened, and he let me go home that afternoon but I had to come back the next morning.

Maksuda/Masuma's testimony tells of her two-year-old daughter's head being scarred even now, and says that she does not get to spend time with her daughter. Maksuda/Masuma lives with her mother and daughter, owns almost nothing, and is still paying off the debt from her hospital stay while giving birth: "I had to go back to work. I am again working from 8:00 a.m. to 10:00 p.m., seven days a week. Now I am earning 2,100 taka a month [$35.14/month; 17 cents an hour]." As with Robina Akhter, Maksuda/Masuma shares intimate details of her life, her working conditions, her family—her pain and her hopes—as part of her testimony. Maksuda/Masuma speaks directly to the people of the United States:

> Now I know that it is you, American people, who buy the clothing we sew in Bangladesh. And I want to ask your help. We don't want a boycott. We need these jobs. But we want the companies to stop beating us and torturing and abusing us. We want one day a week off. I need time to be with my daughter. The companies should pay us our overtime

correctly and not cheat us as they always do. We are willing to work very hard and with good quality. We will work twelve hours a day, from 8:00 a.m. to 8:00 at night, six days a week. But it is wrong to force us to work until 10:00 at night every night, and the all night shifts to 3:00 a.m. are too cruel. Also, the companies should give us our maternity leave with pay as the law says.

Maksuda/Masuma speaks of her hopes for the future if working conditions improve and if her pay were raised to 4,500 taka a month. She says that she could buy milk and food for her baby, pay off her debts, buy a new dress, save some money for when she is older, and buy fish and fruit. She ends her testimony by asking the U.S. audience, "Please don't forget the garment workers in Bangladesh."

Sheik Nazma's testimony serves as both verification and context to the life stories told by Robina Akhter and Maksuda/Masuma: "I know that what these two young workers told you just now is the truth. I too was a child worker. I started in the garment factories when I was 11 years old."[19] Sheik Nazma says, "But do not misunderstand. We are not just sitting around waiting for the companies to give us justice. We are fighting back. But we need your help and solidarity." She describes the unionization efforts of garment workers in Dhaka and their 2003 strike at the Pantex factory outside of Dhaka, which was met by beatings and the police firing at the strikers, resulting in six or seven deaths and many injuries. She says in her testimony, "In the end, some small improvements were won. But it cost the blood of those brave workers."

Sheik Nazma's testimony maintains that Bangladesh has good labor laws in place but that the factory owners do not comply with the laws that are on the books. According to Bangladeshi labor law, workers have the right to maternity leave for three months at full pay. Sheik Nazma says, however, that "95 percent of the factories violate this right," and they are supported by the Bangladeshi state and transnational garment manufacturers. She points to a success story of transnational organizing, where the Bangladesh Workers Solidarity Center and the National Garment Workers Federation began a campaign in Bangladesh:

> Working together, we wrote to all 3,700 garment factories demanding that they respect the maternity leave laws. We organized demonstrations. We marched. We distributed popular education brochures to the workers. We put posters up all over the factory areas. We talked to the media, and we held a conference which even government officials felt they had to attend.

She describes the coordination of the Bangladesh campaign with one carried out by the National Labor Committee in the United States, the result of which was that

> today 19 of the largest apparel companies in the world have signed a pledge that anyone sewing their garments in Bangladesh will be guaranteed her legal maternity leave with full pay. In fact, at our conference, the government Labor Minister even pledged to extend the paid maternity leave to four months. But we will believe the government and the companies only after we see some action.

Sheik Nazma also gives credit to the NLC and to other international organizations who provided help for garment workers after the 2004 floods in Bangladesh, saying, "In Dhaka, tens of thousands of garment workers' homes were under two to three feet of water. Maksuda's house was like that." She thanks the U.S. solidarity community, saying that, with the help of the NLC, Anita Roddick donated $22,000 and other money came in that allowed her organization and others to provide help to the flooded garment workers and their families. She concludes her testimony by saying that international solidarity is needed more than ever; with the January 2005 end of textile and apparel quotas, Bangladesh might lose garment production jobs. Of course, international (and transnational) solidarity is a double-edged sword that sometimes can work to displace or detract from workers' agency in a number of ways. She says,

> In this global economy, international solidarity is more critical than ever. It seems that all of us must struggle together to defend women's and workers rights, fair wages, and the right to organize. This is our only hope. It might seem like nothing to you, but if our garment workers could earn 4,500 taka as a base wage—which is about 37 cents an hour in American dollars—it would make a huge, positive difference in our lives. Also, the workers need one day off a week. These are some of our struggles.

Sheik Nazma was both a child worker in the Bangladeshi garment industry and an early union organizer; she is politically very astute and willing to put herself on the line as part of her organizing work.

All three of the testimonies provided in the NLC tour of the United States, along with the images and testimonies that are featured in *The Hidden Face of Globalization,* have served as contingent interventions—moments of disruption—in the everyday workings of capital. Such testimonies lay bare the day-to-day nature of capitalist production and reproduction and show how discipline and governmentality are often punctuated by violence that belies the structural coherence of hegemonic formations. In *Hegemony and Socialist Strategy,* Laclau and Mouffe argue that "'Hegemony' will be not the majestic unfolding to an identity but the response to a crisis." Specifically, Laclau and Mouffe draw from Rosa Luxemburg and Second International Marxism, as well as from Foucault and Althusser, to theorize hegemony as alluding "to an absent totality, and to the diverse attempts at recomposition and rearticulation which, in overcoming this original absence, made it possible for struggles to be given a meaning and for historical forces to be endowed with full positivity." Laclau and Mouffe point out that "the contexts in which the concept appear will be those of a fault (in the genealogical sense), of a fissure that had to be filled up, of a contingency that had to be overcome."[20]

Such contingent interventions serve as simultaneous fissures and potential excess that hold the possibility of being strategically utilized to overcome such fissures. In *The Power to Choose,* Naila Kabeer points out that the labor market participation of Bangladeshi garment workers cannot be understood in relation to economistic or rational choice theories—they are neither "rational fools" nor "cultural dopes" (16). In Kabeer's discussion of Bangladeshi women garment workers' subjectivities in London and Dhaka, she writes:

> I have sought to analyse their testimonies in relation to the broader context in which they live their lives, some aspects of which may be discernible in these testimonies, but other aspects of which form the unacknowledged conditions in which they make their choices. By grounding the analysis of women's voices in the empirical context of their lives, I have tried to explore their own understanding of the limits embodied by this larger context, and their willingness as well as their ability to transform it.[21]

Insofar as Bangladeshi women are participating in the labor market, they are doing so neither solely because of comparative advantage nor solely because of cultural constraints; they are neither completely "liberated" from tradition (often read as *purdah,* religiously sanctioned seclusion of women) nor are they completely tradition-bound through their labor market participation. Neither their testimony nor the "broader context in which they live their lives" serves the ends of economic or cultural fundamentalism; neither, moreover, is readable within transnational circuits of garment production and protest. In fact, the "broader context" is incommensurable with and irreducible to discourse and circulation as part of transnational organizing and knowledge production. In this book, I am attempting a type of empiricism that reads such broader contexts while at the same time recognizing their unreadability. While I refuse to cede epistemology to the wholly theoretical—and I feel that it would be a disservice to the women who have given me their confidences, who have had confidence in me, to do so—I maintain that evidence, or living proof, is never reducible to the provision of facts or the utilization of case studies in the name of scientific method.

Living Proof, Subjectivity, Citizenship, M-C-M'

The provision of living proof in the form of testimony opens up the possibilities for exposing the fault lines of globalization and showing the contingency of hegemony. Such contingency is laid bare when we place Sheik Nazma's testimony about the violence that meets unionization efforts next to the garment trade advertisement for Bangladeshi export processing zones that tells businesspeople, "For Optimum Profit Invest in EPZs of Bangladesh," with incentives such as "Law forbids formation of labour unions in the zones and strikes are illegal."[22] The side-by-side reading of labor repression and state/paramilitary violence with advertisements for export processing zones where labor unions and strikes are illegal shows the impossibility of seamless "optimum profit" in exploitative productive practices. We can see the contingent nature of hegemony—the uneven balance between "force and consent," to use Gramsci's terms[23]—in the fault lines of legality within garment factories and export processing zones, sites that are part of the nation-state while at the same time serving as juridico-legal outsides. It is these fault lines to which our attention is drawn by women's testimonies and the living proof that they share with us; it is precisely these fault lines to which we must pay attention.

Once we pay attention to such fault lines—and to the living proof provided in testimony by witnesses—how do we account for hegemonic contingencies that, even as they disrupt the practice of difference, create surplus value once they circulate globally? That is to say, once witnesses give testimony that circulates as living proof—of violence, of exploitation, of the longing for recognition on the part of those stepping forward to witness— what happens to subjectivity, citizenship claims, and the reproduction of (global) capital (the creation of M', from Marx's formulas for the reproduction of capital of C-M-C/M-C-M')?[24] Marx theorizes capital production as C-M-C, where C is commodity, which transforms into the money form upon being taken to market and sold; the money is then used to buy another commodity, completing the first circuit. Marx goes on to say that, once we understand that the circuit of capital produces surplus value through labor, the formula shifts to M-C-M', where money is brought to market to buy a commodity that is then transformed through abstract labor power, in which surplus value is extracted, in order to be sold at a profit of M'. Marx argues that, without the production of M' through extracted labor power, capitalism cannot reproduce itself because all of its profit will be consumed by the process of buying commodities.

It is important to point out the impossibility of the subject position of one who provides living proof. It is an impossible subject position whose very circulation depends on its possibility—on the possibility of becoming citizenship, on the one hand, and continuing the circuit of M-C-M', on the other. How is living proof, such as that provided by Rokeya when she tells me "I can't eat" or the testimonies given by Maksuda/Masuma on the NLC tour, where her own statement of her name is not translated, mobilized on behalf of citizenship status? How can the experiences, hopes, and challenges of the children who participate in the schools for former child garment workers or the testimony of Robina Akhter, particularly her statement that "I have never been to a cinema hall. I have never ridden a bike, and I cannot afford a TV or radio," be mobilized as foundations for claims to citizenship? Finally, what does Paril Akhtar's story of the impossibility of garment work, or Sheik Nazma's tales of the state and parastatal violence that meet attempts to unionize, tell us about the stability of M-C-M', the circuit of capital? The problem is one of incommensurability—between that which is included and that which is left out—and the impossibility of understanding classed sites in Bangladesh once they travel along transnational circuits. This relationship is one of double incommensurability because of the impossibility of neatly moving from use- to exchange-value, on the one hand, and the impossibility of translation of Kabeer's "broader context in which they live their lives," on the other.

The incommensurability of use value and exchange value, and of living proof in serving as either, can be thought about through what Dipesh Chakrabarty calls "two histories of capital." In *Provincializing Europe,* Chakrabarty addresses the question of historical difference and the logic of capital through two concepts "inseparable from Marx's critique of capital: that of 'abstract labor' and the relation between capital and history."[25] First, drawing from his earlier work *Rethinking Working-Class History*, Chakrabarty argues: "Labor that is juridically and politically free—yet socially unfree—is a concept embedded in Marx's category of 'abstract labor.' The idea of 'abstract labor' thus combines the Enlightenment themes of juridical freedom (rights, citizenship) and the concept of the universal and abstract human who bears this freedom."[26] Chakrabarty points out that the concept of abstract labor that "is central to Marx's explanation of why capital, in fulfilling itself in history, necessarily creates the grounds for its own dissolution."[27] The provision of living proof—in the forms of testimony and the bodily presence of Third World women as witnesses—lays bare the impossibilities of abstract labor. While Chakrabarty does not—or cannot—theorize gender in his discussion of the two histories of capital, my theorization of living proof shows the limits of capital's, and protest's, abilities to extract surplus value from the bodies of women. Living proof, in fact, can never be completely mobilized as abstract labor or exchange value.

For Marx, abstract labor makes possible the production of surplus value in the circulation of capital. Marx argues, "We see therefore that the addition of new value takes place not by virtue of [a worker's] labour being spinning in particular . . . but because it is labour in general, abstract social labour."[28] I want to discuss the practice of testimony in its becoming abstract social labor—as adding value to the production of antisweatshop activism in the United States and Europe—and what that means for those who provide such abstract labor. This becoming of abstract social labor complicates the idea of living proof and testimony as "acts of love." Marx continues:

> On the one hand, it is by virtue of its general character as expenditure of labour-power in the abstract that spinning adds new value to the values of cotton and the spindle; and on the other hand, it is by virtue of its special character as a concrete, useful process that the same labour of spinning both transfers the values of the means of production to the product and preserves them in the product. Hence a twofold result emerges within the same period of time.[29]

This "twofold result" is also evident in the practice of testimony. The general character of testimony as the "expenditure of labour-power in the abstract" on the behalf of antisweatshop organizing adds new value to the organizing; "its special character as a concrete, useful process" carried out by concrete gendered, raced, postcolonial bodies both "transfers the values of the means of production to the product and preserves . . . the product." The antisweatshop movement needs to produce added value, M', in order to reproduce itself as a movement despite not achieving its stated ends of eliminating worker abuse or becoming a means for worker subjectivity.[30] It is important to theorize garment protest and production as connected through their fundamental—and intimate—dependence on laboring women's bodies. Once sweatshops are eradicated, once the production of M' stops in garment production, the antisweatshop movement itself ceases to be, even as the symbolic, affective value of testimony remains.

Here we can return to Chakrabarty and the question of subjectivity and to abstract labor that is at once "juridically and politically free—yet socially unfree."[31] The provision of living proof—the act of witnessing, the practice of testimony—necessitates this particular combination: those who provide living proof are juridically and politically free; they are subjects able to take part in free speech, yet they are socially unfree, and as such their testimony and their positions as witnesses are valued as living proof of that lack of freedom. Chakrabarty argues for two different histories of capital, History 1 and History 2, in order to develop "a distinction that Marx made between two kinds of histories: histories 'posited by capital' and histories that do not belong to capital's 'life process.'"[32] I would argue that whereas living proof, the act of giving it and the bodies that provide it, belong to History 2, the transnational circulation of testimony—in the form of worker tours and videos aimed at activists and consumers in the United States and Europe—is part of the History 1 of capital and protest. Chakrabarty argues:

> History 2 does not spell out a program of writing histories that are alternatives to the narratives of capital. That is, History 2s do not constitute a dialectical Other of the necessary logic of History 1. To think thus would be to subsume History 2 to History 1. History 2 is better thought of as a category charged with the function of constantly interrupting the totalizing thrusts of History 1.[33]

The attempt to take living proof History 2 and incorporate it into History 1 involves considerable amounts of what Spivak calls epistemic violence. The movement from History 2 to History 1 is one that renders History 2 abstract, exchangeable. As testimony moves transnationally and hegemonically, as in the case of the antisweatshop movement, women's subjectivity is mediated by histories of nation, race, class, sexuality, empire, and gender in ways that make the practice of witnessing and acts of love political impossibilities.

Giorgio Agamben, in *Remnants of Auschwitz,* puts forth what he calls "a kind of perpetual commentary on testimony" in his discussion of position of witnesses, archives, and testimonies of concentration camps. Agamben argues, "At a certain point, it became clear that testimony contained at its core an essential lacuna; in other words, the survivors bore witness to something it is impossible to bear witness to. As a consequence, commenting on survivors' testimony necessarily meant interrogating this lacuna, or, more precisely, attempting to listen to it." Agamben goes on to say that "listening to something absent did not prove fruitless work" and that "For my part, I will consider myself content with my work if, in attempting to locate the place and theme of testimony, I have erected some signposts allowing future cartographers of the new ethical territory to orient themselves."[34] In reading the testimonies provided by garment workers from Bangladesh, El Salvador and New York City in both public and private alongside Agamben's writing on Nazi death camps, I attempt to listen to that which is absent from these accounts. Even as I do so, I know that such an ethical orientation based on knowing these absences is not possible, precisely because they are absences that cannot be filled by representation.

The absent, however, are those who are "drowned"—here Agamben quotes Primo Levi—those whose "death had begun before that of their body." As Agamben points out of those who cannot bear witness:

> the drowned have nothing to say, nor do they have instructions or memories to be transmitted. The witness usually testifies in the name of justice and truth and as such his or her speech draws consistency and fullness. Yet here the value of the testimony lies essentially in what it lacks; at its center it contains something that cannot be borne witness to and that discharges the survivors of authority. The "true" witnesses, the "complete witnesses," are those who did not bear witness and could not bear witness. They are those who touched bottom. . . . The survivors speak in their stead, by proxy, as pseudo-witnesses; they bear witness to a missing testimony.[35]

Just as recipients of living proof must attempt to pay attention to that which is absent, those who provide living proof speak for those who cannot. What subject position is occupied by those who bear witness—those whose lives become living proof?

Living Proof, Justice, and Circuits of Capital

This is an impossible subject position, whose very circulation depends on its possibility—on the possibility of becoming subjectivity, and even citizenship, on the one hand, and continuing the circuit of M-C-M', on the other. What happens when women's bodies and experiences are taken as living proof of history or contention? Can living proof serve as the basis for justice? Here I want to return to my discussion of Mandarin International and the Gap Campaign of 1995 that focused on El Salvador. If Dhaka exemplifies the garment industry as a national developmental model, El Salvador has served as a model for postwar reconstruction and the reinsertion of hegemony in production and protest. Can they also serve as models for justice in global production practices? Here I am referring to Agamben's point, "Almost none of the ethical principles our age believed it could recognize as valid have stood the decisive test, that of an *Ethica more Auschwitz demonstrata*" (13). Can we map antisweatshop protests onto what Agamben points to as this "new ethical territory?"

The national-developmentalist state and the antisweatshop movement alike, in their attempts to put forth such models, foreclose the possibilities for mapping Agamben's new ethical territory. Before the 1995 unionization attempt, lockout, and mass firings at Mandarin International—now called Charter—the National Labor Committee had produced a video, *Zoned for Slavery,* documenting the labor abuses at the Orion factory, located in an EPZ in Honduras. It is offered to the U.S. public so that we can

> Meet the children who work in the sweatshops of Central America. See the armed guards at the factory's gate. Go inside and watch the young workers being searched to prevent them from bringing food to work. Talk to them about the deplorable conditions: low wages, forced birth control, work quotas, long hours and compulsory overtime, denial of education.[36]

Accompanying this description is a photo of Lesly Rodríguez, a fifteen-year-old worker at Orion, at a sewing machine surrounded by piles of clothes to be sewn, side by side with other garment workers with their sewing machines and piles of clothes. The narrative of the video moves between Rodríguez, who begins her day at dawn and works in the maquila to support her mother and younger brother, and the larger political economy of the garment industry. In one segment, the video's narrator tells us that "since the Caribbean Basin Initiative, there has been a 2,400 percent increase in Honduran exports to the United States" and then moves on to describe how "the workers are searched on their way into work to make sure they are not carrying candy, which could stain the fabric."

Zoned for Slavery, while accurately depicting sweatshop conditions in a Central American maquiladora, is a foreshadowing of the Mandarin campaign and the tour of the United States a year later by Viera and Díaz. In fact, the 1994 video laid the foundations for the 1995 tour, setting the Central American sweatshop apart and having it, as with Mitchell's discussion of the colonization of Egypt, enframed. In this case, it is the sweatshop that "was to be ordered up as something object-like. In other words, it was to be made picture-like and legible, rendered available to political and economic calculation . . . to become readable, like a book, in our own such use of the term" (Mitchell, *Colonising Egypt,* 50). In the video, Rodríguez is shown at home, on the bus to work, at her sewing machine, and in her neighborhood with other garment workers, denouncing their abuse by factory management. Orion workers tell interviewer Barbara Briggs that they must make 1,100 shirts a day or 5 embroidered sweaters. They are shouted at and hit and are required to take sweaters home to embroider, otherwise their paychecks will be cut. One worker shown in the video says, "They punish you if they see you talking."

Rodríguez is shown as a child working in a Central American sweatshop, sewing garments for international retailers. The NLC Web site, which features *Zoned for Slavery* along with other videos and publications for sale, advertises, "NLC's video reporters went with their cameras so that we could witness what should not be overlooked." The design on the video cover is of a school notebook, and the video describes kids being picked up to go to work: "Each morning, old American school buses make rounds, picking up kids, as many as can fit on board. The children are taken to work. In 1993, they sewed 77 million garments for sale in the United States."

There is no doubt that the conditions described at Orion are similar to most garment factories. In fact, most of them are still present at Mandarin—with the exception, since the Gap campaign, of forced birth control and compulsory overtime—and at other factories that I visited in El Salvador, Bangladesh, and New York. Forced birth control is especially pernicious in its regulation of women's sexuality as a condition for being granted jobs, as a 1997 report from Human Rights Watch described the situation in Mexican maquiladoras:

> Potential female employees are compelled to take urine tests and answer invasive questions on applications and interviews about their pregnancy status, sexual activity, use of birth control, and menstrual cycles. Those who are pregnant are not hired. Those who have become pregnant are forced to resign, or are subjected to abusive and discriminatory treatment.[37]

Zoned for Slavery, by bringing such violations to the notice of consumers, serves as a counterpoint to the avalanche of advertising images that show young, well-dressed, upper-class (white) people wearing the clothes that are made in garment factories throughout the third world and in the poorest neighborhoods of U.S. cities. Just as an important achievement of the Gap campaign was the end of forced pregnancy tests at Mandarin, the video did indeed help us to "witness what should not be overlooked."

Zoned for Slavery, as both artifact and commodity, also works on several other levels. The video and its accompanying advertising copy and photos serve to normalize the idea of oppressed, gendered, Central American workers in need of salvation by empowered, dollared, North American consumers. The video invites consumers—through the act of buying—to experience factory life and what it means to be a worker. The consumption of the video and the images of exploited workers parallel the act of buying clothes from the Gap and the images of the models wearing the clothes in the advertisements. Relations of consumption and production remain firmly in place, even within the effort to destabilize them. The production process, the staging, and everything that it took to create the video's representations of factory work are left out of the final cut. But how otherwise could workers or activists raise awareness of conditions on shop floors throughout the world?

The final cut of *Zoned for Slavery* provided a script for the Mandarin campaign that followed a year later and for subsequent transnational labor organizing efforts. In this way, the video was useful in demarcating labor violations and educating consumers even as it normalized the very conditions it documented. With that script, and the use of repertoires picked up from 1980s solidarity tactics, the intended audience—U.S.-based consumers— knew what to expect of the conditions at Mandarin. Mitchell points out in his conception of the "world-as-exhibition": "Everything seemed to be set up before one as though it were a model or the picture of something. Everything was arranged before an observing subject into a system of signification (to use the European jargon), declaring itself to be the signifier of the signified."[38]

The script of Viera and Molina's tour was written by the video, by Gap's advertising campaigns, by modernization theory, and by the history of U.S. nation-state building with its particular histories of race, class, and labor organizing. This process of scripting helped us to grasp the happenings at Mandarin as a particular reality, to be conceived and, in this instance, set aside as a problem solved by our having witnessed it.

Transnational campaigns are organized within the context of a complete lack of alternatives. Workers who attempt to organize or defend themselves against violations run up against a capital formation that, while it provides much-needed jobs, is mobile to the point that factories are able to close down in a matter of days in the face of protest. I witnessed the ability of individual factories to cut and run in El Salvador in November 1997 when DINDEX attempted to shut down the day after many of its workers fainted.

I return to the questions with which I began: Can living proof be the basis on which we claim transnational subjectivity? If we provide living proof of our existence, can we then claim citizenship? If one examines the narrative of the campaigns and their resolution, women (and men) present on the factory floors of garment factories throughout the world are shown to us through a set of testimonies that demonstrate what it means to be a garment worker. They are found in the bodies and words of Judith Viera, Lesly Rodríguez, and Ana Maria Romero, in the video images that are left behind, and in the language of agreements and the results of negotiations. They are also represented in each subsequent tour of the United States that replicates and builds on the tours that came before.

Consumers are still invited—in an ironic twist of virtual reality—to purchase the videos that help them to experience the factory floor from the safety of their living rooms, long after the campaigns have ended and everyone has gone back to business as usual. Once the initial outrage has been assuaged by the successful outcome, we can return to the retail outlets that we know and love and consume at even greater levels than before, complacent that we are serving the purpose of social justice by patronizing shops with corporate codes of conduct. The garment factories will keep producing, and the women inside will keep working ten- to twelve-hour days to satisfy the laws of supply and demand while retailers continue to reap profits.

The repertoires of contention employed by the Gap campaign and by the tactics of transnational protest help define what can be said, how it may be said, and who does the talking. This is what Michel Foucault, in *Archaeology of Knowledge,* called a "discursive formation," which is a set of basic conventions that delimit the discursive field of a particular discipline or field of study within which speaking subjects can come to speak.[39] Here I am positing a discursive formation of transnational protest that also defines to whom people talk and upon whom claims are made. On the NLC Web site, contention is carried out, over and over again, against the same companies: Disney, Gap, Kathie Lee, Liz Claiborne, Nike, Ralph Lauren, and Wal-Mart. These companies are the targets of campaigns and are asked to improve the working conditions of their subcontractors—but how are they pushed to enforce such rights? Only by the threat to their brand names and their corporate reputations, and in neither place is there room for the agency, participation, or input of the workers in the factories from which they subcontract production.

By eliminating the worst abuses of women's bodies and work sites, the conditions under which manufacturing regimes operate are normalized and regulated. To borrow from Chakrabarty's use of Marx, the corporate campaigns are also about producing an acceptable discipline that is not tainted by the sweatshop appellation. They produce "uniformity, regularity, order and economy, [within] each individual workshop"[40] and within the industry as a (globalized) whole. It is also about the purification of the brand, the name, and the trademark—about intellectual property as much as about production. In a recent full-page advertisement in *La Prensa Gráfica,* one of

El Salvador's largest national daily newspapers, the government campaign "Nuestro Nuevo El Salvador" stated, in an obvious reference to the international campaigns and the destruction of unionization efforts:

> In 1994, El Salvador did not have a favorable image for national and foreign investment. We have reoriented our international policies in order to have our economic progress recognized and attract investment to the country. El Salvador is now recognized worldwide as an attractive site for investment. Salvadoran and foreign businessmen have invested US$1.795 billion annually between 1994 and 1998. This is double the investment of the previous five years. All of this confidence has translated into 335 thousand new jobs. In 1998, with more and better employment, we are creating a new country: Modern, Democratic, Participatory.[41]

Half of the full-page ad shows a smiling garment worker in front of a machine, sewing garments in the blue color of the national flag. The ad copy is on the blue of the flag and a white background, with the national seal in one corner (Figure 14). As the advertisement exemplifies, the El Salvador brand once more can be marketed to produce investment. Gap Inc. is now sanctified to gather as much profit as possible from its subcontractors in El Salvador and throughout the world. Finally, the National Labor Committee can bank on the legitimacy created by its "success" in El Salvador to carry out other campaigns and gather more funds in the name of women's labor and working conditions throughout the (other) world.

Consumer antisweatshop movements, by focusing protest on the position of workers in these new economic formations, have documented the different strands of production and labor control that run through garment manufacturing. These movements have also worked to improve working conditions and better the lot of garment workers in factories subcontracting throughout the world. However, because of their concern with the politics of images and technology and with influencing corporate policy decisions, they often reproduce the notion that power is created in the uppermost strata of society to be then administered to people living and working as subjects of that power.

The NLC descended—rhetorically and practically—from the 1980s U.S. solidarity movement with Central America. The repertoires of contention employed by the NLC applied the language and tactics of that movement to labor organizing and combined them with the corporate-focused politics of the Clinton years that mimicked the political economy of capital circulation. In this regard, the NLC took on the legacy of solid, dedicated work for social justice of the 1980s solidarity movement in order to make the U.S. government and U.S.-based corporations accountable to the U.S.

Figure 14. Advertisement for the "Nuestro Nuevo El Salvador" (Our New El Salvador) campaign, printed in the national press, features a smiling garment worker sewing clothing the color of the Salvadoran flag. This ad ran to show the Salvadoran public that, despite the claims by antisweatshop activists, the garment industry was thriving in El Salvador with happy, patriotic employees working in great conditions.

consuming public for conditions of production among its subcontractors. At the same time, when battles about people in other parts of the world are waged among U.S.-based participants, they have had the potential to reinforce the notion that agency is based in the United States and that contention occurs only at the heights of political economy. They also potentially reinforce the conception that local conditions are created by global forces rather than through struggles and negotiations in all sites.

My work reinforces Miriam Wells's example of the United Farm Workers' strikes in the lettuce and broccoli fields of California. Wells shows that the attention given to the lettuce boycott and the UFW's organizing had different effects, depending on local conditions at particular strawberry picking sites. Although none of the strawberry pickers were organized, at one site, workers discussed the lettuce organizing and held work stoppages demanding higher pay—which they received. At another site, the workers discussed the situation with the owners, depending on a history of patron-client relations, and eventually got an increase in pay. In a third site, strawberry workers "did not mention the lettuce victory to their Mexican employer." Instead, while they were excited about the potential for "a new era in farm labor," they "continued to labor without complaint until the end of the season." Their wages remained unchanged at the previous year's rate. Wells argues about the need to understand different forms of action—or inaction—through attention to particular locations, histories, and contexts of labor struggle.[42]

While transnational protest calls attention to labor violations and abuse of women, men, and children who make the clothing we all wear, it also replicates a traditional emphasis on the dominant role of U.S. politics and the hegemony of capital accumulation. Because women's (and men's and children's) testimonies move along the same circuits as capital accumulation, from the South to the North, alongside and within garment production commodity chains, we are left with the idea that corporate decision and profit making, and appropriate tactics for labor activists, are products of boardrooms, stock exchanges, and stores rather than of homes, neighborhoods, and production sites. This produces the effect of global-local separation, with the global being read as United States and Europe and the local as everywhere else, by relating protest tactics to media images and granting agency to marketing experts while utilizing conditions on the shop floor and the concerns of garment workers as the material through which images and marketing happen.

The Gap campaign became a battle over the brand name of Gap Inc., of export processing zones, and of El Salvador as a site of garment production.[43] The 1995 campaign was designed to target the profits of Gap Inc. and Mandarin International as well as the advertising image that Gap Inc. represents: of clean, wholesome, upper-class—and, accordingly, innocent—youth. According to one activist, such campaigns, especially if they are directed at the maquila industry, touch almost every sector within El Salvador. Not only do consumer campaigns have an effect on Salvadoran industrialists, landowners, banks, and government officials, but they also affect the corporations themselves and the political economy of the United States and other countries that own factories, such as Taiwan and South Korea. The battle, therefore, is greater than it appears at first glance.[44]

The battle over the branding of garments and their production is more far-reaching, since it touches El Salvador's reliability as a safe bet for investment as well as the success of its peace agreement to ensure stability and productivity in place of civil war, intransigent landowners, and guerrilla movements. The resolution was to rebrand Gap Inc. not only as the purveyor of youthful innocence but also as an organization that was socially conscious and responsible to its workforce, and to rebrand El Salvador as once again a safe, peaceful place for foreign investment. Mandarin and the women who work there were thus rebranded as productive, efficient, and conflict-free, and, as an added bonus, freed of the taint of the sweatshop. In this way, the living proof offered by garment workers—their lives, bodies, and testimonies—once again becomes an impossibility in the everyday practice of capital accumulation and garment production.

Circuits: Stories, Clothing, Capital

The gift of living proof is evidenced in the stories, testimonies, bodies, hardships, hopes, and joys in the lives of garment workers. We can see evidence of living proof in their testimonies before the U.S. Congress and those videotaped for viewing by U.S.- and European-based labor activists. Living proof was also offered to me, a U.S.-based researcher who is now writing about these very women in a book that will circulate in English, published by a U.S. university press, to a mostly academic, mostly English-speaking international readership. I have attempted to address the viabilities, complications, and contradictions in the giving and receiving of living proof and the impossibilities of its movement within the circuits of capital. My work has explored the limits and possibilities of living proof—in its provision, sharing, and circulations. In "Can the Subaltern Speak?," Gayatri Spivak maintains, "This benevolent first-world appropriation and reinscription of the Third World as an Other is the founding characteristic of much third-worldism in the US human sciences today."[45] This appropriation and reinscription takes up living proof, both scripted and unscripted, and begins its circulation as value added in protest, production, and scholarship.

The circuit of capital, M-C-M', is reproduced through the circulation of subaltern narratives and the dual staging and effacement of gendered agency that is central to that circulation. Living proof, however, disrupts such circuits; its provision opens up these circuits and shows their impossibilities and their alterities. It helps us find, as Engin Isin does in *Being Political,* ways to "write histories of citizenship"—along with those of subjectivity and capital—"from the point of view of its alterities in the sense of recovering those solidaristic, agonistic, and alienating moments of reversal and transvaluation, where strangers and outsiders constituted themselves as citizens or insiders and in so doing altered the ways of being political."[46]

Spivak argues, "the staging of the world in representation—its scene of writing, its *Darstellung*—dissimulates the choice of and need for 'heroes,' paternal proxies, agents of power—*Vertretung*." Spivak goes on to argue:

> My view is that radical practice should attend to this double session of representations, rather than reintroduce the individual subject through

the totalizing concepts of power and desire. It is also my view that, in keeping the area of class practice on a second level of abstraction, Marx was in effect keeping open the (Kantian and) Hegelian critique of the individual subject as agent.[47]

This double session circulates as individual subject positions, citizenship claims that are based on the integrity of liberal personhood and the production and reproduction of capital as transnational garment production and protest.

How do we attend to the living proof provided by garment workers in multiple settings, fora, and contexts? Through an explicit engagement with the practice and provision of living proof and testimony in their many forms, an engagement that addresses the presences, absences, stagings, and contexts that are part of living proof. We have to pay attention to those whom we ask to provide proof and to those whom it is impossible to ask. It is essential to keep in mind that living proof is not something that we—or others—own; yet it is something that we engage in, that we give and receive in acts of love. As such, living proof becomes an impossibility that cannot be subsumed—or sublated—into subjectivity, citizenship, or the production of M'.

Epilogue: Gender and the Work of Branding

This study began as an attempt to examine and document the relationship between cross-border protest campaigns for labor rights and the various garment factory floors that have been the focus of transnational organizing. I began with a number of assumptions about the effects of the campaigns in individual garment factories, on labor relations in the industry, and in the lives of the women who were working in the factories. I believed at the outset that the campaigns could give birth to a new politics that would be able to contest globalization by highlighting the everyday lives and struggles of women garment workers. In that initial estimation, transnational labor organizing campaigns would reconfigure—in an explicitly feminist, antiracist, pro-worker way—the discursive and material splits between the first and third worlds.

These were immense political and theoretical expectations, and they went through a number of shifts during the course of my fieldwork and writing. My political position would often vary between a firm belief in the possibilities for transnational protest as one of the few viable alternatives left for labor organizing under the current regime of globalized production practices, and skepticism as to any chance for transnational networks' ability to contest hierarchies within their own organizing paradigms, much less in global production relations. My own ambivalence reflected the hope and disappointment expressed by garment workers with whom I talked, shared stories, observed, and became friends with over the course of my research.

In this volume I have shown that transnational coalitions potentially would contest the very conditions and categories outlined above. Because they are mobilized as global contestations, transnational labor organizing campaigns have reproduced—discursively and materially—a split between the global and the local. The very attempt to protest at the transnational level has manifested itself in media- and consumer-focused protest campaigns carried out against transnational retailers in sites of distribution and marketing. Because localities of protest have been centered in the latter, such sites have been reproduced as privileged; they have been transfigured, in the current political moment, into universal global sites while the factories and neighborhoods and retail spaces outside of the campaigns have been mobilized as particular, aberrant localities of globalization.

Within transnational organizing, the United States, the home base for transnational corporations and retail outlets, cannot be taken as simply another locality within the global. Just as U.S.-based activists are products of their particular localities and their hegemonic positions, retail outlets, centers of activism and protest, and productive spaces inside the United States are particular localities and globalized sites. The ways that relations in sites from El Salvador to New York City, or Bangladesh to San Francisco, are products of their specific localities and of their connections to other localities must be recognized. Otherwise, a hegemonic metanarrative of globalization as finance capital, advertising, and consumption will prevail, while production relations will be relegated to mere occurrences taking place in other sites of globalization.

In order to explore the (re)production of globalization as a hegemonic movement, it is necessary to turn it on its head and look at globalized relations and capital as particular, unstable, and shifting in all of its sites—from factory floors to corporate boardrooms, retail outlets, and advertising outlets. The other side of this reconception of the global is to consider the split between Fordist and post-Fordist modes of labor regulation as dependent on context and locality, rather than as units that are temporally or geographically determined.

The conception of the global-local split also has consequences for the use of the symbolic politics of transnational organizing. I have attempted to analyze the use of symbolic politics in transnational organizing with a focus on the ways in which organizers borrow from signs and symbols of advertising, public relations, and consumption practices. Symbolic politics, however, happens at all levels, not just in advertising, research and development, and consumption practices. Transnational production and transnational politics have drawn on, redeployed, and sometimes shifted particular combinations of signs and symbols in a number of localities—from the shop floor of Mandarin International, the Gap's retail outlets, and neighbor-hoods outside of San Salvador and New York City. I have tried to show how symbolic politics is created and re-created in communities, factory floors, NGO and union offices, and also within Lash and Urry's "economies of signs and symbols."

The use of symbolic politics and the global-local split has had seri-ous implications for the ways in which gender (as it has been articulated through and alongside race, nation, and class) has been utilized and re-produced within the transnational organizing campaigns. I have argued that the new international division of labor in garment production, which has been the focus of a substantial body of literature, is reproduced within transnational labor organizing campaigns. Women's bodies and relations of patriarchy have been central to garment production regimes and their maintenance and discipline on shop floors and in corporate headquarters and public relations firms. Garment producers conceive of women garment workers as fitting into a limited range of positions within the industry. Poor immigrant women in New York City, for example, become unique targets for employment in the city's sweated garment industry for low pay and long hours. Similarly, the bodies and testimonies of women garment workers from Bangladesh, China, El Salvador, Honduras, and Nicaragua are used to appeal to conscientious consumers as part of a larger narrative that is written by U.S. and European activists to contest globalization. Gender, race, nation, and class are used as markers on both sides of transnational politics—in production regimes and in protest campaigns.

However, is transnational protest the audacious democracy celebrated by advocates of the new labor movement? We need to look more closely at the multiple sites, localities, and participants in transnational protest be-fore being able to judge. In order to explore the various sites of the global in transnational protest, I carried out an ethnography that traced the mul-tiple sites of transnational production and protest—from New York City to Dhaka to San Salvador and back—over the course of two years.[1] Through interviews and participant-observation in each site of the campaigns I exam-ined, I traced the transnational relations or, in Burawoy's words, the "global connections" of transnational production and protest in the garment indus-try.[2] In the cases discussed in this study, an overriding commonality is that the transnational structure of the campaigns limits in many ways the extent to which they are able to address labor rights and change conditions on the shop floor. In the end, some working conditions are improved and consumer attention is drawn to the conditions under which clothing is made, but the hierarchies within global production and protest remain firmly in place.

Like globalized production relations, transnational protest has drawn from and built on a configuration of identities that poses some women (poor, suffering, and usually from the third world) exclusively as workers and other women (rich, Northern, and empowered) as consumers. Relations within transnational campaigns have tended to replicate and strengthen differences of gender, race, class, and nationality among participants and to solidify particular identities of participants and target audiences in various locations of protest. I have tried to show how the identities of people both inside and outside the campaigns are deployed as fixed, in geographical and temporal ways, for the duration of the campaign.

The deployment of particular identities depends on a model that features victims of globalization whose only hope of being saved, in turn, lies in transnational politics. Organizing that occurred before the beginning of the transnational campaign was likewise fit into the narrative of the larger campaign. Because struggles, success, and agency were framed as transnational, agency and identity formation in activism could not be considered under other models of protest. In other words, once localized workers, with the support of transnational consumers and activists, fight against global capital, other sites and methods of struggle are necessarily downplayed.

A central target of transnational labor organizing has been the corporate brand and company reputation; the national and local governments' ability to enforce labor rights has been a secondary target. Individual factories, which would historically either close up or lose orders in the face of labor protest, have been pushed to change their production practices through organizers' pressure on the large corporations that subcontract their services. In this way, the politics of transnational protest is always focused at the heights of the corporate and production hierarchy—with local politics, factories, and the nation-state configured as lacking the power to change people's conditions of work and living.

Consumer-targeted protest campaigns, in this way, appear to mark a crisis of politics. Because of the necessity of achieving a degree of flexibility, mobility, and reach comparable to that of global corporations, transnational labor organizing has contested the arenas of consumer culture and capital flows. Citizenship and participation have become linked increasingly with buying power and the ability to boycott and protest labor rights through attacks on brand names, company logos, and corporate reputations, which reinforce the supremacy and integrity of corporate recognition and marketability. In this form of protest, the privileging of consumption demands a reinscription of existing discourses of class, gender, and race, since it is precisely these differences and histories on which consumption relations have depended.

What are the implications of this "citizenship of consumption" for political activism and coalition building around production relations? Primary sites of activism have moved from factory floors and government offices to stock markets, the Internet, and shopping malls. These sites are all within the realm of the private—a realm that can potentially allow consumers unthinkingly to maintain a self-contained world of protest, similar to gated communities and malls. The problematics of corporate and consumer citizenship can be seen in the example of Los Angeles–based apparel manufacturer and retailer American Apparel.

American Apparel has made immense profit on its sweatshop-free branding, bringing in $250 million in sales in 2004.[3] In 2003, however, UNITE HERE charged that American Apparel had been blocking the union from organizing in its factory, saying that American Apparel officials "questioned the loyalty of workers and implied that they could be fined if they joined the union. American Apparel also gathered workers to discuss why a union wasn't needed and printed anti-union T-shirts."[4]

According to a Clean Clothes Campaign report in 2003, American Apparel representatives threatened to arrest union representatives if they did not leave the company parking lot and to close the factory if the workers organized a union. American Apparel also questioned employees about their support for the union, asked its workers to withdraw their union authorization cards, and monitored workers' organizing activities.[5] American Apparel responded by saying that UNITE HERE had misled workers as to union dues and the reasons for organizing. Dov Charney, the CEO of American Apparel, said, "What really happened here is I've broken the sweatshop paradigm, hijacked sweatshops." Charney went on to call UNITE HERE "just another corporate agent."[6] In the end, UNITE HERE and American Apparel settled the matter out of court, and, according to the Clean Clothes campaign Web site, in October 2005 Dov Charney reaffirmed American Apparel's union neutrality pledge that it had signed with the Clean Clothes Campaign in 2002, saying that he had communicated that pledge to the employees. Charney also told Clean Clothes Campaign that he believed in the workers' right to organize and engage in collective bargaining and that he was open to instituting independent monitoring at American Apparel factory sites.[7]

However, the struggle between UNITE HERE and American Apparel points to the problematics of corporate- and consumption-oriented citizenship. American Apparel's Web site includes a description of an undated video called *Legalize L.A.* in which "American Apparel marches with workers to support the legalization of immigrants' rights." The *Legalize*

L.A. video is featured under the "American Apparel Culture" heading. The video shows the Legalize L.A. march and features chants by Latino workers such as "Queremos Trabajo—La Migra al Carajo!" (We want work—to hell with migration officials) and "Sí Se Puede" ("Yes we can," a reference to the United Farm Workers' movement of the 1960s).[8] The description of the video points out that American Apparel supports "the legalization of immigrants' rights," but it does not actually say that it supports the legalization of immigrants' status. The video and the dispute with UNITE HERE point to a corporate culture that plays to leftist and progressive rhetoric but never actually follows through.

Also featured on the American Apparel Web site are gallery shots that critics have called "amateur porn": company employees in various states of undress modeling American Apparel garments. Charney has been taken to court on charges of sexual harassment (which he says are pressed by "disgruntled workers"), and he "decorates stores with covers of Penthouse and Oui magazines from the 70's [and] admits in interviews to engaging in sexual relationships with women who work for him."[9] Charney's and American Apparel's "hipster aesthetic" and progressive rhetoric combined with charges of union busting and sexual harassment show the impossibilities of corporate citizenship. Despite the accusations against Charney and American Apparel, Charney "is often held up as a model for other manufacturers, winning entrepreneurial awards and government commendations for keeping all operations in the United States. He also offers above-minimum wages, health benefits, subsidized lunches and English classes for his workforce, which is mostly Hispanic."[10]

American Apparel is a proponent of vertically integrated manufacturing (VIM), a production process that keeps everything—from design to manufacturing to marketing and retailing—under one roof. The VIM model keeps all operations in the United States and under the umbrella of American Apparel and its CEO. While immigrant and labor activists laud the fact that the labor violations that mark outsourcing and subcontracting are not part of the VIM model—and therefore enable American Apparel to market itself as "sweatshop free"—the VIM model also allows for a kind of corporate culture that makes sure that not only production but also sexual harassment, antiunionism, and structural hierarchies are under the VIM umbrella. In a recent full-page ad on the back of the satirical newspaper the *Onion*, American Apparel featured one of its retail employees, a white woman, lying on the floor wrapped in nothing but a blanket. The ad copy says: "Abby, a retail employee in New York, is wearing our toasty Fleece Airplane Blanket, and nothing else. Made from our supersoft California Fleece, this style comes in 12 colors, online and at our stores." The ad features the name of the company in boldface, with the slogan: "Made in Downtown LA / Vertically Integrated Manufacturing" (Figure 15).[11] The employee featured in the ad is an ideal example of VIM

Figure 15. Advertisement for American Apparel, featuring a retail employee— not a factory employee—unclothed except for the airline blanket that covers her as she is lying on the floor. American Apparel has mixed its antisweatshop message with sexual innuendo, raced and gendered hierarchies, and opposition to union organizing.

production processes: she is both employee and model; she sells the product at the retail site and in the ad. The sexual, gender, class, and race hierarchies that are central to VIM production are also central to the ad; these hierarchies produce and account for the $250 million in sales accrued by American Apparel in the past year.

It remains an open question whether consumer campaigns have the political potential to open up the private sector to public scrutiny and accountability. Certainly, my documentation of some of the pitfalls of transnational network building and a politics of consumption provides a cautionary note. Much of the politics of the transnational depends on particular contexts, localities, and relations among participants in all sites of the campaign. The needed contextualization of transnational organizing and a conception of all localities in the campaigns are difficult to maintain under current conditions.

In transnational labor organizing campaigns, advocacy networks have used various protest tactics to campaign against labor abuses in the garment industry, often without taking into consideration the effects of these politics in all localities of protest. Most of the contention has taken place for a U.S.-based audience of consumers and activists. The protests outside company headquarters, the threat of consumer boycotts, the threatened embargo of imports from companies using child labor, and Internet and e-mail communications have been carried out primarily by activists in the United States and Europe. Media spots and videos have targeted consumers in the United States and Europe and have not been readily available to the garment workers named as the beneficiaries of the protest campaigns. Most of the time, neither have transnational campaigns worked in tandem with struggles and relations in factories and communities. Most promotions for the cross-border campaigns have been in English and therefore not intelligible to most of the garment workers in Bangladesh, El Salvador, and the Chinese- and Spanish-speaking communities in New York City.

Moreover, because the campaigns are planned and implemented in the United States and Europe, the subjects of the campaigns are often left out of tactical planning, negotiations, and the final agreements. This means that the interests that are represented in the corporate campaigns are defined in the U.S.-based offices of activist groups and, like corporate planning within the garment industry, tend to be those of the advocacy networks themselves rather than of the garment workers. A split between globalization and its local manifestations can be seen as a redeployment of those localities— some are mapped at the level of the local, while others are transnational or global. This split raises questions about where agency lies and by whom activism can be carried out—with some sites and practices privileged and others left out of the transnational narrative. Those symbolic politics that are compatible with the forms and symbols of advertising campaigns for the new transnational politics win out over others that would either contest or have nothing in common with public relations demands.

In some cases, transnational organizers stepped in when there had been contention at the grassroots level; in others, organizing was initiated by activists who wanted to contest corporate control, without any previous occurrence of protests in factories or among local organizations. In the case of the anti-child-labor campaign in Bangladesh, the everyday forms of contestation that garment workers—child and adult—engaged in were not recognized as such; the U.S. anti-child-labor campaign resulted in the factory owners' firing of the ten thousand working children under the age of fourteen in the export-oriented garment industry in response to the threatened U.S. boycott of their goods, sparking fears that even more jobs would be lost in the possible boycott of Bangladeshi-made garments. These effects mobilized the children working in the garment industry and their families, bringing people out into the streets to protest the Harkin Bill. In El Salvador, at Mandarin International, the transnational campaign began after organizing had been going on at the factory for several months and hundreds of people were fired for joining the newly formed union. The Kathie Lee campaign built on organizing, literacy, and law classes among women garment workers at the UNITE workers' centers in New York City. The Honduras side of the campaign arose from U.S.-based NGOs' interest in exposing labor practices occurring under the name of a celebrity label— with no previous organizing activities at the factory targeted.

Gender, race, class, and national hierarchies in the campaigns have mirrored those hierarchies mobilized in garment production itself. Women, and often children, are the focus of the campaigns; their everyday working conditions, their lives outside of the factory, and the ways that local meanings and symbols get taken up within production regimes are not addressed in the global arena. Relations among women, men, and children on the factory floor, in retail outlets, and in communities on all sides of the transnational campaigns often are left outside of the realm of protest. They are included when notions of gender and symbolic politics can be utilized in ways that are politically damaging to transnational retailers and without consideration for the ways in which multiple subjectivities are articulated in all sites of protest.

With their focus on the new sweatshop, transnational organizing campaigns have tended not to address the long history of labor organizing among women in their families and communities, on shop floors throughout the world, and in NGO and union centers. By portraying relations under globalization as two-dimensional struggles between transnational corporations and victimized workers in the South, the racial, gender, class, local, and national histories of organizing are neglected. One lesson of the history of the union movement, both inside the United States and internationally, is that it has failed whenever organizers have either ignored questions of gender and race or deliberately played on racist, nationalist, and sexist sentiments in the name of the nation-state or the worker. Historic opportunities for political struggle and local contestations on the grounds of gender, internationalist, anticolonial, and antiracist politics have often been lost in the move to create national, corporate, and union pacts. Thus, opportunities to contest disciplinary mechanisms have been lost in the localities and sites of the EPZ, the garment workers' schools, and even retail and advertising outlets.

The privileging of particular relations and particular tactics of contention and symbolic politics determines which issues are brought to the forefront of transnational campaigns. This privileging has implications for how participation can be carried out, what can be contested, which sites at which moments in time are sites of contention, and which companies will be targeted. It also defines who can participate politically: consumers with buying power, activists with organizing power, workers with the power of production, or some messy combination of all of the above.

Over the course of the growth and expansion of transnational labor organizing campaigns and the surge of transnational campaigns protesting the policies and running of the World Trade Organization (WTO) and the International Monetary Fund (IMF), there has been a learning curve, and consumers, organizers, and activists throughout the world have become better educated about globalization, transnational organizing, and its effects—both intended and unintended. As scholars and activists, we need to keep in mind that globalization, the new international division of labor, involves relations and politics that are in multiple sites, dealing with multiple and sometimes contradictory issues and overlapping identities, subjugations, and subjectivities. We need to grapple with the many-layered negotiations and contestations that are part of a transnational politics. It is necessary to recognize the workings of gendered, raced, and classed hierarchies in the new international division of labor and to focus on the ways in which local practices, relations, affirmations, and contestations of production and consumption regimes are carried out and represented within campaigns that would protest globalization.

Acknowledgments

A project that has been carried out on three continents, in three countries, over the course of many years, and with the help of so many people makes it impossible for me to thank everyone who has contributed to my work and well-being during its course. I hope that all those who have helped me along the way will know how much I appreciate their generosity. The best part of this work I owe to those—named and unnamed—who have read, supported, criticized, and engaged in it over the years; all of the errors are, of course, my own.

I am deeply indebted to all of the garment workers, activists, and organizers who spent hours talking to me and sharing their lives, families, and work. My writing can never do justice to all that they gave me and all that they taught me about work, activism, struggle, and commitment.

I am grateful to my wonderful dissertation advisor and friend, Timothy Mitchell, who has shared with me his advice, encouragement, criticism, patience, and caring, and to my amazing dissertation committee: Christopher Mitchell, Elisabeth Wood, Marilyn Young, and Amrita Basu.

Heartfelt thanks to my former colleagues at New York University's Department of Politics for friendship and support. The Department of Near Middle Eastern Studies and the Hagop Kevorkian Center for Near Eastern Studies provided an area studies home for me. Friends at NYU's International Center for Advanced Studies provided support at every point in the writing process. Thanks to Gayatri Chakravorty Spivak for bringing me toward this project in the first place, and to Lila Abu-Lughod, Judith Adler Hellman, Michael Gilsenan, Bertell Ollman, Mark Roelofs, Mark

Kesselman, Stanley Aronowitz, Javier Auyero, Jane Bayes, Piya Chatterjee, Aldo Lauria, Vijay Prashad, Jackie Smith, Winifred Tate, Dan Bender, Richard Greenwald, Molly Nolan, Mae Ngai, Leti Volpp and Eviatar Zerubavel for reading, commenting, and pushing this work along at various points in the process.

This research was assisted by a fellowship from the International Dissertation Research Fellowship of the Social Science Research Council, with funding provided by the Andrew W. Mellon Foundation. I received financial and administrative support at Rutgers University from the Department of Women's and Gender Studies, Department of Sociology, the Institute for Research on Women, the Center for American Women in Politics, the Center for Cultural Analysis, the Bildner Fellowship for Intercultural Understanding, and the Office of the Vice President for Undergraduate Education, and at New York University from the Pre-Dissertation Fellowship and the Dean's Dissertation Fellowship of the Graduate School of Arts and Science, the Center for Latin American Studies, the Hagop Kevorkian Center for Middle Eastern Studies, the Department of Politics, and the International Center for Advanced Studies.

I offer special thanks to my family in Bangladesh who took care of me and helped me at every step of my fieldwork. I would like to express my gratitude to UBINIG and Shima Das Shimu, the members and organizers of the Bangladesh Independent Garment Workers' Federation, the AFL-CIO Solidarity Center, especially Lydia Sygelakis, Pratima Pal-Majumder of the Bangladesh Institute of Development Studies, and Rehman Sobhan of the Centre for Policy Dialogue. I would also like to thank Hameeda Hossain and Nasreen Khundker for their assistance. I benefited from the help of Rijk van Haarlem, Akky de Cort, and Wahid ur Rahman of the International Labour Organisation, members of the Bangladesh Garment Manufacturers and Exporters Association, and the factory and school monitors who allowed me to travel with them. I am grateful to former U.S. Ambassador to Bangladesh David Merrill and the staff of the U.S. Embassy in Dhaka, Don Hamilton and the management of the Youngone factory, and representatives from UNICEF, the World Bank, and many Bangladeshi government institutions whose representatives I interviewed during my fieldwork.

I extend my sincere appreciation to my dear friend Lotti Silber, who introduced me to El Salvador and to her community and showed me the possibilities of field research in El Salvador. Special thanks also go to Rhett Doumitt of the Solidarity Center, Carolina Quinteros of GMIES, Sharon Phillipps of USAID, to the *Alemanas* and other friends in San Salvador for welcoming me into their lives. I am deeply grateful to Rhina and Olga at

CENTRA for their comradeship and conversation. I benefited from the help and friendship of Daniel García and Jiovanni Fuentes of FEASIES, Marina Rios of MAM, Sergio Chávez of the National Labor Committee, Juan de Dios and the staff of ACILS, Manuel Villanueva and Jennifer Leazer of CISPES, members of the SETMI Directorate, Mark Anner, Francisco Lazo, and Gilberto García of CENTRA, Benjamin Cuellar of the GMIES, and the directors and members of UNTS, CTD, and UTS. Thanks to Pedro Mancía of Mandarin International and to staff members of the U.S. Embassy in San Salvador and the numerous Salvadoran government and industry officials who assisted me in my research.

I am grateful to members and staff of UNITE, the Chinese Staff and Workers' Association, the National Mobilization Against Sweatshops, the National Labor Committee, and the ILO library, all of whom helped me with my research in New York City. I am especially grateful for the help given me by Russell Tan, Greg Simonsmith, Keir Jorgensen, Trinh Duong, Sigmund Shen, Peter Kwong, Ginny Coughlin, Muzzafar Chishti, and Andrew Ross.

I have been fortunate to participate in a number of marvelous workshops and working groups. My heartfelt thanks are extended to the organizers and participants in the Workshop on Neoliberalism at Princeton University, the Princeton Latin American Studies Program Workshop on Inequalities in Latin America, the ICAS/Bilkent Workshop, the Feminist Critical Theory Workshop at the Inter-University Center in Dubrovnik, and the Princeton Institute for International Studies, as well as the SSRC IDRF Program, the Workshop on Contentious Politics and the University Seminar on Labor and Popular Struggles in the Global Economy at Columbia University, the Amsterdam workshop for the International Dissertation Research Fellows, and the Labor Markets Summer Institutes of the German-American Academic Council in Boston and Berlin.

At Rutgers University, I am part of a vibrant feminist community and international studies network. Thanks to all of my colleagues in the Institute for Research on Women workshop on Agency and Social Change, the Center Cultural Analysis workshop on Citizenship, and many others. My IRW writing group (Jennie Brier, Christina Ewig, Robin Greeley, Shuchi Kapila, Waranee Pokpanichwong) read through my work and helped by making numerous suggestions. The South Asian Studies Program and the Latin American Studies Program, as well as the Center for Latino Culture, the Global Studies Program, and the Bildner Fellows Program, have been wonderfully supportive of all aspects of my work. I am grateful to my graduate students for their careful reading, feedback, and suggestions on parts of the book, especially to Soheli Kadiza Azad, Kelly Coogan, Marta Kolarova, Sarasij Majumder, Jane Park, Catherine Sameh, and Elizabeth Woodruff, who carefully commented on parts of this work. Thanks to Michael Siegel of the Department of Geography for making the maps that appear in this volume. Thanks to my wonderful colleagues in women's and gender studies and sociology, who were incredibly supportive over the course of my research and writing, especially to my chair in WGS, Joanna Regulska, Joanne Givand, the administrator of the Department of Women's and Gender Studies, and graduate secretary Margaret Pado. Many thanks to my research assistants, Kathleen Powers and Isra Ali, who read, checked, and collated various drafts of the manuscript. Thanks to my editors at the University of Minnesota Press, Carrie Mullen and Jason Weidemann, who have worked to encourage, push, and support me throughout the process of writing and revising, and to my diligent copy editor, Nancy Sauro.

My whole extended family has supported and loved me unconditionally throughout my education, even when they didn't know quite what the point of all of this was. For my dearest Farhan, I cannot find words to show my gratitude for the love, respect, intellectual and political stimulation, and support he has given me. I send out a prayer that the world will become a better place as my darling daughter Charu grows up and takes her place in it.

Notes

Introduction

1. See, for example, Benería and Roldán, *The Crossroads of Class and Gender;* Benería and Feldman, *Unequal Burden;* Bonacich et al., *Global Production;* and Fernández-Kelly, *For We Are Sold, I and My People.*

2. For example, between 1989 and 1997, Absolut Vodka increased its yearly advertising spending from just under $10 million to nearly $19 million, while between 1984 and 1997, Walt Disney increased its annual spending on advertising from just under $100 million to nearly $1.3 billion. In the past twenty years, McDonald's and Coca-Cola have also exponentially increased their advertising spending. See Klein, *No Logo,* 471; see also Seabrook, *Nobrow.*

3. Gereffi and Korzeniewicz, *Commodity Chains and Global Capitalism;* Keck and Sikkink, *Activists beyond Borders,* 12.

4. For example, when three thousand workers were locked out of Youngone Garments in Dhaka's export processing zone in Bangladesh during July 1997, police and paramilitary troops were called out to disperse the crowd outside the factory. Several workers were injured and hospitalized, and nine others were jailed without charges. Since the factory produces for Nike, international pressure has forced Nike to investigate the jailings and injuries. See chapter 4 for a full discussion of the lockout at Youngone Garments.

5. Keck and Sikkink, *Activists beyond Borders,* 12.

6. See, for example, Green, *Ready-to-Wear, Ready-to-Work;* and Sklar, *Florence Kelley and the Nation's Work.*

7. See, for example, Kwong, *Forbidden Workers;* and Sassen, *The Global City.*

8. See, for example, Mies, *Patriarchy and Accumulation on a World Scale;* and

Majumdar and Chowdury, *The Socio-Economic Condition of Women Workers in the Bangladesh Garments Industry.*

9. See, for example, Lash and Urry, *Economies of Signs and Space;* Sassen, *The Global City;* Harvey, *The Condition of Postmodernity;* Massey, *Spatial Divisions of Labor;* and Lipietz, *Mirages and Miracles.*

10. See, for example, Lefebvre, *The Production of Space;* Soja, *Postmodern Geographies;* and Amin, *Post-Fordism.*

11. See Waters, *Globalization.*

12. Fernández-Kelly, *For We Are Sold, I and My People;* and Bonacich et al., *Global Production.*

13. And, unlike the consumer campaigns to improve working conditions at the beginning of the twentieth century, these campaigns assume that the subjects they are addressing *cannot* be both consumers and workers at the same time. For an interesting discussion of cross-class alliances and consumer boycotts, see Sklar, *Florence Kelley and the Nation's Work,* chapter 7.

14. Tarrow, *Power in Movement;* Smith, Solinger, and Topik, *States and Sovereignty in the Global Economy;* and Berger and Dore, *National Diversity and Global Capitalism.*

15. Sassen, *Globalization and Its Discontents,* xix.

16. Rodrik, *Has Globalization Gone Too Far?* and *The New Economy and Developing Countries.*

17. Mander and Goldsmith, *The Case against the Global Economy;* Barnet and Cavanagh, *Global Dreams;* Korten, *When Corporations Rule the World.*

18. Mitchell, "The Limits of the State," 78.

19. Because the appeals and protests are directed at corporations, or at their high-profile spokespeople such as Kathie Lee Gifford or Michael Jordan, often without taking into consideration factory managers, national labor, human rights and trade laws, or international regimes and organizations, it is then up to the corporations to respond and clean up their acts regarding their labor practices. In this sense, corporations themselves are in dialogue with transnational activist networks and are accorded the final agency with respect to labor rights.

20. Gereffi and Korzeniewicz, *Commodity Chains and Global Capitalism,* 96.

21. Sassen, *The Mobility of Labor and Capital.*

22. Wells, *Strawberry Fields,* xv.

23. Sassen, *The Mobility of Labor and Capital.*

24. For example, GUESS? Inc. shifted production sites from Los Angeles to Mexico in order to destroy a burgeoning unionization and labor rights campaign carried out by UNITE at its Los Angeles factories. For information on UNITE's 1996 "Guess who pockets the difference?" campaign, see http://www.sweatshopwatch .org/swatch/newsletters/2_1.html (accessed September 12, 2000).

25. In a 1995 U.S. Department of Labor survey of forty-eight top U.S. retailers and manufacturers of apparel, thirty-seven retailers provided detailed corporate codes of conduct for labor practices. Companies targeted by the campaigns I examine—Gap Inc., K-Mart, Wal-Mart, and Levi Strauss—all had codes of conduct for labor practices. U.S. Department of Labor, *The Apparel Industry and Codes of Conduct*.

26. Keck and Sikkink, *Activists beyond Borders*, 16. See also Brysk, "Hearts and Minds" and *The Politics of Human Rights in Argentina*.

27. According to figures from the BGMEA, between January 31, 1996, and April 30, 1998, 353 schools were created for the 10,546 former child garment workers, in Dhaka, Narayanganj, Chittagong, Gazipur, and Khulna. A total of 9,743 students were enrolled in the schools. See http://www.bgmea.com/social .htm (accessed September 6, 2000).

28. Here I am recalling Margaret Thatcher's remark about neoliberal globalization, "There Is No Alternative," which became known as the TINA doctrine over the course of her prime ministership. See Mittelman, *Whither Globalization?*, 89.

29. Mitchell, *Questions of Modernity*, 27, xiii.

30. Here I am referring to Gayatri Chakravorty Spivak's critique of knowledge production and marginality in academia in, among other places, *Outside in the Teaching Machine*, 55–59.

1. Children, Schools, and Labored Questions

1. See, for example, Sassen, *The Global City*.

2. I am thinking especially of two phenomena: First, the activism of Craig Keilburger, founder of Free the Children, who at the age of twelve began a protest against child labor and brought schoolchildren from all over the world into the protest. Second, the activism on college and high school campuses over sweatshop production has often exclusively focused on the use of child labor in university athletic wear.

3. For example, in a speech given at the United Nations upon receiving an award for his humanitarian work, ILO director general Juan Somovía stated, "In a world without causes, this is something we can at least think about—eliminating the worst forms of child labor" (October 29, 1999).

4. Foucault, *Power/Knowledge*, 39; italics in original.

5. See Castells, *The Rise of the Network Society;* Lash and Urry, *Economies of Signs and Space*. This calls to mind not only Francis Fukuyama's phrase in *The End of History and the Last Man,* but also Thatcher's TINA politics.

6. Harvey, *The Condition of Postmodernity*.

7. For example, manufacturers who produce in Burma, Indonesia, China, and wartime El Salvador take advantage of repressive regimes to avoid demands by workers regarding factory conditions or labor rights.

8. Mies, *Patriarchy and Accumulation on a World Scale,* 114. See also Fröbel, Heinrichs, and Kreye, *The New International Division of Labor.*

9. Fernández-Kelly, *For We Are Sold, I and My People;* Hossain, Jahan, and Sobhan, *No Better Option?;* International Labor Organization, *La situacion sociolaboral.*

10. Sassen, *The Mobility of Labor and Capital;* Andrew, *No Sweat.*

11. United Students Against Sweatshops (USAS) has joined the antisweatshop movement as a nationwide network of antisweatshop protests and teach-ins on college campuses. USAS, along with NMASS (the National Mobilization against Sweatshops), with its mostly New York City base of college and high school students and other student groups, have made youth groups part of the most vocal opponents of sweatshop labor in the garment industry.

12. Fraser and Gordon, "Civil Citizenship against Social Citizenship."

13. Baud, *Forms of Production and Women's Labour;* Benería and Roldán, *The Crossroads of Class and Gender;* Benería and Feldman, *Unequal Burden;* Chhachhi and Pittin, *Confronting State, Capital, and Patriarchy.*

14. Kabeer, "Cultural Dopes or Rational Fools"; Khundker, "Gender Issues in Export-Based Industrialization in Bangladesh"; Kibria, "Culture, Social Class, and Income Control in the Lives of Garment Workers in Bangladesh."

15. Hossain, Jahan, and Sobhan, *No Better Option?;* Majumdar and Chowdury, *The Socio-Economic Condition of Women Workers in the Bangladesh Garments Industry.*

16. Scheper-Hughes and Sargent, "Introduction: The Cultural Politics of Childhood." See also Stephen, *Children and the Politics of Culture.*

17. For a parallel discussion of the origins of Central American antisweatshop campaigns, see chapter 2.

18. Barnet and Cavanagh, *Global Dreams,* 275–76.

19. Harkin Bill, 1992 S3133, sec. 2 (a)(9).

20. Principle 9 of the Declaration of the Rights of the Child, proclaimed by the General Assembly of the United Nations on November 20, 1959, states, "The child shall not be admitted to employment before an appropriate minimum age; he shall in no case be caused or permitted to engage in any occupation or employment which would prejudice his health or education, or interfere with his physical, mental, or moral development." Quoted in ibid., sec. 2 (a)(1).

21. Ibid., sec. 2 (a)(9).

22. See "Travail des enfants au Bangladesh: Une expérience originale," *Made in Dignity,* no. 8 (November 1996). At http://www.citinv.it/associazioni/CNMS/achivio/strategie/travail_enfba.html.

23. There is some confusion as to whether the date of what is called the Harkin Bill in Bangladesh is the Child Labor Deterrence Act of 1992 or 1993. Some

sources cite 1993 as the date of the act (Razzaque and Rahman, "Harkin's Bill and the Issue of Child Labor"), but in the text of the proposed act that I found in the legislative records, the date is 1992.

24. I have not found the actual report, only references to the report in other publications and in interviews I carried out in Dhaka.

25. For an idea of the way that protectionism and U.S. job creation were to go hand in hand, see an earlier report by Rothstein, *Keeping Jobs in Fashion.*

26. National Labor Committee, *Paying to Lose Our Jobs.*

27. Since 1994, three subsequent volumes were published by the U.S. Department of Labor: volume 2 focused on agricultural imports and the use of forced and bonded labor (1995); volume 3 looked at apparel industry codes of conduct (1996); and volume 4 examined consumer labeling and child labor (1997).

28. *Child Labor and the New Global Marketplace.* Hearing before the U.S. Senate Committee on Labor and Human Resources, Subcommittee on Labor, September 21, 1994.

29. "Background on Garment Workers in Bangladesh," mimeo distributed during a tour of the United States and Canada in 1996 by two BIGU directors, Lovely Yasmin and Nazma Sheikh. The tour was sponsored by AAFLI and UNITE.

30. Since the legal minimum working age according to Bangladeshi labor law is fourteen years, and children as young as six and seven have worked in garment factories and in other areas, it should be noted that some of the people to whom the Wal-Mart representative was referring were between the ages of seven and fourteen.

31. G. Pascal Zachary, "Exporting Rights: Levi Tries to Make Sure Contract Plants in Asia Treat Workers Well," *Wall Street Journal,* July 28, 1994. To Levi Strauss's credit, they also started an on-site schooling program for anyone working at the plants found to be under fourteen. Ironically, when I talked with inspectors and with U.S. Embassy representatives in Bangladesh, underage workers, rather than the people who hired them, were blamed for not knowing their own dates of birth and for not having accurate birth certificates.

32. In its 1992 sourcing guidelines, Wal-Mart outlines its "'Buy American' Commitment: "Wal-Mart has a strong commitment to buy as much merchandise made in the United States as feasible. Vendor Partners are encouraged to buy as many materials and components from United States sources as possible and communicate this information to Wal-Mart. Further, Vendor Partners are encouraged to establish U.S. manufacturing operations." At http://www.walmartstores.com/supplier/vstand_current_standards.html (accessed April 17, 2000). Ironically, Levi Strauss had been accused of using bonded labor in Saipan, capital of the U.S. Commonwealth of the Northern Mariana Islands. Clothing made there is labeled "Made in the U.S.A."

33. From Levi Strauss & Co.'s Web site, cited in Karl Schoenberger, *Levi's Children,* 139.

34. See, for example, Deborah Leipziger, "The Denim Revolution: Levi-Strauss & Co. Adopts a Code of Conduct," *Council on Economic Priorities Research Report,* February 1994 (New York: Council on Economic Priorities).

35. Other companies use different methods. In a telephone conversation with a marketing representative of J. Peterman Company, I was assured, after asking about product sourcing policies and labor conditions, that while Peterman's products were, for the most part, made in India, the consumers would never have to be subjected to traces of the homes (the woman called them "hovels") from which the women worked—or "tea, urine, or food stains" that resulted from working in such places—because the company had invested in a "state-of-the-art cleaning machine that left the clothes as if they had been untouched by human hands." Author's telephone conversation with a J. Peterman Company representative, September 1996.

36. Shirin Akhter and Farida Akhter, "Setting the Agenda on Child Labour in the Bangladesh Garment Industry." At http://www.citinv.it/associazioni/CNMS/archivio/strategie/setting.html (accessed September 30, 1998).

37. Nur Khan Liton, "Fair Deal for the Kids: Harkin's Law Will Do More Harm Than Good for Bangladesh's Working Children," *Dhaka Courier,* September 10, 1993.

38. According to estimates from the U.S. Department of Labor, in its report on *Foreign Labor Trends: Bangladesh, 1994–1995* (Washington, D.C.: U.S. Department of Labor, Bureau of International Labor Affairs, Office of Foreign Relations).

39. Many people, from NGO and union representatives to U.S. Embassy officials, have surmised that factories are moving to EPZs in order to escape the growing threat of unionization in the garment industry—since, according to EPZ bylaws, unionization of the workforce is illegal. Currently, there are ten union federations in Chittagong, with several factories organized—although Dhaka factories remain known for their union-busting stance.

40. BGMEA figures, 1995. From Tabibul Islam, *InterPress Service,* July 18, 1996.

41. Hossain, Jahan, and Sobhan, *No Better Option?,* 100.

42. Author's interview with garment worker, Dhaka, June 1996.

43. Spivak, "Can the Subaltern Speak?," 84.

44. Mitchell, *Colonising Egypt,* 44–45.

45. See http://www.bangladeshgarments.info (accessed August 11, 2004).

46. BGMEA figures, 1996. From Tabibul Islam, *InterPress Service,* July 18, 1996.

47. Pharis Harvey, director of the Child Labor Coalition, in *Workers' Rights News*, August 1995.

48. Author's interview with David Merrill, U.S. ambassador to Bangladesh, Dhaka, August 1996.

49. Author's interview with Wahid ur Rahman, director of the ILO office, Dhaka, Bangladesh, February 1998.

50. ILO's Dhaka office figures, the U.S. Embassy, Dhaka, and the BGMEA, February 1998.

51. It would be useful to study what happens to the children who attended the MOU-mandated schools: where they worked afterward, whether they went on for formal education, whether those who went back into garment production were more likely to join unions, and what their income and earning levels were after the school experiences.

52. I accompanied some inspection tours of factories in various parts of Dhaka, but, although I spent time in several schools, I did not go on school inspection visits with the inspection teams.

53. It is common practice for factories to avoid paying workers' health insurance while still deducting the health insurance fees from monthly wages.

54. U.S. Department of Labor, *The Apparel Industry and Codes of Conduct* lists thirty-seven U.S.-based garment companies with codes of conduct for international labor standards.

55. Marx, *Capital*, 1: 922, 920.

56. According to a 1999 report by the International Labor Rights Fund, *Child Labor in the Soccer Ball Industry: A Report on Continued Use of Child Labor in the Soccer Ball Industry in Pakistan* (http://www.laborrights.org/projects/foulball/foulball.html; accessed August 24, 2006), the use of child labor in soccer ball production in Pakistan continues. The report, citing ILO sources, lists the problems with the program: "Many manufacturers who signed onto the program have not paid dues or provided any details about their stitching centers. . . . [P]articipating employers are still using children. . . . The ILO is not empowered to apply any sanctions to these employers. Soccer ball production may be shifting from Sialkot to nearby, unregulated regions of Pakistan, and some children may be moving from production of soccer balls to production of surgical instruments. In short, we are deeply concerned that soccer ball manufacturers and retailers are using their participation in the program to claim their balls are 'child labor free,' without . . . taking steps to remove children from the production process."

57. As in garments, so in development. Bangladesh, according to economic indicators such as the GDP, is one of the poorest countries in the world and has been often called a fourth world country in the development literature. However, recent World Bank studies have lauded its "enormous" growth potential.

58. Neil Kearney, "Trade in Textiles and Clothing after 2005," 2003. At http://trade-info.cec.eu.int/textiles/documents/153.doc (accessed November 20, 2005).

59. Ibid.

60. Farida Akhter, "Garments aur kono dhurghotona ghotbe na: She nishchoyota ki pete pari?" and Shima Das Shimu, "Garments shilpe dhurghotona norjun shromuk nihojo ahoto aur dhoshotadar dai ke?" *Chinta* (August 28–September 7, 1995).

61. Author's interview with Akky de Kort of the ILO office in Dhaka, January 1998.

62. Fakrul Islam, "Street and Working Children in Bangladesh," *Child Workers in Asia Newsletter* 11, no. 2–3 (April–September 1995). At http://www.cwa .tnet.co.th/Publications/Newsletters/vol11_2-3/v11_2-3_street-children.html (accessed November 20, 2005).

63. And the BGMEA has hired its own Washington lobbyist, former New York representative Stephen Solarz, to defend its interests among U.S. policy makers.

64. Immediately after Bangladesh's independence in 1971, according to the meeting's minute-taker, "A State Department official had told [then–U.S. secretary of state Henry] Kissinger on December 6 that Bangladesh would be 'an international basket case,' to which Kissinger replied, it would 'not necessarily be our basket case.'" Chintito, "15 August 1975: Us and US," *Star Weekend Magazine* (Dhaka), August 15, 2005. At http://www.thedailystar.net/magazine/2005/08/03/ chintito.htm (accessed November 20, 2005).

65. See the ILO *Minimum Age Convention of 1973* (C138), where article 2, points 3–4, state: "The minimum age specified in pursuance of paragraph 1 of this Article shall not be less than the age of completion of compulsory schooling and, in any case, shall not be less than 15 years. Notwithstanding the provisions of paragraph 3 of this Article, a Member whose economy and educational facilities are insufficiently developed may, after consultation with the organisations of employers and workers concerned, where such exist, initially specify a minimum age of 14 years." Article 3, point 1, states: "The minimum age for admission to any type of employment or work which by its nature or the circumstances in which it is carried out is likely to jeopardise the health, safety or morals of young persons shall not be less than 18 years." Convention 138 was ratified by seventy-three countries, including El Salvador and the United States, but not by Bangladesh—or Pakistan or India, all of which are bound to it by their signatures. *C138 Minimum Age Convention, 1973, Convention concerning Minimum Age for Admission to Employment,* at http://www.ilo.org/ilolex/cgi-lex/convde.pl?c138.

66. See Spivak's interview with Sneja Gunew, "Questions of Multi-Culturalism," 60.

67. See Vijay Prashad's critique of the new ILO convention targeting the "worst abuses" of child workers, such as "all forms of slavery [of children], forced or compulsory labor, debt bondage and serfdom, child prostitution, and the use of children in the drug trade," in "Calloused Consciences," 21.

68. Yet reparable; the boycott and the subsequent agreement have hinged on the idea that by getting rid of child labor one could effectively exorcise the demons that plagued and cast a pall over the companies employing them and the clothes they produced in Bangladesh.

2. Organizing in Time of (Post)War

1. Luis Enrique Mejía Godoy is one of the founders of the Nicaraguan *nueva canción*.

2. In this case, repertoires of contention included calls for boycotts, protests at company headquarters and retail outlets, attempts to influence the brand name as a protest tactic, worker tours and witnessing, and coordination of consumer-directed protests with organization on the shop floor.

3. The campaign was carried out in support of workers' organizing in two factories, one of which was Mandarin International in El Salvador. I focus on the Mandarin International case rather than that of Orion Apparel in San Pedro Sula, Honduras, because Mandarin International became the central focus of the U.S. campaign and the subsequent negotiations with Gap Inc.

4. See, for example, the *First Public Report of the Independent Monitoring Group of El Salvador*, from April 1997 (San Salvador, Independent Monitoring Group, http://gmies.org.su/gmies/FirstGMIESPublicReportApril1997.doc7); and Bob Herbert's "A Sweatshop Victory," *New York Times*, December 22, 1995. See also Andrew Ross, *No Sweat* (New York: Verso, 1997).

5. And, by extension, its implications for labor organizing in Central America and in sweatshops throughout the world.

6. I am grateful to Bertell Ollman for pointing out to me the various levels at which the campaigns could work. Ollman was careful to pinpoint the various political implications of organizing with targets here (among consumers and workers in the United States), as opposed to there (in factory floors throughout the world).

7. Nike Inc., "Nike Code of Conduct." At http://www.nike.com/nikebiz/gc/mp/pdf/English.pdf (accessed June 28, 2006).

8. The literature on repertoires of contention is, by now, extensive, but the concept was first presented by Charles Tilly in *From Mobilization to Revolution*. He argues, "[C]ollective action usually takes well-defined forms already familiar to participants, in the same sense that most of an era's art takes on a small number of established forms" (143). He goes on to say: "A population's repertoire of collective action generally includes only a handful of alternatives. It generally changes slowly,

seems obvious and natural to the people involved. It resembles an elementary language" (156).

9. See Krupat, "From War Zone to Free Trade Zone," 64.

10. NLC, "National Labor Committee History." At http://www.nlcnet.org/History.htm (accessed August 16, 2000).

11. National Labor Committee, *Free Trade's Hidden Secrets*, iii.

12. Smith, Chatfield, and Pagnucco, *Transnational Social Movements and Global Politics*, 44.

13. Keck and Sikkink, *Activists beyond Borders*, 45.

14. Ibid.

15. Smith, *Resisting Reagan*, 231–32.

16. Ibid.

17. This effect of global-local split is part of the process that Mitchell calls "enframing," part of a process of disciplining people and practices outside the order of modernity. Mitchell looks at village plans and the construction of barracks, operating "by conjuring up a neutral surface or volume called 'space.'" Mitchell, *Colonising Egypt*, 44.

18. For more about prison labor and garment production, see Farhan Haq, "United States: Captive Labor Force," *Kathmandu Post*, March 12, 1997; see also Eric Schlosser, "The Prison-Industrial Complex," *Atlantic Monthly*, December 1998, 51–77. Lash and Urry ask: "How should we understand the recent and sharp growth of an ever more 'impacted' ghetto in the inner cities of the USA and the UK? What about the recent qualitative increase in streams of migrants working legally or illegally in the sweatshops of the clothing industries of various global cities? What about the 'nimble-fingered' immigrant (and native) women peopling routine assembly from Orange County to Scotland's Silicon Glen? How is it that there are increasing numbers of homeless people filling the streets of London, New York and Paris?" *Economies of Signs and Space*, 145.

19. Ong, *Spirits of Resistance and Capitalist Discipline;* Benería and Feldman, *Unequal Burden;* and Rowbotham and Mitter, *Dignity and Daily Bread*.

20. For an interesting examination of the importance of context, socioeconomic, temporal, geographical, and historical, in determining forms and occurrences of women's activism, see Basu's *Two Faces of Protest*. Basu compares instances of women's activism and protest in one village in Maharashta and one village in West Bengal.

21. National Labor Committee, *Zoned for Slavery*. The hearing took place before the U.S. Senate Committee on Labor and Human Resources, Subcommittee on Labor, on September 21, 1994, and included garment and footwear workers from Honduras, Bangladesh, Brazil, and California, along with anti-child-labor activists and experts on labor, unions, and children's welfare. I examine this hearing, and its effects, at length in chapter 1.

22. Anner, *La maquila y el monitoreo independiente en El Salvador.*

23. Author's interview, San Salvador, October 1997.

24. Author's telephone interview with Mike Prokash, New England CISPES, September 1997.

25. Author's interview with Mark Anner, GMIES, New York City, January 1998.

26. Author's interview with a member of SETMI's directorate, San Salvador, November 1997.

27. Author's interview with SETMI leader, San Salvador, November 1997.

28. Author's interviews with SETMI members, San Salvador, October and November 1997, and "Golpean a Trabajadora," *Diario Latino* (San Salvador), February 9, 1995.

29. Author's interview with SETMI member, San Salvador, November 1997.

30. Press releases from the National Labor Committee, May 18, 1995, and June 28, 1995. Bob Hebert, "Children of the Dark Ages," *New York Times,* July 21, 1995.

31. National Labor Committee, memo to "key contacts," February 9, 1995.

32. "Golpean a Trabajadora," *Diario Latino* (San Salvador), February 9, 1995, 1.

33. Author's interview with Pedro Mancía, director general of Mandarin International, San Salvador, July 1998.

34. Author's interview with member of SETMI's directorate, San Salvador, October 1997.

35. Bob Hebert, "Children of the Dark Ages."

36. Author's interview with SETMI member, San Salvador, November 1997.

37. According to its Web site, Gap Inc. replaced its vendor code of conduct, "Sourcing Principles and Guidelines," created in 1993, with a "Code of Vendor Conduct" in 1996 in the wake of the 1995 labor conflict at Mandarin International factory in El Salvador (http://www.gapinc.com/public/SocialResponsibility/sr _ethic_cvc.shtml).

38. Author's interview with SETMI member, San Salvador, November 1997.

39. Author's interview with SETMI leader, San Salvador, October 1997.

40. The El Salvador independent monitoring program was never carried out. Author's interview with Francisco Lazo, San Salvador, November 1997.

41. "Trabajadores: Violando derechos laborales en silencio," *Co-Latino,* May 30, 1996, 11 (my translation).

42. Author's interview with SETMI leaders, San Salvador, November 1997.

43. "Trabajadores," 11. In various interviews with SETMI members, they affirmed the human rights advocate's assessment of the situation at Mandarin International and cited Calderón's denouncement of them as traitors.

44. Author's interview with member of SETMI's directorate, San Salvador, October 1997.

45. Anner, *La maquila y el monitoreo independiente en El Salvador.*

46. Gap Inc. also hired its own monitor in El Salvador, Gene Palumbo, a journalist present at the negotiations, who informs the company about the Mandarin International situation and the implementation of the Gap code of conduct.

47. Author's interviews with SETMI workers, San Salvador, October 1997.

48. Author's interview with Francisco Lazo, San Salvador, November 1997.

49. According to Carolina Quinteros, from the GMIES, they are currently negotiating with Gap Inc. to monitor its newly contracted production in two other factory sites in El Salvador. Author's interview with Carolina Quinteros, June 1998.

50. According to the Labor Code of El Salvador, a factory union can be incorporated with the affiliation of thirty-five members but cannot engage in collective bargaining until its membership reaches 51 percent of those employed at a given site.

51. Author's interview with member of SETMI's directorate, San Salvador, October 1997.

52. GMIES, "Primer Informe Publico," in Anner, *La maquila y el monitoreo independiente en El Salvador* (my translation).

53. The factory doors continued to be locked during the workday in order to prevent theft, break-ins, or sabotage, according to the management, who said there are guards to open the door if necessary. However, I was inside the factory in November 1997 and was not able to leave; it took me fifteen minutes to find a guard to unlock a door. The locked doors would prevent the quick exit of the factory's more than five hundred workers in the event of fire or severe air contamination.

54. See Melissa Connor, Tara Gruzen, Larry Sacks, Jude Sunderland, and Darcy Tromanhauser, "The Case for Corporate Responsibility: Paying a Living Wage to Maquila Workers in El Salvador," a study for the National Labor Committee (May 14, 1999). At http://www.nlcnet.org/elsalvador/sipareport.htm (accessed August 22, 2000).

55. According to the same IADB country study, consumer prices in El Salvador had risen 10.6 percent in 1994, 10.1 percent in 1995, and 9.7 percent in 1996. See Ladislao Brachowicz and Carlos P. Lecaros Zavala, "El Salvador: Situación económica y prospectos," *Inter-American Development Bank,* March 1999, 12. At http://www.iadb.org/regions/re2/sep/es-sep.htm (accessed August 21, 2000).

56. Author's interview with Judith Viera, November 1997.

57. Author's interview with SETMI leader, San Salvador, November 1997.

58. See chapter 4 for a discussion of discipline and dependence in the industry and in the campaigns.

59. "Una sola zona franca visualiza Calderón Sol," *La Prensa Gráfica,* January 2, 1995, 4A (my translation).

60. Tellingly, I have never been searched upon entering or exiting any of the

factories and export processing zones that I have visited in El Salvador, nor have any of the academics or professionals whom I have seen enter or with whom I have entered the factory premises.

61. Farhan Haq, "Sweatshops, Government Lash Out at Unions."

62. Campaign for Labor Rights Action Alerts, December 5, 1996, "Salvadoran President Calls Labor Leaders Traitors; Salvadoran Right Wing and Newspapers Attack CISPES" (http://www.hartford-twp.com/archives/47/208.html).

63. Carolina Quinteros, Gilberto Garcia, Roberto Gochez, and Norma Molina, "Dinamica de la Actividad Maquila y Derechos Laborales en El Salvador," mimeo, Centro de Estudios del Trabajo (CENTRA), San Salvador, 1998.

64. The National Labor Committee recently opened an office in El Salvador to keep up with the union movement and the labor situation on the ground. They have hired Sergio Chávez, a former unionist and labor specialist, to coordinate with them on local labor situations for their work in Central America. This seems to be an attempt to avert some of the problems of communication that arose in their campaigns in El Salvador, Honduras, and Nicaragua.

65. Duncan Green, "The Asian Garment Industry and Globalisation," *CAFOD Policy Papers,* November 1998. At http://www.cafod.org.uk/garment_industry .htm (accessed August 23, 2000).

66. Author's interview with SETMI leader, San Salvador, November 1997. This view was confirmed by interviews with members of the GMIES and the Mandarin International management.

67. In Bangladesh, there is a similar dilemma with regard to monitoring. After the MOU to eliminate child labor in the export-oriented garment industry, the ILO, the government of Bangladesh, and the factory owners association set up a program of monitoring for compliance. The monitors who inspect factories for child labor are not authorized to look for or report on other violations of health, safety, or labor codes.

68. For an excellent history of AIFLD in Central America, especially of its involvement in El Salvador during the 1980s, see Barry and Preusch, *AIFLD in Central America.*

69. Part of the reformation of the AFL-CIO's international offices was the closing of all of its Central American offices in early 1997. El Salvador was opened as the Central American headquarters of the Solidarity Center of the AFL-CIO in September 1997, and people with histories of labor activism in unions and NGOs were put in place in El Salvador and Guatemala. By the end of 1997 the last FBI agent was retired from the AFL-CIO's Solidarity Center in Mexico.

70. For an excellent discussion of the labor movement in the transition to democracy in El Salvador, see Fitzsimmons and Anner, "Civil Society in a Postwar Period."

71. Irma Patricia Cruz, "La Industria de Maquila en El Salvador: El Desarrollo

Socioeconómico y su Impacto en la Población Económicamente Activa Femenina," Universidad de El Salvador, San Salvador, 1998, 42. Cited in Connor et al., "The Case for Corporate Responsibility," 10 (see note 54).

72. ILO, "El Caso de El Salvador," in *La Situación Sociolaboral en las Zonas Francas y Empresas Maquiladoras del Istmo Centroamericano y República Dominicana*, ACTRAV, Proyecto RLA/94/MO9/NOR, 1996. Cited in Connor et al., "The Case for Corporate Responsibility," 10 (see note 54).

73. Author's interview with Marina Ríos, San Salvador, June 1998.

74. Fitzsimmons and Anner, "Civil Society in a Postwar Period," 124.

75. Author's interviews with maquila workers, San Salvador, August 1998.

76. Author's interview with SETMI members, San Salvador, November 1997.

3. The Ideal of Transnational Organizing

1. UNITE joined the Hotel Employees and Restaurant Employees International Union to form UNITE HERE on July 8, 2004. UNITE HERE "represents more than 450,000 active members and more than 400,000 retirees throughout North America." UNITE HERE, "What Is UNITE HERE?" At http://www.unitehere.org/about/ (accessed November 22, 2005).

2. Wal-Mart's Kathie Lee label was linked to sweatshops in Nicaragua later in 1996, in New York City in 1997, and in El Salvador in 1999.

3. See, for example, the discussion of the role of the AAFLI in Bangladesh in chapter 1 and that of the AIFLD in El Salvador in chapter 2.

4. See Putnam and Feldstein, *Better Together;* Putnam, *Bowling Alone;* and Putnam, *Democracies in Flux.*

5. See Harvey, *A Brief History of Neoliberalism* and *The Condition of Postmodernity.*

6. Gompers's "pure and simple" unionism was marked by anticommunism and a politics of focusing on bread-and-butter issues rather than an interest in changing societal relations in any large-scale way. For a discussion of Gompers's legacy, see Buhle, *Taking Care of Business.* For discussions of race, immigration, and the U.S. labor movement, see Xiaolan Bao, "'Holding Up More Than Half the Sky': A History of Women Garment Workers in New York's Chinatown, 1948–1991" (Ph.D. diss., New York University, 1991); Davis, *Prisoners of the American Dream;* R. D. G. Kelley, *Hammer and Hoe;* and Kwong, *Forbidden Workers.*

7. National Labor Committee, "Kathie Lee Fashions Made by Child Labor," March 1996. At http//www.uniteunion.org/sweatshops/sweatshoparchive/kathielee/kathielee.html (accessed February 10, 2000).

8. Krupat, "From War Zone to Free Trade Zone."

9. Farhan Haq, "Sweatshop Dispute Snares Television Host," wire report from InterPress Service, May 2, 1996.

10. Ibid.

11. Ibid.

12. Suyapa Nolasco was cited in Charles Kernaghan's April 29, 1996, testimony about Global Fashions. Wendy Díaz toured the United States in the summer of 1996 and testified in front of the U.S. Congress about conditions at Global Fashions. Lesly Rodríguez was featured in the 1994 video *Zoned for Slavery,* Judith Viera toured the United States with the NLC during the 1995 Gap campaign, and Nazma Akhter testified in front of Congress about the use of child labor in Bangladesh's garment industry. The Fundación Salvadoreño de Desarrollo Económico y Social (FUSADES) ad featuring Rosa Martínez, describing her as "more than just colorful . . . one of El Salvador's best buys," is reprinted in Ross, *No Sweat,* 88. FUSADES was funded by USAID to develop El Salvador's postwar economy through export-oriented garment production.

13. Cited in Ross, *No Sweat,* 62.

14. "Labor Pains: Kathie Lee Gifford Learns the Hard Way That Sweatshops Are Flourishing Again in American Cities," *People,* July 10, 1996, 59.

15. Ibid. The Variety Cody Gifford House and Cassidy's Place are now supported through the Cody Foundation, set up by Gifford in her son's name.

16. Krupat, "From War Zone to Free Trade Zone," 61.

17. U.S. histories of race, gender, and class allow Gifford the space to redeem herself in ways that Michael Jordan, for example, cannot. Although he was targeted briefly for labor violations in producing the Nike sneakers that bore his name, Jordan could not, as a rich African American man who made his money as a basketball player, cry on television and defend himself. This was an avenue open only to Kathie Lee Gifford as a white woman television personality who touted her love for children.

18. Haq, "Sweatshop Dispute Snares Television Host."

19. Author's telephone interview with Barbara Briggs of the National Labor Committee, April 14, 2000.

20. Ibid.

21. See chapter 2 for a discussion of Wal-Mart's "Made in America" response to the activism around its production practices and use of child labor in Bangladesh.

22. Haq, "Sweatshop Dispute Snares Television Host."

23. Harvey, *The Condition of Postmodernity,* 149–50.

24. Massey, *Spatial Divisions of Labor.*

25. According to Kathie Lee Gifford's calculations, her signature line brought Wal-Mart more than $300 million a year. Rob Howe, "Labor Pains," *People,* June 10, 1996, 65.

26. National Labor Committee, *Paying to Lose Our Jobs,* 29.

27. Danna Harman, "Outsourcing Gets Closer to Home with CAFTA," *USA*

Today, November 7, 2005. At http://cf.us.biz.yahoo.com/usat/051107/13212809. html (accessed November 28, 2005).

28. The Caribbean Basin Initiative was initiated by the Reagan administration "to foster the growth of productive, self-sustaining income and job producing private enterprise in developing countries." Its rationale was described by then–vice president George Bush: "We want to maintain a favorable climate for foreign investment. . . . CBI will not only provide direct incentives for this investment, but encourage follow-on investment" (Ross, *No Sweat,* 81). For a more detailed discussion of USAID's role in infrastructure building for the CBI, see chapter 4.

29. Geoff Dwyer, "Kathie Lee'll Mend City Sweatshop Ways."

30. Ibid.

31. Howe, "Labor Pains," 58.

32. Ibid., 65.

33. U.S. Department of Labor, Office of Public Affairs, "OPA Press Release: Seo Fashions Found Owing More Than $47,000 in Wages, $22,000 in Fines to 45 Workers Making Garments for Walmart Stores," May 30, 1996.

34. Virginia Breen, William K. Rashbaum, and Jere Hester, "The Giffords Give Cold, Hard Cash to Sweatshop Workers," *Daily News,* May 24, 1996.

35. Ibid.

36. Krupat, "From War Zone to Free Trade Zone." The Rubenstein firm no longer represents Kathie Lee Gifford. Gary Lewi of Rubenstein Associates pointed out that when he attended the negotiations in Washington, D.C., "Rubenstein was the only PR firm" there. Of all of the celebrity endorsers of clothing lines, Lewi said, Gifford was the only one who cared enough [about the effect of sweatshops on her name] to hire a public relations consultant (author's telephone interview with Gary Lewi, April 17, 2000).

37. Jay Mazur, UNITE Media Advisory, "UNITE President Issues Statement on Kathie Lee Gifford Controversy Following Daily News Expose," May 23, 1996.

38. Gramsci, *Prison,* 366–67.

39. Mazur, UNITE Media Advisory, May 23, 1996.

40. *Late Night with David Letterman,* "New Items from the Kathie Lee Gifford Product Line," July 6, 1996. At http://cbsnews.cbs.com/network/tvshows/ mini/lateshow/topten/lists/19960606.shtml (accessed June 4, 1999).

41. New York State Governor's Office, press release, "Governor Pataki Proposes Legislation to Crack Down on Sweatshops," May 30, 1996. At http://www .state.ny.us/governor/press/may 30_4.html (accessed June 4, 1999). In addition to the "hot goods" proposal, Pataki also announced that state attorney general Dennis Vacco had filed a single charge of failing to pay wages in Manhattan Criminal

Court against the president and agent of Seo Fashions, punishable by up to one year in jail and a $10,000 fine.

42. Ibid.

43. Krupat, "From War Zone to Free Trade Zone," 60.

44. Press release, "Statement Following a Meeting at the Residence of Archbishop Cardinal O'Connor," June 6, 1996. At http://www.uniteunion.org/sweatshops/sweatshoparchive/kathielee/kathielee.html (accessed February 10, 2000).

45. Ibid.

46. Ibid.

47. Ibid.

48. Ibid.

49. Ibid.

50. In fact, the National Labor Committee, UNITE, and the Workers' Centers in New York City also serve as backdrops in the background of this debate.

51. At http://www.walmartstores.com/supplier/vstand_031898_nlc.html (accessed April 17, 2000).

52. Press release, "Statement Following a Meeting at the Residence of Archbishop Cardinal O'Connor."

53. Krupat, "From War Zone to Free Trade Zone," 61.

54. Ibid.

55. William J. Clinton and Robert Reich, "Statement on Fair Labor Practices, Washington, D.C.," August 2, 1996. Available from CIS Congressional Universe (accessed April 10, 2000).

56. In 1995, as Clinton notes in his speech, more than seventy people were discovered "working in virtual slavery behind barbed wire in a garment factory in El Monte, California." This discovery, he goes on to say, "awakened Americans to the fact that some of the clothes and shoes they buy are manufactured by people who work under deplorable conditions. The well-documented episode involving Kathie Lee Gifford also awakened many people to this problem." Ibid.

57. Ibid.

58. Author's interviews with unionists and labor activists familiar with the independent monitoring project in Honduras during 1997 and 1998.

59. U.S. Department of Labor, Office of Public Affairs, "OPA Press Release: Reich Praises Bonewco Fashions for Paying More than $40,000 in Back Wages and Penalties Owed by Sweatshop That Produced Kathie Lee Line," July 11, 1996.

60. Author's interview with Trinh Duong of the CSWA, New York City, July 1997.

61. Kwong, *Forbidden Workers,* 123–24. The New York State Labor Department was acting under the "hot goods" initiative promoted by Governor Pataki and the Giffords, mentioned earlier.

62. Ibid., 124.

63. Ibid.

64. Daniel Vila, "UNITE Continues the Fight v. Brand Name Sweat Shops," *People's Weekly World,* September 14, 1996.

65. Kwong, *Forbidden Workers,* 124.

66. Although in 1998 and 1999, the Gifford line was cited in campaigns for subcontracting to factories with poor working conditions in El Salvador and in New York City.

67. Jessop, "Reflections on Globalisation and Its (Il)Logic(s)," 19.

68. Charles Kernaghan, "Why I Picked on Kathie Lee & Co.," New York *Daily News,* June 21, 1996.

69. Ibid.

70. Ibid.

4. Disciplining Bodies

1. Thanks to Srirupa Roy and Jayati Lal for helping me formulate the guiding questions of this chapter.

2. See Lasn, *Culture Jam.*

3. National Labor Committee, *Wal-Mart's Shirts of Misery,* report published July 1999, 1.

4. "Corporate Watch Interview with Julie Su, Asian Pacific American Legal Center." At http://www.corpwatch.org/trac/feature/sweatshops/elmonte.html (accessed April 25, 2000).

5. John F. Lyons, "The Triangle Shirtwaist Factory Fire," *Journal for Multi-Media History* 2, no. 1. At http://www.albany.edu/jmmh/vol2no1/trianglefire.html (accessed December 1, 2005).

6. Asian-American Free Labor Institute, "Working People to Death," 1994, informational flyer.

7. Author's interview with Lydia Sygelakis, AAFLI representative in Bangladesh, Dhaka, July 1996. See also Govinda Shil, "Frustration Creeps In As Factory Inspectors Face an Enormous Task," *Daily Star,* August 3, 1997; Tabibul Islam, "Garment Industry Indifferent to Workers' Plight," InterPress Service, July 18, 1996.

8. Author's interview with Russell Tan about garment factories in Sunset Park, Brooklyn, New York City, May 1996.

9. Author's interview with Carolina Quinteros, December 1999. See also the National Labor Committee's *Mickey Mouse Goes to Haiti.*

10. Author's interview with Oscar Darío Trujillo, San Salvador, November 1997. Darío, a former U.S. Marine of Colombian descent, worked on security issues for the U.S. Embassy in El Salvador at the height of the conflict in 1981. After

leaving the Marines, Darío stayed on in El Salvador and worked as a consultant to garment factories and export processing zones on security and surveillance measures to guard against worker sabotage and union activity. In our interview, Darío talked about the fact that the tactics he had learned during the war had made him marketable as a consultant for garment manufacturers.

11. See U.S. Department of Labor, *The Apparel Industry and Codes of Conduct*. Codes of conduct are listed in appendix C, 124–207.

12. Ibid. I am drawing from the codes of conduct of Dayton Hudson Corp., Dillard Department Stores, Family Dollar Stores, Fruit of the Loom, and Gap Inc.

13. Author's interview with general manager of Brothers Fashions, Dhaka, January 1998.

14. Author's interview with Lydia Sygelakis, AAFLI Bangladesh, Dhaka, June 1996.

15. Taylor, *The Principles of Scientific Management,* 7.

16. Ibid., 41, 38.

17. Ibid., 59–60.

18. Ibid., 96.

19. Ibid., 140.

20. Author's interview with the managers of Ornob Garments, Dhaka, July 1996.

21. *Recintos fiscales,* literally "fiscal enclosures," are bonded areas certified by the Salvadoran government that fall under the same tax and legal exemptions as the country's export processing zones. Legislación Laboral Salvadoreña, Código de Trabajo, Constitución Política, Ley de Fomento a las Exportaciones, Ley de Zonas Francas y Recintos Fiscales (El Salvador, 1994).

22. Sheila McClear, "End to Garment Quota System Spells More Competition, More Poverty," in *Labor Notes,* February 2005, at http://www.labornotes.org/archives/2005/02/articles/a.html (accessed January 13, 2006).

23. Author's interview with Arturo Carías, San Salvador, October 1997.

24. Author's visit to Youngone Garments in February 1998. These systems of gauging production levels are monitored in similar fashion throughout Dhaka's garment factories. All subsequent discussion of Youngone, unless otherwise noted, is based on this thirteen-hour-long visit to the factory.

25. Nike's code of conduct. At http://www.nikebiz.com/labor/code.shtml (accessed May 5, 2000).

26. Author's interview with Don Hamilton, Dhaka, February 1998. All quotes in this section are from this interview, unless otherwise noted.

27. Mitchell, *Colonising Egypt.*

28. Bourdieu, *Outline of a Theory of Practice,* 190–91.

29. Ibid.

30. Ibid., 191.

31. Ibid.

32. Ibid.

33. See http://www.cleanclothes.org/news/newsletter8.htm (accessed May 11, 2000).

34. Ibid.

35. Byrne, *El Salvador's Civil War*, 95.

36. Fitzsimmons and Anner, "Civil Society in a Postwar Period."

37. The six EPZs were American Park in Santa Ana, El Pedregal in Camalapa, El Progreso in Santa Tecla, Export Salva in Colón, San Bartolo in Soyapango, and San Marcos in San Marcos. All are located near highways, shipping ports, and airports for quick transport. ISTU, FUSADES, CASATUR, *Destination El Salvador: The Official Visitor Guide to El Salvador* (ABC International Publishing, 1996).

38. "Crecen exportaciones de maquila," *El Diario de Hoy*, March 31, 1997, 38.

39. Organización Internacional del Trabajo/International Labor Organization, *La Situación Sociolaboral en las Zonas Francas y Empresas Maquiladoras del Istmo Centroamericano y República Dominicana* (Proyecto RLA/94/MO9/NOR: ILO, 1996), 115–16.

40. The CBI was begun under the Reagan administration and designed to be a foreign aid program that would encourage private investment as the key to stabilization in the Central American and Caribbean region. The CBI "called for the elimination of import duties for certain products from the region . . . and financial assistance aimed to enhance the region's business climate." It promoted the combination of U.S. investment, export promotion, and strengthening the private sector in order to foster economic development. See Barry and Preusch, *The Soft War*, 34–35.

41. Segovia, "The War Economy of the 1980s," 41. Between 1985 and 1989, $1.848 billion in economic aid was allocated to El Salvador, 91.5 percent of the amount requested by the Reagan administration. See Byrne, *El Salvador's Civil War*, 142.

42. Rosa, *AID y las Transformaciones Globales en El Salvador*.

43. The National Labor Committee, *Paying to Lose Our Jobs*, 50.

44. Rosa, *AID y las Transformaciones Globales en El Salvador*, 80.

45. "Una sola zona franca visualiza Calderón Sol," *La Prensa Gráfica*, January 2, 1995.

46. Ibid.

47. FUSADES, *Destination El Salvador*, 90 (see note 37).

48. Ibid., 89.

49. "Trabajadores: Violando derechos laborales en silencio," *Diario Co-Latino*, May 30, 1996.

50. "Golpean a trabajadora," *Diario Co-Latino,* February 9, 1995.

51. "Muere de dolor al no darle permiso para ir al ISSS," *Diario Co-Latino,* March 6, 1994.

52. Quinteros et al., *Dinámica de la actividad maquiladora y derechos laborales en El Salvador,* 52–58.

53. Alejandro Cantor, "Derechos Humanos y las Maquilas," *La Voz* 3, no. 27 (1995): 4.

54. Quoted in U.S. Department of State, *1999 Country Reports on Human Rights Practices: El Salvador,* at http://www.state.gov/www/global/human_rights/ 1999_hrp_report/elsalvad.html (accessed May 18, 2000).

55. Marisol Ruíz and Gilberto García, *Condiciones Laborales de Mujeres y Menores en las Plantas de la Maquila Coreana y Taiwanesa en El Salvador,* Working Paper, February 1995 (San Salvador: Centro de Estudios del Trabajo CENTRA, 1996), 47–48; my translation.

56. Author's interview, San Salvador, December 1997.

57. Ruíz and García, *Condiciones Laborales de Mujeres y Menores,* 48.

58. Author's interview with Marina Ríos, San Salvador, April 1998.

59. Mark Anner, "¿Hacía la sindicalización de los sindicatos?" *Estudios Centroamericanos* 573–574 (1998): 599–613; my translation. In my own interviews with union leaders in El Salvador, several would disparage other groups while pointing to their own work in the factories and their own international connections. Communication and interunion solidarity is often replaced by gossip, and the factories remain unorganized.

60. Ruíz and García, *Condiciones Laborales de Mujeres y Menores,* 48.

61. For discussions of AIFLD in El Salvador, see Barry and Preusch, *The Soft War,* 242; Armstrong and Shenk, *El Salvador;* Diskin and Sharpe, *The Impact of U.S. Policy in El Salvador, 1979–1985;* and Byrne, *El Salvador's Civil War.*

62. Barry and Preusch, *The Soft War,* 243. AIFLD was expelled from El Salvador in 1973, after the right wing and government elite labeled the unions supported by AIFLD "communist." It did not return until 1980.

63. Montgomery, *Revolution in El Salvador,* 192–93.

64. Barry and Preusch, *The Soft War,* 245.

65. COSDEMA, "Verdades en la Maquila," published in *La Prensa Gráfica,* December 10, 1996.

66. Author's interview with Marina Ríos of MAM, San Salvador, April 1998.

67. "Las zonas francas no son zonas de libertad," *Diario Co-Latino,* n.d.

68. Alejandro Cantor, "Derechos Humanos y las Maquilas," *La Voz* 3, no. 27 (1995): 5.

69. See Freedman and Brooks, "Globalized Chinese Capital in Central America."

70. Abu-Lughod, "Romance of Resistance."

71. Harvey, *The Condition of Postmodernity*, 156; emphasis mine.

5. Women First?

1. For discussions of such gendered, raced, classed, and local practices, see Ong, *Spirits of Resistance and Capitalist Discipline;* Mies, *Patriarchy and Accumulation on a World Scale;* Fernandez-Kelly, *For We Are Sold, I and My People;* and Rowbotham and Mitter, *Dignity and Daily Bread.*

2. Gilroy, *The Black Atlantic*, 68–69.

3. Lisa Lowe, "Work, Immigration, Gender: The New Subjects of Cultural Politics," in Lowe and Lloyd, *The Politics of Culture in the Shadow of Capital*, 360.

4. For a view of a shop floor that is gendered male, see Burawoy, *Manufacturing Consent.* For views of segregated shop floors, some masculine and some feminine, see Taylor, *The Principles of Scientific Management.* For discussions of the "feminization" of shop floors, the workforce and the labor market, see Piore, *Birds of Passage;* Braverman, *Labor and Monopoly Capital;* and Fröbel, Heinrichs, and Kreye, *The New International Division of Labour.* For a male-centered view of the possibilities for organizing, see Hardt and Negri, *Empire;* and Hardt and Negri, *Multitude.*

5. Author's interviews with DINDEX workers, San Salvador, November 11, 1997; "Intoxicación masiva en maquila," *La Prensa gráfica* (San Salvador), November 12, 1997, 4 (my translation); "Intoxicación Masiva," *El Diario de Hoy* (San Salvador), November 12, 1997, 1–3 (my translation); "Update: Salvadoran Workers Poisoned by Carbon Monoxide," CISPES Alert, December 8, 1997.

6. "Intoxicación masiva en maquila," 4.

7. Author's interview with DINDEX workers, San Salvador, November 11, 1997.

8. CISPES Action Alert, December 7, 1997.

9. "Trabajadoras no tenían certificados del ISSS," *La Prensa Gráfica* (San Salvador), November 12, 1997, 4 (my translation).

10. "Víctimas dadas de alta," *El Diario de Hoy* (San Salvador), November 13, 1997, 6 (my translation).

11. "Salud procederá legalmente contra maquiladora DINDEX," *El Diario de Hoy* (San Salvador), November 13, 1997, 6 (my translation).

12. "Víctimas dadas de alta," 6.

13. "Desmayos y pánico en la factoría," *El Diario de Hoy* (San Salvador), November 12, 1997, 3 (my translation).

14. "Sin conocerse causa de intoxicación," *La Prensa Gráfica* (San Salvador), November 13, 1997, 6 (my translation).

15. "Salvadoran Workers Poisoned by Carbon Monoxide," CISPES Action Alert, December 8, 1997.

16. "Sin conocerse causa de intoxicación," 6.

17. "Intoxicación masiva en maquila," 4.

18. "Salud procederá legalmente contra maquiladora DINDEX," 6 (my translation).

19. "Intoxicación masiva en maquila," 4.

20. "Interiano asegura que 'hubo exageración,'" *La Prensa Gráfica* (San Salvador), November 13, 1997, 6 (my translation).

21. "Trabajadores no tenían certificados del ISSS," 4.

22. "Hay un olor extraño," *El Diario de Hoy* (San Salvador), November 12, 1997, 3 (my translation).

23. "Salud procederá legalmente contra maquiladora DINDEX," 6.

24. Article 30, Item 10 of the Labor Code of El Salvador states: "It is prohibited that management reduce, directly or indirectly, the salaries that they pay, by either supplementing or reducing social welfare benefits that should be administered to their workers, except when there is legal cause." (Ricardo Mendoza Orantes, ed., *Codigo de Trabajo con Reformas Incorporadas,* República de El Salvador, 1997), 17 (author's translation).

25. Ong, *Spirits of Resistance and Capitalist Discipline.*

26. "Víctimas dadas de alta," 6.

27. "Piden investigar intoxicación," *El Diario de Hoy* (San Salvador), November 14, 1997, 2 (my translation).

28. CISPES Action Alert, "Salvadoran Workers Poisoned by Carbon Monoxide," December 8, 1997.

29. Ibid.

30. Ibid., 1.

31. Author's interview with garment factory owner, Dhaka, June 30, 1996.

32. Author's interview with garment factory manager, Dhaka, July 6, 1996.

33. Author's interview with garment factory owner, Dhaka, July 15, 1996.

34. Hossain, Jahan, and Sobhan, *No Better Option?,* 64–65.

35. Pratima Paul-Majumder and Sharifa Begum, "Upward Occupational Mobility among Female Workers in the Garment Industry of Bangladesh," prepared for UNDP (UN Development Programme), Dhaka (Bangladesh Institute of Development Studies: December, 1994), 25–26.

36. Author's interview with factory manager, Dhaka, July 20, 1996.

37. Author's interview with factory manager, San Salvador, November 14, 1997.

38. Author's interview with garment factory owner, Dhaka, July 15, 1996.

39. Author's interview with garment factory owner, Dhaka, July 18, 1996.

40. Kabeer, "Cultural Dopes or Rational Fools?," 151.

41. Ibid., 153.

42. Author's interviews with garment workers, San Salvador, October 20, 1997.

43. Gilroy, *The Black Atlantic,* 68–69. For an in-depth discussion of the antislavery debate and its relationship to capitalism, see Bender, *The Anti-Slavery Debate.*

44. Brown, *States of Injury,* 97.

6. Living Proof

1. Spivak, *Outside in the Teaching Machine,* 3, 5.

2. Author's interview with Paril Akhtar, Dhaka, June 1996. The original quote in Bangla from Akhtar is "chutti dai na, poisa dai ne—bolen ki 6 diben, kinto 3 achbe." All translations from Bangla to English are my own.

3. Ibid. The original quote in Bangla from Akhtar is "Bangladesh labor law kothai? Amarke garments posondo kori. Kinto garmentser chakri hoi na."

4. Author's interview with garment worker Rokeya, Dhaka, July 1996. The original quotes in Bangla are "Ami khete pari na" and "Dine, ami shudu ekta kola khete pari. Kobe ami garmentser kaj kori, amar pet kharap hue jai."

5. Ibid. The original quote in Bangla is "Ami Dhakate takbo kinto, jodi amar poribarer dorkar."

6. Auyero, *Contentious Lives,* 197.

7. Jelisaveta Blagojevic, "Taking the Place of Love: The Borderlines of Subjectivity," paper presented at the postgraduate course Feminist Critical Analysis: Boundaries, Borders, and Borderlands, at Interuniversity Centre, Dubrovnik, Croatia, May 24–29, 2004.

8. Ahmed, *The Cultural Politics of Emotion,* 195.

9. Lila Abu-Lughod, "Other Differences: Feminism Meets Culture and Class in the Middle East," lecture given at the Institute for Research on Women, Distinguished Lecture Series, Rutgers University, October 16, 2003.

10. McLagan, "Human Rights, Testimony, and Transnational Publicity," 2.

11. *Child Labor and the New Global Marketplace: Reaping Profits at the Expense of Children?* Hearing before the U.S. Senate Committee on Labor and Human Resources, Subcommittee on Labor, Washington, D.C., September 21, 1994.

12. National Labor Committee, *The Hidden Face of Globalization,* back cover description of the video.

13. National Labor Committee, "The Human Face behind the Global Economy Bangladesh Workers' Tour," U.S. tour, September 28–October 27, 2004. At http://www.nlcnet.org/campaigns/bangtour/oldinfo.shtml (accessed November 11, 2005).

14. National Labor Committee, "Maksuda Sheds Tears at Boston College, Boston, MA" and "Robina Demonstrates How She Was Hit with the Wal-Mart

Pants She Sewed. Brandeis University, Waltham MA." At http://www.nlcnet.org/campaigns/bangtour/photos.shtml (accessed November 11, 2005).

15. National Labor Committee, "Testimony from Robina Akhter, Factory Worker from Bangladesh." At http://www.nlcnet.org/campaigns/bangtour/robina.shtml (accessed November 11, 2005).

16. Ibid.

17. Ibid.

18. National Labor Committee, "Testimony of Masuma, Factory Worker from Bangladesh." At http://www.nlcnet.org/campaigns/bangtour/maksuda.shtml (accessed November 11, 2005).

19. National Labor Committee, "Testimony of Sk. Nazma, President of the Bangladesh Center for Worker Solidarity." At http://www.nlcnet.org/campaigns/bangtour/sknazma.shtml (accessed November 11, 2005).

20. Laclau and Mouffe, *Hegemony and Socialist Strategy*, 7.

21. Kabeer, *The Power to Choose*, 52.

22. Bangladesh Export Processing Zones Authority, "For Optimum Profit Invest in EPZs of Bangladesh," promotional flyer, n.d.

23. Gramsci, "Notes on Italian History," 169.

24. Marx, "The General Formula of Capital," in *Capital*, vol. 1, chapter 4.

25. Chakrabarty, *Provincializing Europe*, 50.

26. Chakrabarty, *Rethinking Working-Class History*.

27. Chakrabarty, *Provincializing Europe*, 50.

28. Marx, *Capital*, 1: 308.

29. Ibid., 308–9.

30. See Spivak, "Can the Subaltern Speak?" 277, for a discussion of class-in-itself and class-for-itself.

31. Chakrabarty, *Provincializing Europe*, 50.

32. Ibid.

33. Ibid., 66.

34. Agamben, *Remnants of Auschwitz*, 13.

35. Ibid., 34.

36. From the NLC's home page advertising *Zoned for Slavery* for $12. Another video offered for sale on the home page is *Mickey Mouse Goes to Haiti*, which asks the question, "What is it like to work in a Haitian factory sewing Disney children's clothing?"

37. Human Rights Watch, "Stop Discrimination in Mexican Maquiladoras," May 1997. At http://www.hrw.org/hrw/campaigns/wrp-mexico/alert2a.html (accessed August 23, 2000).

38. Mitchell, *Colonising*, 12.

39. Foucault, *Archaeology of Knowledge*, 45. I am extremely grateful to Kelly

Coogan for guiding me to the connection between my argument and that of Foucault's in *Archaeology of Knowledge*.

40. Chakrabarty, *Rethinking Working-Class History*, 19.

41. *La Prensa Gráfica*, San Salvador, June 21, 1998; my translation.

42. Wells, *Strawberry Fields*, 190.

43. Even its appellation is a question of brand name. By calling it the Gap campaign, we are to understand that the factory in question produces Gap clothing, and that Gap Inc. is (exclusively) responsible for the working conditions at the factory. In fact, Mandarin produces only a small part of Gap's clothing and Gap is but one of several manufacturers who subcontract from Mandarin and from the San Marcos EPZ.

44. Author's interview with Manuel Villanueva of CISPES, San Salvador, October 1997.

45. Spivak, "Can the Subaltern Speak?" 289.

46. Isin, *Being Political*, 276–77.

47. Spivak, "Can the Subaltern Speak?," 279.

Epilogue

1. See Marcus, "Ethnography in/of the World-System."

2. See Burawoy et al., *Global Ethnography*, 30.

3. Mireya Navarro, "His Way Meets a Highway Called Court," *New York Times*, July 10, 1995, sec. 9, 1.

4. Patrick J. Cliff, "American Apparel Is Sweatshop Free but Needled by a Union," *Columbia News Service*, March 1, 2004. At http://www.jrn.columbia.edu/studentwork/cns/2004-03-01/501.asp (accessed December 6, 2005).

5. Clean Clothes Connection, "Update on American Apparel." At http://www.cleanclothesconnection.org/AmericanApparel.htm (accessed December 6, 2005).

6. Cliff, "American Apparel Is Sweatshop Free but Needled by a Union."

7. Clean Clothes Connection, "Update on American Apparel."

8. At http://www.americanapparel.net/gallery/galleryCulture.html (accessed December 6, 2005).

9. Navarro, "His Way Meets a Highway Called Court."

10. Ibid.

11. American Apparel advertisement, *Onion*, November 24–30, 2005, 36.

Bibliography

Abu-Lughod, Lila. "Romance of Resistance: Tracing Transformations of Power through Bedouin Women." *American Ethnologist* 17, no. 1 (1990): 41–55.

Ackers, Peter, Chris Smith, and Paul Smith. *The New Workplace and Trade Unionism*. New York: Routledge, 1996.

Adorno, Theodor. *Critical Models: Interventions and Catchwords*. New York: Columbia University Press, 1998.

Agamben, Giorgio. *Remnants of Auschwitz*. New York: Zone Books, 2002.

Aggarwal, Pradeep. *Economic Restructuring in East Asia and India*. New York: St. Martin's, 1995.

Aglietta, Michel. *A Theory of Capitalist Regulation: The US Experience*. London: New Left Books, 1979.

Ahmed, Sara. *The Cultural Politics of Emotion*. New York: Routledge, 2004.

Akhter, Farida. "Garments aur kono dhurghotona ghotbe na: She nishchoyota ki pete pari?" *Chinta*, August 28–September 7, 1995.

Alejandro, Roberto. "Impossible Citizenship." In *Citizenship after Liberalism*, ed. Karen Slawner, Mark Denham, and Peter Long. New York: Peter Lang, 1998.

Alliez, Eric. *Capital Times: Tales from the Conquest of Time*. Minneapolis: University of Minnesota Press, 1996.

Amin, Ash, ed. *Post-Fordism*. Cambridge: Blackwell, 1994.

Anner, Mark Sebastian. *La maquila y el monitoreo independiente en El Salvador*. El Salvador: Grupo de Monitoreo Independiente, 1998.

Applebaum, Herbert. *Construction Workers, U.S.A.* Westport, Conn.: Greenwood Press, 1999.

Appelbaum, Richard, and Peter Dreier. "SweatX Closes Shop." *Nation,* July 1, 2004, 1–4.

Armbruster-Sandoval, Ralph. "Globalization and Transnational Labor Organizing: The Honduran Maquiladora Industry and the Kimi Campaign." *Social Science History* 27, no. 4 (2003): 551–76.

Armstrong, Robert, and Janet Shenk. *El Salvador: The Face of Revolution.* Boston: South End Press, 1982.

Arrighi, Giovanni. *The Long Twentieth Century: Money, Power, and the Origins of Our Times.* New York: Verso, 1994.

Auyero, Javier. *Contentious Lives.* Durham, N.C.: Duke University Press, 2003.

Bahl, Vinay. *The Making of the Indian Working Class.* New Delhi: Sage, 1995.

Banerjee, Nirmala. *Indian Women in a Changing Industrial Scenario.* New Delhi: Sage, 1991.

"Bangla Floods Claim Nearly 300 Lives." *Hindu,* July 26, 2004.

Barnet, Richard, and John Cavanagh. *Global Dreams: Imperial Corporations and the New World Order.* New York: Simon and Schuster, 1994.

Barry, Tom and Deb Preusch. *AIFLD in Central America: Agents as Organizers.* Albuquerque, N.M.: Resource Center, 1990.

———. *The Soft War.* New York: Grove Press, 1988.

Basu, Amrita. *The Challenge of Local Feminisms: Women's Movements in Global Perspective.* Boulder, Colo.: Westview Press, 1995.

———. ed. *Two Faces of Protest: Contrasting Modes of Women's Activism in India.* Berkeley: University of California Press, 1992.

Baud, I. S. A. *Forms of Production and Women's Labour: Gender Aspects of Industrialization in India and Mexico.* New Delhi: Sage, 1992.

Bender, Thomas, ed. *The Anti-Slavery Debate.* Berkeley and Los Angeles: University of California Press, 1992.

Benería, Lourdes, and Shelley Feldman. *Unequal Burden: Economic Crises, Persistent Poverty, and Women's Work.* Boulder, Colo.: Westview Press, 1992.

Benería, Lourdes, and Martha Roldán. *The Crossroads of Class and Gender: Industrial Homework, Subcontracting, and Household Dynamics in Mexico City.* Chicago: University of Chicago Press, 1987.

Benko, Georges, and Alain Lipietz. *Les régions qui gagnent.* Paris: Presses Universitaires de France, 1992.

Berger, Suzanne, and Ronald Dore, eds. *National Diversity and Global Capitalism.* Ithaca, N.Y.: Cornell University Press, 1996.

Bergquist, Charles, ed. *Labor in the Capitalist World-Economy.* Beverly Hills, Calif.: Sage Publications, 1984.

Bernstein, Nina. "Invisible to Most, Immigrant Women Line Up for Day Labor." *New York Times,* August 15, 2005.

Björkman, James Warner. *The Changing Division of Labor in South Asia.* River-dale, Md.: Riverdale, 1986.

Block, Fred. *Postindustrial Possibilities: A Critique of Economic Discourse.* Berkeley: University of California Press, 1990.

Blunt, Allison, and Gillian Rose, ed. *Writing Women and Space: Colonial and Post-colonial Geographies.* New York: Guilford Press, 1994.

Bolin-Hort, Per. *Work, Family, and the State: Child Labor and the Organization of Production in the British Cotton Industry, 1780–1920.* Lund, Sweden: Lund University Press, 1989.

Bonacich, Edna, Lucie Cheng, Norma Chinchilla, Nora Hamilton, and Paul Ong. *Global Production: The Apparel Industry in the Pacific Rim.* Philadelphia: Temple University Press, 1994.

Boris, Eileen. *Home to Work: Motherhood and the Politics of Industrial Homework in the United States.* New York: Cambridge University Press, 1994.

Boris, Eileen, and Elisabeth Prugl, ed. *Homeworkers in Global Perspective: Invisible No More.* New York: Routledge, 1996.

Bosniak, Linda. "Citizenship." In *Oxford Handbook of Legal Studies,* ed. Peter Carne and Mark Tushnet. Oxford: Oxford University Press, 2003.

Bourdieu, Pierre. *The Logic of Practice.* Stanford, Calif.: Stanford University Press, 1990.

———. *Outline of a Theory of Practice.* New York: Cambridge University Press, 1977.

Boyce, James K., ed. *Economic Policy for Building Peace: The Lessons of El Salvador.* Boulder, Colo.: Lynne Rienner, 1996.

Boyer, Robert, ed. *Capitalismes fin de siècle.* Paris: Presses Universitaires de France, 1986.

Braverman, Harry. *Labor and Monopoly Capital.* New York: Monthly Review Press, 1974.

Brinton, Mary C. *Women and the Economic Miracle: Gender and Work in Postwar Japan.* Berkeley: University of California Press, 1993.

Brown, Wendy. *States of Injury.* Princeton, N.J.: Princeton University Press, 1994.

Brysk, Alison. "Hearts and Minds: Bringing Symbolic Politics Back In." *Polity* 27 (Summer 1995): 559–85.

———. *The Politics of Human Rights in Argentina: Protest, Change, and Democra-tization.* Stanford, Calif.: Stanford University Press, 1994.

Budd, Leslie, and Sam Whimster, ed. *Global Finance and Urban Living: A Study of Metropolitan Change.* New York: Routledge, 1992.

Buhle, Paul. *Taking Care of Business: Samuel Gompers, George Meany, Lane Kirk-land, and the Tragedy of American Labor.* New York: Monthly Review Press, 1999.

Burawoy, Michael. *Manufacturing Consent*. Chicago: University of Chicago Press, 1979.

————. *The Politics of Production: Factory Regimes under Capitalism and Socialism*. London: Verso, 1985.

Burawoy, Michael, Joseph A. Blum, Sheba George, Zsuzsa Gille, Teresa Gowan, Lynne Haney, Maren Klawiter, Steven H. Lopez, Seán Ó Riain, and Millie Thayer. *Global Ethnography: Forces, Connections, and Imaginations in a Global World*. Berkeley and Los Angeles: University of California Press, 2000.

Burt, Ronald S. *Structural Holes: The Social Structure of Competition*. Cambridge, Mass.: Harvard University Press, 1992.

Byrne, Hugh. *El Salvador's Civil War: A Study of Revolution*. Boulder, Colo.: Lynne Rienner, 1996.

Bythell, Duncan. *The Sweated Trades: Outwork in Nineteenth-Century Britain*. New York: St. Martin's Press, 1978.

Castells, Manuel. "Four Asian Tigers with a Dragon Head." In *States and Development in the Asian Pacific Rim*, ed. R. Appelbaum and J. Henderson. Newbury Park, Calif.: Sage, 1992.

————. *The Rise of the Network Society*. Cambridge, Mass.: Blackwell, 1996.

Cavendish, Ruth. *Women on the Line*. London: Routledge and Kegan Paul, 1982.

Chakrabarty, Dipesh. *Provincializing Europe: Postcolonial Thought and Historical Difference*. Princeton, N.J.: Princeton University Press, 2000.

————. *Rethinking Working-Class History: Bengal, 1890–1940*. Princeton, N.J.: Princeton University Press, 1989.

Chapkis, Wendy, and Cynthia Enloe. *Of Common Cloth: Women in the Global Textile Industry*. Washington, D.C.: Transnational Institute, 1983.

Chhachhi, Amrita, and Renée Pittin, ed. *Confronting State, Capital, and Patriarchy*. New York: St. Martin's Press, 1996.

Clark, Alice, ed. *Gender and Political Economy: Explorations of South Asian Systems*. New York: Oxford University Press, 1993.

Cohen, Michael A. *Learning by Doing: World Bank Lending for Urban Development*. Washington, D.C.: World Bank, 1983.

Cohen, Stephen S., and John Zysman. *Manufacturing Matters: The Myth of the Post-Industrial Economy*. New York: Basic Books, 1987.

Cohn, Samuel. *When Strikes Make Sense—And Why: Lessons from Third Republic French Coal Miners*. New York: Plenum Press, 1993.

Cunningham, Jonathan. "Sweatshop Labour in Hip-Hop Apparel." *Wordmag.com* (2005), at http://www.laborrights.org/press/sweatshops_hiphop_0705.htm.

Danesh, Abol Hassan. *The Informal Economy: A Research Guide*. New York: Garland, 1991.

Davis, Mike. *Prisoners of the American Dream*. New York: Verso, 1990.

Deyo, Frederic C. *Beneath the Miracle: Labor Subordination in the New Asian Industrialism*. Berkeley: University of California Press, 1989.

Dicken, Peter. *Global Shift: The Internationalization of Economic Activity*. New York: Guilford Press, 1992.

Diskin, Martin, and Kenneth Sharpe. *The Impact of U.S. Policy in El Salvador, 1979–1985*. Institute of International Studies, Policy Papers in International Affairs 27. Berkeley: University of California Press, 1986.

Dude, Arindrajit, and Ken Jacobs. "Hidden Cost of Wal-Mart Jobs: Use of Safety Net Programs by Wal-Mart Workers in California." Briefing Paper Series, University of California Berkeley Labor Center. Berkeley: University of California Press, 2004.

DuGay, Paul. *Consumption and Identity at Work*. Thousand Oaks, Calif.: Sage, 1996.

Enloe, Cynthia. *Bananas, Beaches, and Bases: Making Feminist Sense of International Politics*. Berkeley: University of California Press, 1990.

Ernst, Daniel R. *Lawyers against Labor*. Urbana: University of Illinois Press, 1995.

Escobar, Arturo. *Encountering Development: The Making and Unmaking of the Third World*. Princeton, N.J.: Princeton University Press, 1995.

Ewen, Stuart. *PR! A Social History of Spin*. New York: Basic Books, 1996.

Featherstone, Mike, Scott Lash, and Roland Robertson. *Global Modernities*. London: Sage, 1995.

Felski, Rita. *The Gender of Modernity*. Cambridge, Mass.: Harvard University Press, 1995.

Fernandes, Leela. *Producing Workers: The Politics of Gender, Class, and Culture in the Calcutta Jute Mills*. Philadelphia: University of Pennsylvania Press, 1997.

Fernández-Kelly, María Patricia. *For We Are Sold, I and My People: Women and Industry in Mexico's Frontier*. Albany: SUNY Press, 1983.

Fine, Ben, and Ellen Leopold. *The World of Consumption*. New York: Routledge, 1993.

Firat, A. Fuat, and Nikhilesh Dholakia. *Consuming People: From Political Economy to Theaters of Consumption*. New York: Routledge, 1998.

Fitzsimmons, Tracy, and Mark Anner. "Civil Society in a Postwar Period: Labor in the Salvadoran Democratic Transition." *Latin American Research Review* 34, no. 3 (1999): 103–28.

"Floods in Relentless Fury." *Daily Star* 5, no. 60 (2004): 1–2.

Foucault, Michel. *Archaeology of Knowledge*. New York: Pantheon, 1982.

———. *Power/Knowledge: Selected Interviews and Other Writings, 1972–1977*. New York: Pantheon, 1980.

Franzosi, Roberto. *The Puzzle of Strikes: Class and State Strategies in Postwar Italy*. New York: Cambridge University Press, 1995.

Fraser, Nancy, and Linda Gordon. "Civil Citizenship against Social Citizenship." In *The Condition of Citizenship,* ed. Bart Van Steenbergen, 90–107. Thousand Oaks, Calif.: Sage, 1994.

Freedman, Amy, and Ethel Brooks. "Globalized Chinese Capital in Central America." *Asian Pacific Perspectives* 1, no. 1 (May 2001): 23–31.

Frenkel, Stephen, and Jeffrey Harrod. *Industrialization and Labor Relations: Contemporary Research in Seven Countries.* Ithaca, N.Y.: ILR Press, 1995.

Fröbel, Folker, Jürgen Heinrichs, and Otto Kreye. *The New International Division of Labor.* New York: Cambridge University Press, 1980.

Frundt, Henry J. *Refreshing Pauses: Coca-Cola and Human Rights in Guatemala.* New York: Praeger, 1987.

Fukuyama, Francis. *The End of History and the Last Man.* New York: New Press, 1992.

Garten, Jeffrey E. *The Big Ten.* New York: Basic Books, 1997.

Gereffi, Gary, and Miguel Korzeniewicz, ed. *Commodity Chains and Global Capitalism.* Westport, Conn.: Praeger, 1994.

Gilroy, Paul. *The Black Atlantic.* Boston: Harvard University Press, 1993.

Goldberg, Ellis. *Tinker, Tailor, and Textile Worker.* Berkeley: University of California Press, 1986.

Gootenberg, Paul. *Imagining Development.* Berkeley: University of California Press, 1993.

Gorz, André. *Strategy for Labor: A Radical Proposal.* Boston: Beacon Press, 1967.

Gramsci, Antonio. "Notes on Italian History." In *Selections from the Prison Notebooks,* trans. Quentin Hoare and Geoffrey Nowell Smith. New York: International Publishers, 1971.

———. *Prison Notebooks.* New York: International Publishers.

Green, Nancy. *Ready-To-Wear, Ready-to-Work: A Century of Industry and Immigrants in New York.* Durham, N.C.: Duke University Press, 1997.

Guha, Ranajit, and Gayatri Chakravorty Spivak, ed. *Selected Subaltern Studies.* New York: Oxford University Press, 1988.

Hakim, Catherine. *Key Issues in Women's Work.* London: Athlone, 1996.

Hanagan, Michael P. *The Logic of Solidarity.* Urbana: University of Illinois Press, 1980.

Hanagan, Michael, Leslie Page Moch, and Wayne Te Brake, ed. *Challenging Authority: The Historical Study of Contentious Politics.* Minneapolis: University of Minnesota Press, 1998.

Hardt, Michael, and Antonio Negri. *Empire.* Cambridge, Mass.: Harvard University Press, 2001.

———. *Multitude: War and Democracy in the Age of Empire.* New York: Penguin, 2004.

Hartmann, Betsy, and James K. Boyce. *A Quiet Violence: View from a Bangladesh Village*. London: Zed Press, 1983.

Harvey, David. *A Brief History of Neoliberalism*. New York: Oxford University Press, 2005.

———. *The Condition of Postmodernity*. Cambridge, Mass.: Blackwell, 1989.

———. *Justice, Nature, and the Geography of Difference*. Cambridge, Mass.: Blackwell, 1996.

———. *Spaces of Hope*. Berkeley: University of California Press, 2000.

Haynes, Douglas, and Gyan Prakash, ed. *Contesting Power: Resistance and Everyday Social Relations in South Asia*. Berkeley: University of California Press, 1992.

Ho, Laura, Catherine Powell, and Leti Volpp. "(Dis)Assembling Rights of Women Workers along the Global Assembly Line: Human Rights and the Garment Industry." *Harvard Civil Rights–Civil Liberties Law Review* 31 (1994): 383–414.

Hossain, Hameeda, Roushan Jahan, and Salma Sobhan. *No Better Option? Industrial Women Workers in Bangladesh*. Dhaka, Bangladesh: University Press Limited, 1990.

Hsiung, Ping-Chun. *Living Rooms as Factories: Class, Gender, and the Satellite Factory System in Taiwan*. Philadelphia: Temple University Press, 1996.

Iglesias Prieto, Norma. *La flor más bella de la maquiladora*. Mexico, D.F.: Frontera, 1985.

International Labor Organization (ILO). *La situación sociolaboral en las zonas francas y empresas maquiladoras del istmo centroamericano y República Dominicana*. Geneva: ILO, 1996.

Isin, Engin F. *Being Political*. Minneapolis: University of Minnesota Press, 2002.

Jessop, Bob. "Reflections on Globalisation and Its (Il)Logic(s)." In *Globalisation and the Asia-Pacific,* ed. Kris Olds, Peter Dicken, Philip F. Kelly, Lily Kong, and Henry Wai-chung Yeung. New York: Routledge, 1999.

Kabeer, Naila. "Cultural Dopes or Rational Fools? Women and Labour Supply in the Bangladesh Garments Industry." *European Journal of Development Research* 3, no. 1 (1991): 133–60.

———. "Globalisation, Labour Standards and Women's Rights: Dilemmas of Collective Action in an Interdependent World." *Global Social Policy* 4, no. 2 (2004): 153–69.

———. *The Power to Choose*. New York: Verso, 2000.

Karim, M. Bazlul. *Participation, Development, and Social Structure*. New York: University Press of America, 1994.

Keck, Margaret, and Kathryn Sikkink. *Activists beyond Borders: Transnational Advocacy Networks in International Politics*. Ithaca, N.Y.: Cornell University Press, 1998.

Kelley, Florence. *The Notes of Sixty Years*. Ed. Kathryn Kish Sklar. Chicago: Charles H. Kerr, 1986.

Kelley, Robin D. G. *Hammer and Hoe*. Chapel Hill: University of North Carolina Press, 1990.

Khundker, Nasreen. "Gender Issues in Export-Based Industrialization in Bangladesh." Mimeo, in *Centre for Policy Dialogue Report No. 11*. Dhaka, Bangladesh, 1995.

Kibria, Nazli. "Culture, Social Class, and Income Control in the Lives of Garment Workers in Bangladesh." *Gender and Society* 9, no. 3 (1995): 289–309.

King, Anthony. *The Bungalow: The Production of a Global Culture*. New York: Oxford University Press, 1995.

———. *Culture, Globalization, and the World-System: Contemporary Conditions for the Representation of Identity*. Binghamton, N.Y.: SUNY Binghamton Press, 1991.

Klass, Morton. *From Field to Factory: Community Structure and Industrialization in West Bengal*. Philadelphia: Institute for the Study of Human Issues, 1978.

Klein, Naomi. *No Logo: Taking Aim at the Brand Bullies*. New York: Picador, 1999.

Knox, Paul, and John Agnew. *The Geography of the World Economy*. New York: Edward Arnold, 1994.

Korten, David C. *When Corporations Rule the World*. San Francisco: Berrett-Koehler, 1995.

Krupat, Kitty. "From War Zone to Free Trade Zone." In *No Sweat: Fashion, Free Trade, and the Rights of Garment Workers*, ed. Andrew Ross. New York: Verso, 1997.

Kumar, Nita. *Women as Subjects*. Charlottesville: University Press of Virginia, 1994.

Kwong, Peter. *Forbidden Workers*. New York: New Press, 1997.

———. *The New Chinatown*. New York: Hill and Wang, 1996.

Laclau, Ernesto, and Chantal Mouffe. *Hegemony and Socialist Strategy*. New York: Verso, 1984.

Lash, Scott, and John Urry. *Economies of Signs and Space*. Thousand Oaks, Calif.: Sage, 1994.

———. *The End of Organized Capitalism*. Madison: University of Wisconsin Press, 1987.

Lasn, Kalle. *Culture Jam: The Uncooling of America*. New York: Eagle Brook, 1999.

Lauria-Santiago, Aldo, and Leigh Binford, ed. *Landscapes of Struggle: Politics, Society, and Community in El Salvador*. Pittsburgh: University of Pittsburgh Press, 2004.

Lefebvre, Henri. *Critique of Everyday Life*. New York: Verso, 1992.

———. *The Production of Space*. Cambridge, Mass.: Blackwell, 1991.

Levinson-Estrada, Deborah. *Trade Unionists against Terror.* Chapel Hill: University of North Carolina Press, 1994.

Lipietz, Alain. *Mirages and Miracles: The Crises of Global Fordism.* London: New Left Books, 1977.

Lowe, Lisa. *Immigrant Acts.* Durham, N.C.: Duke University Press, 1996.

Lowe, Lisa, and David Lloyd. *The Politics of Culture in the Shadow of Capital.* Durham, N.C.: Duke University Press, 1997.

Maier, Linda, and Isabel Dulfano, ed. *Woman as Witness: Essays on Testimonial Literature by Latin American Women.* New York: Oxford University Press, 2004.

Majumdar, Pratima Paul, and S. Chowdury. *The Socio-Economic Condition of Women Workers in the Bangladesh Garments Industry.* Dhaka: Bangladesh Institute of Development Studies, 1991.

Mander, Jerry, and Edward Goldsmith, eds. *The Case against the Global Economy: And for a Turn toward the Local.* San Francisco: Sierra Club Books, 1996.

Marcus, George. "Ethnography in/of the World-System: The Emergence of Multi-Sited Ethnography." *Annual Review of Anthropology* 24 (1995): 95–117.

Marx, Karl. *Capital,* vol. 1. New York: Penguin Classics, 1990.

———. "Economics and Politics in the Labor Movement." In *The Marx-Engels Reader,* ed. Robert C. Tucker. New York: W. W. Norton, 1978.

Massey, Doreen. *Spatial Divisions of Labor,* 2nd ed. New York: Routledge, 1995.

McLagan, Meg. "Human Rights, Testimony, and Transnational Publicity." *Scholar and Feminist Online* 2, no. 1 (2003): 2.

Meyer, Mary K., and Elisabeth Prugl, ed. *Gender Politics in Global Governance.* New York: Rowman and Littlefield, 1999.

Mies, Maria. *Patriarchy and Accumulation on a World Scale.* London: Zed Press, 1986.

Mitchell, Timothy. *Colonising Egypt.* Berkeley: University of California Press, 1991.

———. "The Limits of the State: Beyond Statist Approaches and Their Critics." *American Political Science Review* 85, no. 1 (March 1991): 78.

———. ed. *Questions of Modernity.* Minneapolis: University of Minnesota Press, 2000.

Mittelman, James. *Whither Globalization? The Vortex of Knowledge and Ideology.* New York: Routledge, 2004.

Mitter, Swasti, ed. *Computer-Aided Manufacturing and Women's Employment: The Clothing Industry in Four EC Countries.* New York: Springer-Verlag, 1991.

Momsen, Janet H., and Vivian Kinnaird, ed. *Different Places, Different Voices: Gender and Development in Africa, Asia, and Latin America.* New York: Routledge, 1993.

Moneta, Carlos, and Carlos Quenan, ed. *Las Reglas del Juego.* Buenos Aires: Corregidor, 1994.

Montgomery, Tommie Sue. *Revolution in El Salvador: From Civil Strife to Civil Peace*. Boulder, Colo.: Westview Press, 1995.

Mudie-Smith, Richard. *Sweated Industries*. New York: Garland, 1980.

Mukerji, Chandra. *From Graven Images: Patterns of Modern Materialism*. New York: Columbia University Press, 1983.

———. *Territorial Ambitions and the Gardens of Versailles*. New York: Cambridge University Press, 1997.

Nasreen, Gitiara. *Work, Space, and Fabrics: Locations and Locutions of Bangladeshi Women in a Changing World*. Ph.D. diss., University of Hawai'i, 1998.

National Labor Committee. *Free Trade's Hidden Secrets: Why We Are Losing Our Shirts*. New York: NLC Press, 1993.

———. *The Hidden Face of Globalization: What the Corporations Don't Want Us to Know*. Video. New York: Crowing Rooster Arts, 2003.

———. *Mickey Mouse Goes to Haiti: Walt Disney and the Science of Exploitation*. New York: Crowing Rooster Arts, 1994.

———. *Paying to Lose Our Jobs*. New York: National Labor Committee, 1992.

———. *Zoned for Slavery*. Video. New York: Crowing Rooster Arts, 1994.

Ness, Immanuel. *Immigrants, Unions, and the New U.S. Labor Market*. Philadelphia: Temple University Press, 2005.

Nielsen, Michael E. "The Politics of Corporate Responsibility and Child Labour in the Bangladeshi Garment Industry." *International Affairs* 81, no. 3 (May 2005): 559–80.

Offe, Claus. *Disorganized Capitalism: Contemporary Transformations of Work and Politics*. Cambridge, Mass.: MIT Press, 1985.

Offe, Claus, and Helmut Wiesenthal. "Two Logics of Collective Action: Theoretical Notes on Social Class and Organizational Form." *Political Power and Social Theory* 1 (1980): 67–115.

Okely, Judith. *Own or Other Culture*. New York: Routledge, 1996.

Olds, Kris. *Globalisation and the Asia Pacific: Contested Territories*. New York: Routledge, 1999.

Ong, Aihwa. *Flexible Citizenship*. Durham, N.C.: Duke University Press, 1999.

———. *Spirits of Resistance and Capitalist Discipline*. Albany: SUNY Press, 1987.

Ong, Paul, Edna Bonacich, and Lucie Cheng. *The New Asian Immigration in Los Angeles and Global Restructuring*. Philadelphia: Temple University Press, 1994.

Pahl, R. E., ed. *On Work: Historical, Comparative, and Theoretical Approaches*. New York: Basil Blackwell, 1988.

Parr, Julian, and Sumi Dhanarajan. *In Focus 6: Stitching Values Together: Implementing Core Labour Standards through Management Training in the Bangladesh Ready-Made Garment Sector*. London: Corporate Social Responsibility Forum, 2002.

Parreñas, Rhacel Salazar. *Servants of Globalization*. Stanford, Calif.: Stanford University Press, 2001.

Paus, Eva, ed. *Struggle against Dependence*. Boulder, Colo.: Westview, 1988.

Payer, Cheryl. *Lent and Lost: Foreign Credit and Third World Development*. New York: Zed Books, 1991.

Peck, Jamie. *Work-Place: The Social Regulation of Labor Markets*. New York: Guilford Press, 1996.

Peet, Richard, ed. *International Capitalism and Industrial Restructuring: A Critical Analysis*. Boston: Allen and Unwin, 1987.

Peterson, V. Spike, and Anne Sisson Runyan. *Global Gender Issues*. Boulder, Colo.: Westview, 1999.

Piore, Michael. *Birds of Passage*. New York: Cambridge University Press, 1979.

Portes, Alejandro, and Alan Stepick. *City on the Edge: The Transformation of Miami*. Berkeley: University of California Press, 1993.

Portes, Alejandro, Manuel Castells, and Lauren A. Benton. *The Informal Economy: Studies in Advanced and Less Developed Countries*. Baltimore: Johns Hopkins University Press, 1989.

Prakash, Gyan. "Writing Post-Orientalist Histories of the Third World: Perspectives from Indian Historiography." *Comparative Studies in Society and History* 32, no. 2 (1990): 141–68.

Prashad, Vijay. "Calloused Consciences: The Limited Challenge to Child Labor." *Dollars and Sense*, September/October 1999, 21–23.

———. "From Plantation Slavery to Penal Slavery." *Economic and Political Weekly*, September 9, 1995, 2237–41.

———. "No Sweat." *Public Culture* 10, no. 1 (1997): 193–99.

Putnam, Robert D. *Bowling Alone: The Collapse and Revival of American Community*. New York: Simon and Schuster, 2001.

———. *Democracies in Flux: The Evolution of Social Capital in Contemporary Society*. New York: Oxford University Press, 2004.

Putnam, Robert D., and Lewis Feldstein. *Better Together: Restoring the American Community*. New York: Simon and Schuster, 2003.

Quinteros, Carolina, Gilberto García, Roberto Góchez, and Norma Molina. *Dinámica de la Actividad Maquiladora y Derechos Laborales en El Salvador*. San Salvador: CENTRA and AFL-CIO Solidarity Center, 1998.

Rahim, M. Abdur, and Sarwar A. Chowdhury. "Deluge Instills Shortfall Fear in Exporters." *Daily Star* 5, no. 60 (2004).

Rajchman, John, ed. *The Identity in Question*. New York: Routledge, 1995.

Rancière, Jacques. *The Nights of Labor: The Worker's Dream in Nineteenth-Century France*. Philadelphia: Temple University Press, 1989.

Razzaque, Mohammad Abdur, and Mohammad Anisur Rahman. "Harkin's Bill and the Issue of Child Labor: Replicability of Recently Signed MOU between ILO, UNICEF, and BGMEA in the Non-Tradable Sector in Bangladesh." *Journal of Social Studies* 73 (1996).

Rodrik, Dani. *Has Globalization Gone Too Far?* Washington, D.C.: Institute for International Economics, 1997.

————. *The New Economy and Developing Countries: Making Openness Work.* Washington, D.C.: Overseas Development Council, 1999.

Roldán, Martha. *The Crossroads of Class and Gender: Industrial Homework, Subcontracting, and Household Dynamics in Mexico City.* Chicago: University of Chicago Press, 1987.

Rosa, Hermán. *AID y las transformaciones globales en El Salvador.* Managua: Coordinadora Regional de Investigaciones Económicas y Sociales, 1993.

Ross, Andrew, ed. *No Sweat: Fashion, Free Trade, and the Rights of Garment Workers.* New York: Verso, 1997.

————. *Universal Abandon? The Politics of Postmodernism.* New York: Verso, 1997.

Rothstein, Richard. *Keeping Jobs in Fashion.* Washington, D.C.: Economic Policy Institute, 1989.

Rowbotham, Sheila, and Swasti Mitter, eds. *Dignity and Daily Bread: New Forms of Economic Organizing among Poor Women in the Third World and the First.* New York: Routledge, 1994.

Said, Edward. *Orientalism.* New York: Vintage, 1979.

Sassen, Saskia. *The Global City: New York, London, Tokyo.* Princeton, N.J.: Princeton University Press, 1991.

————. *Globalization and Its Discontents.* New York: New Press, 1999.

————. *The Mobility of Labor and Capital.* New York: Cambridge University Press, 1988.

————. "Whose City Is It? Globalization and the Formation of New Claims." In *Cities and Citizenship,* ed. James Holston. Durham, N.C.: Duke University Press, 1999.

Scheper-Hughes, Nancy, and Carolyn Sargent. "Introduction: The Cultural Politics of Childhood." In *Small Wars: The Cultural Politics of Childhood,* ed. Scheper-Hughes and Sargent, 1–33. Berkeley: University of California Press, 1998.

Schmiechen, James A. *Sweated Industries and Sweated Labor: The London Clothing Trades, 1860–1914.* Urbana: University of Illinois Press, 1984.

Schoenberger, Karl. *Levi's Children: Coming to Terms with Human Rights in the Global Marketplace.* New York: Atlantic Monthly Press, 2000.

Scott, Alison MacEwen. *Divisions and Solidarities: Gender, Class, and Employment in Latin America.* New York: Routledge, 1994.

Scott, Allen J., and Michael Storper. *Production, Work, Territory: The Geographical Anatomy of Industrial Capitalism.* Boston: Allen and Unwin, 1986.

Scott, Gregory Shawn. *Sewing with Dignity: Class Struggle and Ethnic Conflict in the Los Angeles Garment Industry.* Ph.D. diss., University of California, Santa Barbara, 1998.

Scott, James. *Weapons of the Weak: Everyday Forms of Peasant Resistance.* New Haven, Conn.: Yale University Press, 1985.

Seabrook, John. *Nobrow: The Culture of Marketing, the Marketing of Culture.* New York: Alfred A. Knopf, 2000.

Segovia, Alexander. "The War Economy of the 1980s." In *Economic Policy for Building Peace: The Lessons of El Salvador,* ed. James K. Boyce. Boulder, Colo.: Lynne Reinner, 1996.

Seidman, Gay. *Manufacturing Militance: Workers' Movements in Brazil and South Africa, 1970–1985.* Berkeley: University of California Press, 1994.

Sen, Gita, and Caren Grown. *Development Crises and Alternative Visions.* New York: Monthly Review Press, 1987.

Shaull, Wendy. *Tortillas, Beans, and M-16s.* London: Pluto Press, 1990.

Shima Das Shimu. "Garments shilpe dhurghotona norjun shromuk nihojo ahoto aur dhoshotadar dai ke?" *Chinta,* August 28–September 7, 1995.

Siim, Birte. *Gender and Citizenship: Politics and Agency in France, Britain, and Denmark.* Cambridge: Cambridge University Press, 2000.

Sivaramakrishnan, K. "Crafting the Public Sphere in the Forests of West Bengal: Democracy, Development, and Political Action." *American Ethnologist* 27, no. 2 (1999): 431–61.

Sklar, Kathryn Kish. *Florence Kelley and the Nation's Work.* New Haven, Conn.: Yale University Press, 1995.

Smith, Christian. *Resisting Reagan.* Chicago: University of Chicago Press, 1996.

Smith, David A., Dorothy J. Solinger, and Steven C. Topik. *States and Sovereignty in the Global Economy.* New York: Routledge, 1999.

Smith, Jackie. "Characteristics of the Modern Transnational Social Movement," In Jackie Smith, Charles Chatfield, and Ron Pagnucco, eds., *Transnational Social Movements and Global Politics,* 42–58. Syracuse, N.Y.: Syracuse University Press, 1997.

Soja, Edward W. *Postmodern Geographies.* New York: Verso, 1989.

Southall, Roger, ed. *Trade Unions and the New Industrialization of the Third World.* Pittsburgh: University of Pittsburgh Press, 1988.

Spivak, Gayatri Chakravorty. "Can the Subaltern Speak?" In *Marxism and the Interpretation of Culture,* ed. Cathy Nelson and Lawrence Grossberg. Urbana: University of Illinois Press, 1988.

————. "Can the Subaltern Speak?" In *Colonial Discourse and Post-Colonial Theory,* ed. Patrick Williams and Laura Chrisman. New York: Columbia University Press, 1994.

————. *A Critique of Postcolonial Reason.* Cambridge, Mass.: Harvard University Press, 1999.

————. *Outside in the Teaching Machine.* New York: Routledge, 1993.

————. "Questions of Multi-Culturalism." In *The Post-Colonial Critic: Interviews, Strategies, Dialogues,* ed. Gayatri Chakravorty Spivak and Sarah Harasym. New York: Routledge, 1990.

Standing, Hilary. *Dependence and Autonomy: Women's Employment and the Family in Calcutta.* New York: Routledge, 1991.

Stephen, Sharon, ed. *Children and the Politics of Culture.* Princeton, N.J.: Princeton University Press, 1995.

Sternlieb, George, and James W. Hughes, eds. *America's New Market Geography.* New Brunswick, N.J.: Rutgers University Press, 1988.

Tarlo, Emma. *Clothing Matters: Dress and Identity in India.* Chicago: University of Chicago Press, 1996.

Tarrow, Sidney. *Power in Movement.* New York: Cambridge University Press, 1998.

Taylor, Frederick Winslow. *The Principles of Scientific Management.* New York: Norton, 1967.

Thompson, E. P. *The Making of the English Working Class.* New York: Vintage, 1966.

Thompson, Ginger. "Fraying of a Latin Textile Industry." *New York Times,* March 25, 2005, C1–C4.

Tilly, Charles. "Contentious Repertoires in Great Britain, 1758–1834." *Social Science History* 17, no. 2 (1993): 253–80.

————. *From Mobilization to Revolution.* Reading, Penn.: Addison-Wesley. 1978.

Tribe, Keith. *Land, Labor, and Economic Discourse.* London: Routledge and Kegan Paul, 1978.

Trouillot, Michel-Rolph. "The Anthropology of the State in the Age of Globalization." *Current Anthropology* 42, no. 1 (2001): 125–33.

Turpin, Jennifer, and Lois Ann Lorentzen, eds. *The Gendered New World Order.* New York: Routledge, 1996.

"Two-thirds of Bangladesh under Water." *Sydney Morning Herald,* July 27, 2004, 1.

U.S. Department of Labor. *The Apparel Industry and Codes of Conduct: A Solution to the International Child Labor Problem?* Washington, D.C.: U.S. Department of Labor, 1996.

————. *By the Sweat and Toil of Children,* vol. 1, *The Use of Child Labor in U.S.*

Manufactured and Mined Imports. Washington, D.C.: U.S. Department of Labor, 1994.

———. *DOL-ILO Conference on Advancing the Campaign against Child Labor*. Washington, D.C.: U.S. Department of Labor, 2000.

Volpp, Leti. "Asian Women and the 'Cultural Defense.'" *Harvard Women's Law Journal* 17 (1994): 57–101.

———. "Blaming Culture for Bad Behavior." *Yale Journal of Law and the Humanities* 12, no. 89 (2000): 89–116.

———. "The Citizen and the Terrorist." *UCLA Law Review* 49 (2002): 1575–600.

———. "Feminism versus Multiculturalism." *Columbia Law Review* 101, no. 118 (2001): 1181–218.

Walton, Mary. *Car: The Drama of the American Workplace*. New York: W. W. Norton, 1997.

Walzer, Michael. "Citizenship." In *Political Innovation and Conceptual Change*, ed. Terrence Ball, James Farr, and Russell L. Hanson, 211–19. Oxford: Cambridge University Press, 1989.

Ward, Kathryn, ed. *Women Workers and Global Restructuring*. Ithaca, N.Y.: Cornell University Press, 1990.

Waring, Marilyn. *If Women Counted*. New York: Harper and Row, 1988.

Waters, Malcolm. *Globalization*. New York: Routledge, 1995.

Wells, Miriam J. *Strawberry Fields: Politics, Class and Work in California Agriculture*. Ithaca, N.Y.: Cornell University Press, 1996.

Williams, Patrick, and Laura Chrisman. *Colonial Discourse and Post-Colonial Theory: A Reader*. New York: Columbia University Press, 1994.

Wolf, Eric R. *Envisioning Power: Ideologies of Dominance and Crisis*. Berkeley: University of California Press, 1999.

Wood, Elisabeth Jean. *Insurgent Collective Action and Civil War in El Salvador*. New York: Cambridge University Press, 2003.

World Bank. *Bangladesh: Recent Economic Developments and Priority Reform Agenda for Rapid Growth*. Dhaka, Bangladesh: World Bank, 1995.

Worsley, Peter. *The Three Worlds: Culture and World Development*. London: Weidenfeld and Nicolson, 1984.

Zald, Mayer N., and John D. McCarthy. *Social Movements in an Organizational Society*. New Brunswick: Transaction Books, 1987.

Index

AAFLI (Asian-American Free Labor Institute), 6, 7, 16, 85, 105, 139

AALC (African-American Labor Center), 105

aberrance: discourse of, 3, 16, 25, 34, 58, 60, 61, 132

abolitionist movement: roots of garment worker tours of Unites States in, 116, 117, 132

Absolut Vodka, 177n2

abstract labor: Marx's category of, 150–51, 152

Abu-Lughod, Lila, 142, 198n70, 200n9

accountability for corporations: lack of public, 49, 50

accountability politics, xxvi

achievements of transnational campaigns, xxvii. *See also* Bangladesh, anti-child-labor campaign in; El Salvador, NLC-Gap campaign in; Kathie Lee campaign

activism: primary sites of, 167

activists: privileged agency of, xxvi

ACTWU (Amalgamated Clothing and Textile Workers Union), 30, 115

advertising/advertisement, xxviii, 9, 34, 60, 82, 83, 116; for American Apparel, hierarchies central to VIM in, 168–70; for Bangladeshi export processing zones, 149; billboards in Bangladesh, 12, 14; commodified image in, xv–xvi; for direct investment in Bangladesh, 16; images, 68, 113, 137; NLC videos of labor violations as counterpoint to, 155–56; "Nuestro Nuevo El Salvador" advertising campaign, 158, 159; spending, 177n2

AFL-CIO, 6, 29, 110; complicity in supporting U.S. foreign policy and trade initiatives, 67; NLC criticism of, 30; Solidarity Center of, 50–51, 139, 189n69

African-American Labor Center (AALC), 105

Agamben, Giorgio, 152–53, 154, 201n34

58; living proof of abusive, 143–46; NLC video documenting, 35, 58, 154–55, 191n12; origins of "industrial capitalist" in, 20; other working conditions excluded due to focus on, 19–20, 21–22, 24–25; proliferation of reports on, 7; in soccer ball production in Pakistan, 21, 183n56. *See also* Bangladesh, anti-child-labor campaign in

Child Labor Coalition, xxiv, 6, 16, 20

Child Labor Deterrence Act of 1992, 6–7, 9–10, 11, 24–25, 180, 180n23

Child Labor in Soccer Ball Industry: A Report on Continued Use of Child Labor in Soccer Ball Industry in Pakistan (ILRF), 183n56

Chinese Staff and Workers Association (CSWA), 76

Chinta (UBINIG journal), 135, 136

Chittagong, Bangladesh: garment production in, 12

Chowdury, S., 178n8, 180n15

Christian Democratic Party (El Salvador), 110

circuit of capital (M-C-M'), 149–53: disrupted by living proof, 161; surplus value produced through labor in, 149–50, 151

circuits of subjectivity, 138

CISPES (Committee in Solidarity with the People of El Salvador), 47, 48, 125

citizenship: celebrity-citizenship as privileged site from which to act, 60–61; of consumption, 167; corporate good, xxx, 56, 75; living proof and citizenship claims, 149–53; stages of, 4–5

"Citizenship and Social Class" (Marshall), 4–5

civil citizenship, 4

civil society: "global" and cross-border, xv

Clean Clothes Campaign, 103, 167

Clinton, William J., 6, 55, 74–75, 79, 80, 158, 193n55, 193n56; "new unionism" in era of, 55–56

CLR (Campaign for Labor Rights), 125

CNTS (Centro Nacional de Trabajadores Salvadoreños), 52

Coca-Cola, 177n2

CODEH (Committee for Defense of Human Rights in Honduras), 57

codes of conduct for labor practices, corporate, xxiii, 8, 9, 29, 179n25; as accepted tools for specifying labor rights at various levels of commodity chain, 49; Gap Inc. Code of Vendor Conduct, 39, 40, 41, 187n37; globalized rectification of sweatshop abuse through, 86–87; monitoring compliance with, 49–50. *See also* monitoring programs, independent

Cody Foundation, 191n15

cold war unionism, 56

collective action: repertoire of, 185n8

collective bargaining, 49, 50

colonialism: origins of "industrial capitalist" in, 20; salvation in solidarity's name as reenactment of, 24

Colonising Egypt (Mitchell), 15, 154

Committee for Defense of Human Rights in Honduras (CODEH), 57

Committee in Solidarity with the People of El Salvador (CISPES), 47, 48, 125

commodification of images, xv

commodity chains, xvi; labor flows

ETHEL C. BROOKS is assistant professor of women's and gender studies and sociology at Rutgers University.